MW01043226

A LIFE OF PURPOSE

THE GUIDE TO LIVING YOUR HIGHER SELF

STEPHEN WARREN

BALBOA.
PRESS
A DIVISION OF HAY HOUSE

Balboa Press books may be ordered through booksellers or by contacting:

Balboa Press
A Division of Hay House
1663 Liberty Drive
Bloomington, IN 47403
www.balboapress.com
1 (877) 407-4847

Because of the dynamic nature of the Internet, any web addresses or links contained in this book may have changed since publication and may no longer be valid. The views expressed in this work are solely those of the author and do not necessarily reflect the views of the publisher, and the publisher hereby disclaims any responsibility for them.

The author of this book does not dispense medical advice or prescribe the use of any technique as a form of treatment for physical, emotional, or medical problems without the advice of a physician, either directly or indirectly. The intent of the author is only to offer information of a general nature to help you in your quest for emotional and spiritual well-being. In the event you use any of the information in this book for yourself, which is your constitutional right, the author and the publisher assume no responsibility for your actions.

Any people depicted in stock imagery provided by Thinkstock are models, and such images are being used for illustrative purposes only. Certain stock imagery © Thinkstock.

Printed in the United States of America.

ISBN: 978-1-4525-8622-9 (sc)
ISBN: 978-1-4525-8621-2 (e)

Balboa Press rev. date: 11/19/2013

DEDICATION

To my family members with the hope that they
each find their own Purpose in life.

CONTENTS

ACKNOWLEDGMENTS

You, as part of the collective whole of humanity, serve as my primary motivation for writing this book. If it were not for all of our interactions with each other, none of us would possess the knowledge of who we are, what we want and how we are going to get there. Thus, this book is based almost entirely upon everyone that I have ever met, talked to, learned from or read about. *You*, therefore, have inspired me to think about the many facets of Purpose and how it should be guiding our lives. To that end, I must first thank *You* for helping me write this book.

God, the creator of all mankind, certainly deserves the highest acknowledgment. God has given me the total responsibility and freedom for determining how purposeful my life will be. Not only does He get all the credit for the person I am, He is ultimately responsible for my opportunity to think, feel, react and question all of my self-beliefs about life and how it should be lived. My ultimate self-empowerment comes from God, and I thank Him for this privilege to make my life what I choose it to be.

My Family will always receive an immediate indebtedness for this book. Each of them has provided me with such uniquely interesting behavior to study… and I say that with total loving admiration of their strong personalities and unrelenting advice, whether I have asked for it or not. But most importantly, they have given me the opportunity to be myself, having accepted me as I am rather than trying to make me somebody I am not. Their unselfish and unconditional love is the greatest gift I will ever hope to receive.

PREFACE

My life began in 1986. That was the year that I lost everything - my family, my company, a million dollars, my health, and my mind!

IT WAS THE BEST YEAR OF MY LIFE!

I wouldn't take anything now for that experience. In order for me to find it all, I had to lose it all. It was the only way I could learn who I really was and get on track for rediscovering my purpose and real inner peace. This was also God's way of whacking me between the eyes with an invisible two-by-four, and saying *Wake Up, You Fool!*

Until then, I was too stubborn to figure out for myself that I was on a collision course with disaster. After five years of eighty-hour work weeks with no vacation, I had lost touch with my family, my friends, myself and, indeed, my very soul. I had literally lost myself!

Outwardly, I appeared to have everything associated with a successful life: married with two great kids, a half-million dollar home, luxury cars in the garage, club memberships and the prestige of being President of a company based in Washington, D.C. To this point in my life I had never experienced any real failure. I held graduate degrees from top universities, received promotions every other year, gained industry wide recognition and possessed all the luxury items that normally come with success. I had a future with no imaginable limits.

Then the ambulance showed up!

I had been patiently sitting on a couch in a stranger's office where I had a planned business meeting. As I awaited my clients to appear for our scheduled appointment, a rush of panic suddenly consumed me. I instantly felt that I couldn't breathe. My heart began pounding. I was sweating, dizzy, and felt the greatest sense of doom that I had ever experienced in my life. I knew this was the big one – a cardiac arrest, that my *successful* life was over.

The paramedics said I was lucky, that it wasn't a heart attack after all. They had me sign a release and told me to go see my doctor. I was so shaky I had to call my wife to come and get me. A few hours later and the diagnosis was delivered: Stress! I was having a classic panic attack. Acute Anxiety Disorder.

"Not me!" I protested. *"That's for weak wimps! I'm in charge here!"*

The doctor insisted I was doing too much; taking on too many things; that I was the guy on the old Ed Sullivan Show trying to keep all the plates spinning; that I had a significant bodily reaction to pressure and work overload. He lectured me on the stressors in my life, told me to relax, learn to cope and change my perspective on things. He then gave me a prescription for Xanax and sent me on my merry way.

I instantly felt defeated. The panic attacks increased in frequency and intensity over the next few weeks. Then depression set in. My wife told me to be strong, that it was simply mind over matter. I tried, but it only got worse. I ate the tranquilizers like candy, chained smoked and drank myself to sleep. I was basically existing in a semi-vegetated state, seldom leaving the confines of a dark room.

A month later my wife told me *"Get Out!"*

Needing income, I half-heartedly began a management job with a bank in Florida. I thought moving to a sunny paradise might help but quickly discovered the stress of working was too much while trying to get my life back together. Before long, I wasn't able to even get out of bed. I couldn't think, walk, talk, or do anything!

The panic attacks were now increasing in frequency, occurring at least every two hours. I tried counseling. Again, the verdict was stress, burnout, anxiety, depression, and any other label that says you can't deal with reality.

I became more and more detached from the real world and often heard strange voices in my head. In my worst moments I felt like I was floating above the ground while seeing imaginary things crawling on the walls. I thought I was going mad and even contemplated suicide.

LIFE WAS A LIVING HELL!

This went on for over a year. There were moments when I thought I was getting better, but then I would have setbacks that made me feel there would never again be any hope. Ever!

I didn't know where to turn. A highly recommended psychologist was of some value. He began to make me understand the problem and to believe that there was hope. But he couldn't fix it for me. *"You have to do it for yourself,"* he said.

Easier said than done. I still couldn't find any solutions. The harder I tried, the further away and more elusive the answers became. I became financially depleted and my physical health was an equal mess. I was in complete despair the day I walked into a church in the middle of the afternoon and told God that He was my last hope.

"Please either take the pain away or take my life away. Your choice!" I pleaded.

I sat by myself in the pew for an hour waiting for an answer. There wasn't one. But strangely enough, I began to feel a little better for at least asking God for spiritual help and guidance.

As I left the church, I felt different. I won't say a miracle occurred or that my problems immediately went away, but as I walked out of the church into the bright Florida sunshine, a smile came across my face. It felt good to smile, something I hadn't done in over a year.

It wasn't much, but it was a start. I drove to a library and spent the day reading. I read about the problems I had. Some of it was very dry and technical, but some of it was uplifting. The more I read, the more consumed I became on the subject of stress, worry, anxiety, agoraphobias, panic, burn out, depression, and everything else that I thought I had.

I checked out a dozen books and spent the next week reading. Then I went to bookstores and bought every book I could find relating to positive thinking, general life management and finding purpose and meaning in your life. I learned about relaxation techniques and meditation. I absorbed Eastern religious philosophy at the same time that I studied the Bible. I analyzed time management and goal setting. I read about drug treatment and modern psychological treatments.

I went from the scientific to the occult, from modern medicine to astrology. I looked at mysticism and existentialism, biofeedback and neurolinguistic programming. I attended seminars and had numerous discussions with professionals in the trade. I went to every corner of knowledge available, looking for my answers.

Essentially, I was earning my own PhD. in life planning and management. The more I studied, the more aware I became of the issues affecting me, and the possibilities for hope. I practiced different techniques. Some worked; some didn't. I learned that millions of people are affected in varying degrees by the same problem. At least I didn't feel alone anymore, especially as I met and talked to others who shared my experiences.

I was now fully on the path of self-discovery and self-renewal. My approach was holistic, including total lifestyle changes, from nutrition to exercise, from self-awareness training to spiritual training, from practicing meditation to yoga, from setting goals to analyzing my value system. It was actually an enjoyable experience to embrace new principals and ideals to live by. The rough days became fewer and fewer. The old feelings did resurface from time to time but I had developed new tools and skills to deal with them.

Within a year my calm attitude surprised my friends and family. I decided to go see the psychotherapist I had visited before. He was amazed at my transformation. He now saw me leaning back, relaxed and self-confident in his office. "*You know…*" he began to speak, but then hesitated as if studying this new person sitting in front of him. Still staring at me in disbelief he said, "*You used to grit your teeth and set on the edge of your chair when you saw me. But now you seem so calm and confident… like you have renewed your purpose in life!*"

Since then I have remained disciplined in my approach, but the process has become natural and easily maintained. There hasn't been a single recurrence of severe panic or anxiety, and fortunately, depression now seems like an ancient malady. I do still have my fair share of negative stress but the good news is that I have learned to manage it. When I now sense it trying to invade my body and mind, I flip a few switches and it's gone.

My self-discovery has now been going on for more than twenty five years since my life appeared so completely lost. I've learned that this process will never end, that real inner peace and happiness depends on gaining an awareness of our highest values and living each day with great purpose. I hope you will now join me and make your life all that it can gloriously be…

INTRODUCTION

"Well…" she began speaking in a thoughtful tone. *"I think it's… well, uh,… like getting a new home to live in!"*

Maria, a Cuban exile and close friend had just finished reading the original manuscript for *A LIFE OF PURPOSE*.

"I don't understand!" My perplexed look was obvious to her.

"Do you know how your life seems to get a fresh start when you move into a new home?"

"Well, yes… I guess so." I tried not to show my anxiousness of her opinion of the book.

"After reading it…" she paused, then smiled broadly, *"I now feel my life has a new home to live in!"*

My effort in writing *A LIFE OF PURPOSE* was immediately gratifying as it had touched one person, motivating her to seek a new purpose for her life. My elation over Maria's review is due to my belief that we each spend precious little time and energy thinking about what is necessary to build a meaningful and purposeful life. I feel that most of us simply *allow life to happen* rather than *making life happen*! We tend to be unaware of our hidden motives, going about our daily motions while seldom stopping to think about who we are, where we are going, and why we do what we do!

While I realize this is a harsh indictment of how most of us tend to manage our lives, my motivation for writing this book was to challenge people into thinking about what could be different about their lives going forward. If we do not discover and live our Purpose, then I believe we should not complain if our lives turn out to be less meaningful than we had hoped for. While this may seem an unpopular notion to many of us, the fact is if we don't *Wake Up* and choose how our lives will be lived, something or somebody else is going to decide for us. I believe that we can make our lives happen with a conscious Purpose, and that it is our individual right and obligation to do so. Anything less would be our acceptance of fate while we missed the wonderful opportunity to choose our own destiny.

One of my most enjoyable challenges is to get people to really think about what makes them do the things they do. I made my son really angry his senior year in high school when I put him on the hot seat by questioning his life's Purpose. Our conversation went something like this:

"Guess what Dad? I made the Principals honor roll!" He said gleefully.
"That's great!" I gave him a high-five. *"But why did you do that!"*
"Huh?"
"I mean, why did you feel it was important to make such good grades?"
"Well, I thought that was what you wanted me to do!"
"I'm very pleased and proud of you… but is that what you wanted to do?"
"Of course!"
"Why?"
"So I can get into a good college."
"Why do you want to get into a good college?"
"So I can get a good job!"
"Why do you want to get a good job?"
"So I can make lots of money!"
"Why do you want to make lots of money?"
"So I can buy a nice car!"
"Why do you want a nice car?"
So I can meet more girls!
"So…" I said with suspicion. *"You are telling me that you made good grades so you can meet more girls?"*

Admittedly, this was an argumentative, if not an underhanded way of getting my son to think about the hidden purposes behind his actions. The drill I put him through was not designed to get him to admit that his Purpose in life was to meet more girls, but rather to think about his real motivation for what he is doing each day of his life.

Lest you are assuming by now that I am the quarrelsome type, you should know that it is really my sincere love for life that makes me the way I am. I just feel that it is too beautiful to be wasted. I also care about people and their potential and want them to care more about themselves and the lives that they choose to lead. The problem is that we all have the tendency to think superficially, to quickly accept the surface explanations for our choices and decisions rather than deeply explore that which really drives us to action. If we were more consciously aware of our reasons for doing anything, we would have the focus and self-confidence to know and pursue what we are really seeking in life.

Thus, *A LIFE OF PURPOSE* is designed to get you thinking about what is really important to you. It gives you the tools and the framework for putting together your own life plan of action. I don't do this for you. I'm simply a facilitator who gets you to come up with the answers to some really tough questions.

My friend Maria told me she had to sit the book down at the end of each page because she found the words troubling and perplexing. Yet, she also said she found them to be inspiring and inviting. Yes, I invite you to think for yourself and to be perplexed also! Out of your confusion will emerge wonderful, inspiring insights about yourself. You will think about things that you have never thought about before while gaining a greater awareness of who you are along the way.

While this book will challenge your mind, it is not an esoteric academic piece. Our university and public libraries are full of intellectual manuals and dissertations on the arcane science of human behavior. I know because I have read enough of them to know that they rarely help anybody. Also, our national chain bookstores have enough self-help psychology books to choke an army of our society's neurotic, over-achieving souls.

So what makes *A LIFE OF PURPOSE* any different from these other success-oriented self-help books?

First - the framework for this book actually emerged from my experiences in the corporate world. After reading *umpteen* management books and attending company seminars on everything from sales and marketing to strategic planning, I found that businesses, from large to small, were all beginning to embrace the concept of Purpose. Every innovative company wants to know why they are in business, where there are heading and how they are going to get there. Thus, they spend several days each year, usually at some retreat where they can avoid phones and emails, to contemplate their Purpose and literally draft a philosophy for their existence.

From these marathon sessions, they create a *Mission Statement*, an *Action Plan* and something similar to *A Commitment to Excellence*. Even the subject of *Corporate Values* is now showing up in company annual reports. For those of you who have participated in these corporate planning sessions, you will see many familiar terms and concepts as you read about personal life planning in this book. My assumption, however, is that the vast majority of us have never been through the exercise of considering Mission Statements, Values Elicitation, Vision Analysis or Action Planning at the corporate level, and thus, have never applied these concepts to our personal lives.

Second – *A LIFE OF PURPOSE* emerged from educational materials for *The Whitestone Project*, an online forum and workshop that promotes and shares life management strategies. Thousands of questions have been asked, hundreds of ideas have been discussed and literally uncountable hours have been spent in pondering life's Purpose and how to bring greater meaning to our lives. Thus, *A LIFE OF PURPOSE* was written for laypersons as a guide book, the objective being to enlighten the simple and perplexed souls that we all are. My personal belief and sincere hope is that we can each live a happier and more meaningful life if we just had a little reference resource to help us collect our thoughts from time to time.

Third - this book is mostly common sense, something we all need more of. It does not break new ground, at least not in the academic sense. This is perhaps a painful thing for any author to admit, but in my case it doesn't matter. While writing this treatise on creating and living a purposeful life, it was never my intent to impress philosophers or psychological scholars on how my insights would advance human understanding of the complexities of life. I will, pun intended, leave that impossible task up to the motivational speakers of the world.

Fourth - *A LIFE OF PURPOSE* is *not* a motivational self-help book, at least not in the traditional sense. While you possibly discovered it in the self-help section of your local bookstore, it could have also been located among philosophy, religion, psychology or even the new age books. The reason for this book's split personality is that it doesn't neatly fit in the long line of formula-based books that tell you how to lose weight, budget your time, find your next love, raise your kids or manage your boss.

Everyone is looking for the quick fix to their problems - the new idea, tool, skill, program, method, procedure, technique, recipe or secret code that will unlock the mysteries of life and give us a simple solution to whatever troubles us. For this reason alone, we have a plethora of books, CD's, audio & videotapes and even planning calendars that offer the magic elixir that we all crave. As long as we keep buying that miracle tonic, someone will formulate, package and sell it to us. I know this to be true because I own tons of this stuff myself.

The reason that self-help books seldom work is simple: We *Seek the Help* before we *Seek the Self*. We really want something or somebody else to hold our hand or do it for us. However, without first knowing the hidden motivations of our *Self*, we will never effect any significant or lasting change in our life. Absolutely, positively nothing will happen without first uncovering our Purpose. The fact is that we cannot passionately pursue nor achieve anything worthwhile unless we have a compelling reason to do so.

Many self-help books have wonderful ideas and techniques for improving the quality of our lives. But unfortunately, they soon collect dust on our bookshelves because we don't really understand why we wish to change, grow, learn, improve, renew or become a more complete person. They may lead us to the water, but we must first know why we need a drink. Until we know what we are here for, what we want, where we are going and are committed to the journey, no self-help book ever written will get us there.

Fifth - A LIFE OF PURPOSE, while incorporating certain spiritual and biblical principles is not exclusively Christian-based. By design, this book includes Christianity as a source of purpose and as a key value to a meaningful life. As a Christian myself, I certainly appreciate the power of faith and make every effort to live a life that reflects God's purpose for me. However, I firmly believe that God gave us free choice as to how we will live our lives. The Christian belief that our *Self* is subjugated to God is well-understood and accepted but within that principle there also exists the need to conduct our lives in the specific ways that we individually choose. The term *Self-Centered* may have negative connotations to many Christians, but that term should not be considered as a synonym for *Selfish*.

My intentions and purpose for this book is simply to accept God's *Grand Plan* for us as an opportunity to transform our mortal *Self* to the highest levels we can achieve during our earthly existence.

A LIFE OF PURPOSE is broken into two parts. I suggest you first read it in the order that it was written, as concepts evolve and build upon each other. Once you have learned the general framework of thought, you can go back and jump around as much as you wish. The flow of thought goes from the general to the specific, then back to the general as we attempt to unify and organize everything into a clear structure. Also, as this book is derived from seminar materials, this is the way we would naturally learn and progress in a class-type environment.

Part One is essentially a short-course on Purpose. In this section, we actually get more questions than answers. This section is designed to provoke thought and discussion and to lubricate our minds into thinking about the meaning of our lives. Only after understanding what is most important to us, should we proceed to *Part Two* and put the demands upon our *Self* to actually achieve it.

Part Two takes our Purpose and puts it to work. Here we learn how to create and live a balanced, self-managed and purposeful life. This section deals with self-empowerment through understanding basic life skills and personal planning techniques. Obviously, each subject covered is only a primer and not intended to be all-inclusive. You can find volumes that have been written on every aspect of life management. Thus, where I speak briefly about time and stress management, you could easily find encyclopedic references to study. My intent is not to overwhelm you on any subject area, but rather to prod you into making your own conclusions as to what areas of your life need to be awakened and given more attention.

I believe you will find that *A LIFE OF PURPOSE* is a mosaic of meaningful ideas, not a dissertation on life. You have plenty of time to work that out by yourself. What I hope you gain from this book is a framework of thought, a basic structure that will hold the building blocks to help you organize and create for yourself the life you seek. You will make your own destiny by filling in the details as your future unfolds;

and hopefully, this book will convey a roadmap that will be simple and easy for you to follow.

My goal is to give you a new viewpoint, much like Robin Williams offered his students in the movie, *The Dead Poets Society*. When he asked all of his students to get up and stand on their desks, they came to realize that their previous views had changed, that everything looked different from their higher perspective. In order for us to transform to lives of greater significance, we need to change our point of view, to see our lives from a different and higher perspective.

As I shared with you in the *Preface*, I had my own little world of confusion, anxiety, stress and lack of purpose to conquer. As I set about the task of figuring it all out, I came across a multitude of books, seminar materials, manuals, and even tidbits off the Internet that spoke to some aspect of purposeful living. I also received wise counsel from students, seminar leaders and professionals from the worlds of religion, psychology, medicine and philosophy. I hope that I have recognized throughout this book the majority of these key influences whom I have heavily borrowed from. I have agreed with some of these sources. I have also disagreed with just as many on their principles and *hypothetical facts* as to how we should live our lives.

No doubt, everyone has an opinion. We are all fortunate that so many people are at least thinking about this subject. I know that I am much wiser for their ideas. But the point is that there is no single path to enlightenment. It would be wondrous if some *touchy-feely* dialogue from a self-help book or motivational speaker could convince us that we've discovered the definitive answers. Unfortunately, that conviction never seems to work for the long-term. Also, compassionate hand-holding from friends, family and neighbors, while well-intentioned, will have little impact on our true self-awareness nor enable our personal responsibility for self-renewal or change. In the end, we must each decide our own path. Unfortunately, there is no other approach.

Of all the potential roads to take, I am sharing the one that isn't the shortest nor the easiest to navigate. However, it works for me as the direction is straightforward and has a clear destination. You should not rely exclusively on it but rather borrow from it as I have from others. The important thing is to be searching… To be questioning… To be seeking…

To be gaining your own awareness… And to realize that your path through life, with all of its twists and turns, is exactly what makes it so interesting. Have fun on your journey and take great joy, not just in your own self-discovery, but also in the trip itself!

PART ONE

Our Quest for Purpose and Meaning

This is the true joy in life,
  the being used for
a purpose recognized by
  ourselves as a mighty one;
one being thoroughly worn
  out before we are thrown
on the scrap heap; the being a force
  of nature instead of a feverish,
selfish little clod of ailments and grievances
  complaining that the world will not
devote itself to making us happy...

George Barnard Shaw

PROLOGUE

To be what we are, and to become what we are capable of becoming, is the only end in life.

Robert Louis Stevenson

The quest for Purpose has been a dilemma, if not an illusion for most of us. Without question, its pursuit is a worthy objective, but also a very ambitious and frustrating one. We all seek meaning in our life. We also desire happiness, personal achievement and self-fulfillment. But unless we know what we are truly seeking, we will likely come up short in our quest.

The good news, however, is that we can each discover a unique Purpose to guide us through life. While our quest will be challenging, we can find precisely that which we are seeking, including great life success and achievement. But we must first know where to begin our search… and that place is within ourselves.

Part One of this book takes us on our journey into the *Self*. We will actually ask more questions than we will receive answers. However, as we begin to understand *who we are, what we want and where we are going*, our answers will become clear. *Part Two* will tell us how to get there, but we must first have a starting point. That is, we must determine our Purpose for the life we are living now - *Today!*

All too often, we think of *Today* as just something that we must pass through. But it is much more than just another twenty-four hour period of our life. It is our *Present* - the most precious commodity we all possess for the fulfillment of our *Self*. If we view *Today* in any other way than that wonderful opportunity to *make life happen*, then we will have missed the whole point of living. The choice is ours to make *Today* the starting point for a purposeful life.

But to accomplish this requires a deep personal understanding of our inner *Self*, basically our beliefs and values which collectively define our Purpose. We like to think that if our Purpose were only revealed to us, we would be highly successful and all of our dreams and aspirations would come true. But unfortunately, no one has told us our Purpose. Nor should they! The fact is that we must each decide for ourselves what a purposeful life would be. The good news is that by knowing our *Self*, we will know our Purpose and what is most important to us... and with these insights, we will be prepared to unequivocally pursue life's rewards.

But what is it that will make life rewarding? Significant? Successful?

Many of us believe that the doors to life success will magically open once we possess those things that we normally associate with personal or individual success - fame, fortune, power and prestige being the major prerequisites to a happy and successful life. But unfortunately, we often find upon their attainment that a major void still exists within us. Basically, we discover that *being rich* is not the same thing as *living a rich life.* Thus, we become confused in our quest with these mixed and conflicting definitions of the term *success,* all the while pursing more elusive and unsatisfactory goals.

In the end, we will find that there is really only one lasting definition of *success* that will work for all of us: *Self-Fulfillment Through the Actualization of Our Purpose.* Life success is simply being, *All that you can be!* It is a state of mind that says we know who we are, what we want and are actively pursuing it throughout life with great enthusiasm and excitement. This is the realm of the *Higher Self,* that state of being that is congruent with our Purpose. This passionate form of living our *Higher Self* allows us to blissfully feel in control of our life, where we are committed to *making it happen!*

Also, as we pursue our *Higher Self,* we will know that it was the journey and not the outcome that becomes our greatest reward. By living our Purpose, we will be aware that we are *doing the right thing the right way at the right time.* Our rewards will then automatically emanate from our purposeful choices and decisions. When our actions are congruent with our Purpose, we will discover the full manifestation of our *Higher Self,* where we are taking complete control of our own destiny.

Part One, therefore, attempts to unravel life's most complex questions. What is my Purpose? What is the meaning and Value of my life? Who am I? What is my true potential? What Vision do I have and which Mission will guide me through life? How do I determine my own destiny? *Part One* sets the stage for our self-empowerment, where we will learn the power of self-choice and self-determination. We will take self-mastery to its highest form, unlocking and releasing the full power of the *Higher Self.*

Our ultimate reward will be the realization of our life's meaning, a state of being where we are consciously aware of and actively living our Purpose. In *Part One*, we ask the tough questions about *who we are, what we want, where we are going, and how we are going to get there.* We will probe our inner needs and expectations about life. Once we have firmly grasped these self-concepts, *Part Two* will tell us how to put our new insights to work in our daily lives. We will learn about life planning, mental mastery, goal and time management, and the *Unifying Principles* that will ensure our ultimate happiness and fulfillment. Most importantly, we will manifest our unique Purpose into a self-guided tour through life. We will again *make life happen* and truly begin to live - with great Purpose!

...Let's have a wonderful journey!

CHAPTER ONE

What Is Our Purpose?

Unraveling Life's Complex Secret

"Our only obligation in any lifetime is to be true to ourselves."
Richard Bach

WHAT PURPOSE IS THERE?

The knowledge of our Purpose is the definitive dilemma of our life. If we knew our Purpose, we would know precisely what we are seeking and even how to attain it. With a defined Purpose, our time would never be expended on meaningless activities. Our life would have tremendous conviction and resolve and every thought and action would have a clear reason behind it. We would feel confident that whatever happens was supposed to happen as everything would always fit in perfect harmony with the Grand Plan. Our journey would be magically transformed and we could effortlessly guide ourselves toward the ultimate life. Yes, knowing our Purpose would be a wondrous event... akin to having the secret to life itself!

Maybe we should seek out that mystical guru on the mountaintop for our answers. Then again, maybe we should ask why we even want to get out of bed in the morning...

But here we are, still getting out of bed each morning... but do we really know why? Do we have any compelling reason to arise and face our daily challenges? Do we really know for what clear purpose we are here experiencing the feeling of being alive, productive and worthwhile? While painful to acknowledge, let's be honest - for most of us the purpose at work in our daily lives is a complete and dark mystery, about as well understood as theoretical physics.

And there is a valid reason for this: As model human beings, we have become masters of *busyness*, more preoccupied with the *process* of life than with the *objective* of it. As typical for most of us, we roll out of bed, shuttle off to our jobs, return home in the evening to sort through our junk mail, do our house chores, debate with our children, pay our bills and then go online to surf the Internet. That is, we are living a *normal* life just like everyone else. And while there may be nothing wrong with leading a *normal* life, there is a question that beckons: *Am I living with any conscious awareness of why I do what I do each day other than that is what I'm supposed to do?*

It is likely that many of us will admit that our daily life operates much like our computers. We hit *ctrl-alt-del* each morning to re-boot ourselves and then go into the world with the same basic programs that have been running the same way every day, automatically and blindly repeating our patterned routines without questioning what actually lies behind what we are doing. Thus, we exist largely on the basis of what these programs tell us, remaining focused upon that which is most expected, expedient and convenient.

The unfortunate result of this cybernetic living is that we may discover that we disregarded the very Purpose of life itself, that we have been simply *doing life* rather than *living life?* In today's complex world of disorienting change, competing values, technological demands and incessant pressures for instant gratification, it is not uncommon to find ourselves directionless and perplexed as to the bigger picture of life. However, by not setting our own self-designed and self-charted course, our life will have succumbed to its own level of meaning, providing nothing more than whatever it turns out to be. In essence, we will have allowed *life to happen* without any conscious awareness of *why it is happening* or even *how it should be happening.*

That won't ever happen to me!

The idea that we are just *getting through life* without *actually living it* will make us feel disturbed, if not a little irritated. We would naturally prefer to believe that we are living on a higher plane of existence; that we are in a continuing quest for greater human accomplishment. We obediently set our goals, employ planning schedulers to lead us through our tasks and then measure our success by ticking off the gains on our checklist of material achievements.

We may even compel ourselves to act by creating certain feelings of guilt or obligation, and along the way, validate our *humanness* by experiencing some deep emotions, exhibiting certain passions or even attaining some form of spiritual awareness. Most assuredly, we will even insist that we know why we get out of bed, go to work, have children and pay our bills. Our reasoning is that we have learned to function like model humans - because that is the way we are *supposed* to act!

But despite our good intentions and all of our *busyness*, can we truthfully state that we know what we passionately live for? Is our inner drive truly motivated by anything deeper than what we have been programmed or taught to do? Are our decisions controlled by our strongest convictions and desires or rather by what we deem to be socially acceptable? Are we doing what we know to be most important or only that which we have learned from our parents, our teachers, our clergy and even our legal system? Can we legitimately claim that we know who we are, why we are doing what we are doing, and for what Purpose we are sensing our experience and rationale for life.

From time to time, we should hit the pause button and look deep within ourselves to answer:

Have I ever relied upon my Purpose as the basis for anything that I have done in life?

Have I ever put my Purpose to work in planning the life I will lead?

If asked to state my unique Purpose in life, could I respond with anything more than a blank and perplexed stare?

Can I recall when I last made an informed choice or decision based on the knowledge of my specific Purpose?

Do I know for what Purpose I will choose to do anything different in the future than what I have done in the past?

Again, most of us will struggle with these difficult questions. While there is, in fact, no *normal* and clearly acceptable state of existence for anyone, it is highly *normal* to not know the Purpose for which we choose to exist and act in the specific ways that we do. As creatures of habit, we tend to forget what matters most while permitting our lives to run on automatic pilot, reacting to daily events more from stimulus/response than from any purposeful decision-making. However, by not living with a directed Purpose, we will find ourselves running through it much like Forrest Gump… simply running without knowing why we are running… or to where we are running. We are just running!

But my life is just going to happen anyway - *normal or not* - and I can't change that!

It is true that we can choose to accept what life throws at us and concede ourselves to whatever happens. But it is equally true that we can choose a higher path through life. We can, in fact, challenge ourselves to question what is *normal* and what could be *different* going forward. We don't need to keep running, just to stay in the race that never seems to have a finish line. And we don't need to destine ourselves to a life that is *just happening* - simply because it is *supposed to.*

If our life is not everything we want it to be, we can immediately seize new opportunities for change, recognizing the freedom that we have to make new choices. We can challenge ourselves to determine the most compelling reasons to live with more passion and meaning. And we can stir our souls to take charge, to *make our lives happen* our way with a persuasive sense of Purpose.

Wait a minute! How could I possibly know what my life should be?

Obviously, we are not going to give up our comfort zone of *normalcy* without some complaint. We probably perceive living more purposefully with some bewilderment. And more than likely, we have a certain degree of angst and suspicion about this. After all, it is much easier to live without having to think about it and it is much less demanding to take a *normal* and routine path through life.

Perhaps it's not even our fault that we don't live with more Purpose. No one has given us the means for discovering it nor have we been given access to the right doors to open. And besides, where should we look for it anyway? How could we expect to discover what is missing from our life when we can't even find our car keys!

There is no doubt that for some of us life may be going along reasonably well. We may have been blessed with money, good health and overall success. We would hardly see the point of giving our Purpose much meaningful thought if we don't really need it. If there is no valid reason to bring our Purpose into focus why not just let it hang in our psychological closet, hidden away like the umbrella that only comes out when it begins to rain. There's really no need to worry about something as esoteric as our Purpose if life is good… right?

It is certainly an option to accept life without any question or concern. And it is true that we can march through it and never consider if there could have been more to it. But let's keep in mind that willful blindness to life's possibilities has a consequence. When it turns out differently than what we had expected or hoped for, we cannot then protest, *I never found my Purpose!* And if we forever wander in circles and then look back on all the years that so quickly passed, it will then be too late to ask, *What Purpose did my life serve?*

The inescapable fact is that the vast majority of us will at some point question the Purpose of life. Whether prince or pauper, healthy or ill, joyful or depressed, almost all of us will ultimately question the reasons why our life turned out the way it did. We may go days, months or even years when all seems to be great with the world, then… *Wham!* We experience a major upheaval and the entire world seems to be tilted on its axis. We will be left hanging, feeling out of control and out of Purpose. Or we may be coasting along just fine with nothing major happening, each day looking much like the day before, then… *Pffff!* Like a balloon, the air is let out of us and every little event becomes a major chore. Thus, our crises and misfortunes, whether minor or major, will eventually arise and beckon us to find a greater reason for what we are doing with our life.

What if I have a Purpose but can't recognize it? And much less live it!

It is characteristically human to question life - for what it is, and for what it is not. We may ultimately lament our failures and shortcomings and then blame our fate on the circumstances in which we lived. But it is indisputable that by not living our Purpose, we will certainly not experience all that life has to offer us. Our final reward for living without Purpose will be to miss out on life itself. Myles Munroe, the Bahamian minister tells us, *Purpose doesn't make life easy. It makes it possible.* We may, therefore, find it difficult to accept our Purpose abandoning us when we face the greater reality that we had abandoned it.

It is somewhat ironic that we all desire greater life meaning and significance yet do so little to actually influence that happening. After all, we do have free choice so it would seem that we could choose to live with more Purpose. Therefore, should we not ask which would be the better alternative: consciously pursuing our own dreams and passions with a strong conviction of Purpose or simply rolling the dice? If we choose the latter, we will undoubtedly march through our entire life without ever attaining any awareness, application and benefit of our real Purpose. Our rewards will have been based upon the whims of fate instead of our own initiative. And our highest wants and aspirations will be left unheeded since we failed to recognize and make them part of our reality.

I still don't see why knowing my Purpose will make any difference!

Everything clearly has a Purpose behind it. Would we even attempt to perform a useful life if we perceived no benefit in doing so? Would our family, our homes and our society be worth any effort if we could not recognize any Purpose for them? Would even the air we breathe have any Purpose if our survival were not the underlying benefit? The fact is that our Purpose is always functioning, even when we are unconscious of its presence. It serves us like a guardian angel, silently sitting on our shoulders and leading us forward in directions that we may not always consciously know.

And whether we accept it or not, our Purpose is the basis for everything that we do, think or feel. While we may not be able to label all of our actions in purposeful terms, our Purpose is the subliminal force that guides us in every aspect of our life. It determines whom we marry, where we work, what we wear, where we live, and even what we eat. In fact, nothing will happen without a Purpose attached to it.

So let's imagine what our lives would be like if we were consciously aware of and in total control of our Purpose. How valuable and worthwhile would our lives become if we could channel the collective Purpose behind all that we do? Would we not feel, see or sense everything more intensely if we controlled and commanded the power of Purpose in our life? What could we achieve, acquire or enjoy if we took our Purpose out of the closet and made it the conscious reason for all of our choices and decisions? Would we not become more productive, more efficient and more fully manifested as complete and total human beings if we only knew *why* we do what we choose to do?

We, therefore, cannot escape the need for finding our reason to live with greater Purpose. As Montaigne told us, *No wind favors him who has no destined port.* If we do not attempt to base our life on any chosen Purpose, we can only expect to receive that which we have chosen to receive. Nothing more and nothing less!

The promise for each of us is that if we clearly understand our Purpose, we will automatically know what we want, where we will find it and even how to attain it. It will answer all of our questions about ourselves and our destiny, while showing us the right path through life. It will make us live more fully, more completely and with the satisfaction of knowing that we are living with the power and full knowledge of that which truly motivates us.

Our Purpose should then become the living, breathing, self-actualizing set of beliefs that governs and regulates our entire lives. Our Purpose, is in fact, the total inspiration for our life, the force that provides us the drive to make *life happen* the way we choose it to happen.

WHY HAVE A PURPOSE?

Purpose provides us hope and inspiration.
Purpose gives us an intended, clear direction.
Purpose offers us promise for the future.
Purpose teaches us our values and goals.
Purpose provides us a daily roadmap to follow.
Purpose puts passion into our life.
Purpose gives us control of our destiny.
Purpose is the total source of our spirituality.
Purpose sustains our commitment to achieve.
Purpose creates our self-confidence and self-esteem.

Purpose provides meaning and significance to our life.
Purpose is the basis for our happiness and joy.
Purpose focuses our efforts and gives us perseverance.
Purpose creates productivity by managing time for us.
Purpose provides us balance and harmony.
Purpose is the source of our strength and inner peace.

Is finding my Purpose my responsibility?

Here's the dilemma… and the opportunity. It is our individual responsibility to search for it ourselves. It is lying there quietly, waiting to be discovered through our own hearts and minds. To know our Purpose, we will have to ask the difficult questions about our lives and then have the courage to make equally difficult choices. We must ask *What Purpose is there for me? What is behind my intentions and my behavior?* And it will not suffice to simply state our Purpose. It is more critical that we ask ourselves: *Why will I live my life this way?*

We must know exactly what we want from life and be prepared to pursue it with unequivocal intent and passion. We must accept great responsibility for this enlightenment. By accessing this wisdom, we will be required to actually live it. By connecting with our supreme motivation, we will be required to make profound decisions, adopt new attitudes and consciously chart our own path in this world. It is, therefore, up to each of us to make it the decisive force in our behavior, that is, to accept and manifest our specific Purpose in everything that we do.

But why is this so complicated?

Unfortunately, we always make our quest more problematic than it should be. Each of us attribute different meanings to the concept of Purpose and take different paths to find it. Also, we are usually unaware of it even when it should be plainly obvious. The reason is that we tend to view Purpose much like the energy that is hidden in a light bulb. Something is obviously behind the scenes making it work but we don't really know what it is. Or like the airplane that flies, the computer that computes or even the heart that beats inside us, we know there must be some internal force that makes our life function as it does, but we don't really know why. We do, however, have the personal obligation to find out. It won't come to us. We have to go and look for it!

Most of us would agree this is a major task to undertake, much less fulfill. What is it that will motivate us to actually live on a higher, more conscious plane of awareness? And since we are not born with the knowledge of our Purpose, who will tell us what this secret force really is? Unfortunately, no one will. Nor should they! Our Purpose is entirely up to us to discover. It is simply laying dormant, waiting for its own *Wake-Up Call*. And if we heed that call, we will find that our Purpose and life itself becomes much less complicated and much more rewarding. The wonderful promise is that we can each gain a total awareness of the true meaning of our life… and we can realize everything that we have ever hoped for.

How do I define my Purpose?

The quest for Purpose has been one of the longest pursuits of mankind, beginning with man's first breath on Earth. The reason why few of us ever know our Purpose is predictable and understandable. Our inquiries about Purpose are seldom addressed by our parents or teachers. Likewise, our church leaders wrap the issue of Purpose entirely around spiritual concepts, rarely relating it to the complexities of daily living. Undoubtedly, our Purpose has deep spiritual roots, but we seldom dig deep amongst these roots to uncover it for ourselves.

Our search usually begins by asking others about their Purpose, but we are quickly confounded by the answers we receive. As our entire western culture has ignored Purpose as a valid life skill, we receive a variety of divergent answers depending upon whom we ask. Almost everyone defines their Purpose subject to their own unique situations and perspectives. They usually develop definitions that reflect their emotional needs which in turn provides a large assortment of equally confusing responses.

Webster defines Purpose as *to aim, to intend, to plan… the object for which something exists or is done.* Using that definition, some of us will say they are passionate, *My only purpose is to love and be loved.* Some of us are materialistic, *My life would be complete if I only had that house or boat.* Some of us are altruistic, *My purpose in life is to help others.* And some of us are purely self-serving, *My purpose is simply to enjoy the good life and have a great time.* With all of these unique Purposes swirling around us, it is no wonder that we are bewildered when defining our own Purpose.

Naturally, we could look to spiritual references for a definition of our Purpose. From the Christian perspective, we learn that God's Purpose is for us to *believe, follow, repent, and accept* in order to attain our heavenly salvation. Certain Eastern religions tell us our Purpose is to attain continually higher levels of earthly perfection until we are one with the universe and attain Nirvana. Virtually every religious persuasion connects our Purpose to a form of earthly living that will prepare us for another life. They don't, however, give us the keys to unlock the unique Purpose that lies within each of us, that compelling reason to make us exuberantly and intensely motivated about our life today.

Okay, what should I be searching for?

We should begin by asking ourselves some tough questions. For many of us, this may be the first time that we have had this self-dialogue. As Plautus told us, *Hardly one man in ten knows himself.* However, this personal conversation with ourselves is crucial to understanding how and why we think the way we do.

Let's begin by first asking "**Why we are who we are?**"

Why am I here doing what I do every day?
Why do I care about myself, my family and my health?
Why do I even bother facing the challenges of each day?
Why do I feel the way I do?
Why do I act the way I do?
Why do I choose a certain career?
Why do I believe in what I do?
Why do I love or hate certain things?
Why do I worry, feel anxious or get depressed?
Why do I get excited or inspired?
Why do I care about my future?
Why do I feel anything makes any sense?

As children, we are full of these *Why?* questions. Unfortunately, as adults we quit asking *Why?* preferring instead to say *Because!* or *Why Not?* Maybe the answers became too difficult for us to comprehend, or maybe we could no longer explain them to the less complicated minds of children. But we can answer every *Why?* question if we possess the knowledge of one thing: Our Purpose! All of our answers are based entirely on Purpose; the intrinsic reason for all that exists. Love! Work! Beliefs! Actions! War! Peace! Death! Hope! Beauty! Despair! Freedom! God! Even computers, cars, ice cream, and toilet paper! We will ultimately discover that everything has a Purpose, but most importantly – Ourselves!

By asking *Why?* we are more precisely asking the question, *What Purpose is there for me?* The question of *Why?* is answered by thinking about our highest needs and expectations and beginning to understand what truly motivates us to live. We should refuse to accept *Because!* or *Why Not?* as sufficient answers to guide us in life. We must seek the answer to *Why?* as the knowledge of our Purpose would be the most important thing we could know about ourselves.

Why am I here?

In this book about Purpose, we must distinguish between the religious definition of Purpose from our earthly definition of Purpose. That is, *God's Purpose* for us versus *Our Purpose* for ourselves. It is understood that in most religions they are one in the same. Whether Christian, Muslim or Jew, we are told that we are here on earth for the sole purpose of worshiping and serving God. That point is not being debated in this book. Rather, the context of the word Purpose used throughout this book is not about God's Purpose for us but rather the unique Purpose we choose for ourselves and the manner in which we will individually govern our daily lives.

Many of us believe that the final answer to the *Big Purpose* question **Why am I here?** will not even be answered in our lifetime. Perhaps at death, this mystery will be solved. Beforehand, we may be given clues or scriptural reasons for our lives, but we will never be completely certain as to God's *Grand Plan* for our own unique existence. After all, that would be His plan, not ours. Many hope to receive the big revelation from our Creator upon transcending an earthly presence, but until then the problem remains for each of us to uncover the purposeful reasons for being here at this moment - living, breathing, doing whatever it is that we choose to do today.

We could even consider accepting the belief of some progressive New Age proponents that we were born with a Purpose, that we were called to Earth because of some void that existed, a need that only we could fulfill. They assert that we actually chose to come here and take human form, such that we could manifest our spiritual being. Many of them believe that we chose our parents, our culture and our destiny before we were even born. And even if we accepted this, the problem still exists that we suffered instant amnesia at our moment of birth, thus forgetting the reasons we chose to come here in the first place.

Our *Big Purpose* question becomes even more difficult at each successive stage of our lives. As children we ask this of our parents as soon as we are old enough to recognize our own uniqueness. Later, as college students we go off searching for our *true identity*, another generic label for Purpose. At middle age, we endure the proverbial midlife crisis and discover that our life's Purpose is coming up short. And finally in old age, as we lay on our deathbed, we ask once more, *What Purpose did my life serve?* Is it little wonder that our true Purpose always seems to be just beyond our grasp?

Some of us may wake up along the way, have the big revelation as to their pre-chosen Purpose and then go on to a very significant and meaningful life. This will be a wonderful occurrence for the lucky few that are blessed with this insight or awakening. But for the rest of us, even if we were granted our Purpose beforehand, we will not in our normal course ever uncover it. Perhaps we will not be listening or we prefer to be deaf and blind to our possibilities. Or maybe we simply lack faith. But regardless of the reason, if our pre-chosen Purpose is not evident, we must still choose a definitive and unique Purpose for our life at present.

And we already know what it is. It quietly resides within our own hearts and minds, patiently waiting for the *Wake-Up Call*. We simply need to listen to and believe in ourselves. We already possess this knowledge; it is simply a matter of responding to it.

So what am I living for?

If we look at our Purpose as our most compelling reason for living a full and rewarding life, the *Big Purpose* question needs to be rephrased from ***Why am I here?*** (that ultimately only God can answer) to ***What am I here for?*** (that only we can answer). If we cannot discern exactly why God originally wanted us here, we must still decide what we will do with the life that God has given us - our own plan for the time that we are here.

Therefore, the answer to our unique Purpose is unequivocally up to each of us. The definition that we choose will be based entirely upon those forces that motivate us to action. It will not be divined through tea leaves, tarot cards, or other astrological forces; it will be revealed only by searching for what is missing in our lives and for what motivates us to achieve, grow and live our life to its fullest?

In many respects, the answer to our Purpose now becomes easier as we no longer have to wait for some higher divine or psychic force to tell us what it is. Indeed, most of us would be waiting a long time for that to come. We must decide for ourselves what will make life more meaningful and significant for us - Today! We can either look at our Purpose in life as a riddle with no solution or we can take the initiative and develop a self-directed Purpose of our own design.

The self-discovery of our Purpose is not complicated, yet its pursuit will challenge us greatly. If we do not accept this challenge, we will have given up our rights to fate and chance. However, life must not be quietly conceded to others or to the circumstances that surround us when we have the power to control the outcome.

This places direct responsibility where it belongs, upon our own shoulders. We have the freedom to make our lives as purposeful as we choose them to be. Our Purpose - our reason to live and to enjoy happiness, prosperity, and ultimate fulfillment - then becomes our choice. Once we unlock our Purpose and consciously decide to live it, we will have discovered the secret to a productive life. We will know who we are, what we want, where we are going, and how we will arrive there. That is our Purpose.

CHAPTER TWO

What Is The Right Thing?
My Great Expectations

A musician must make music, an artist must paint, a poet must write, if he is to be ultimately at peace with himself.
Abraham Maslow

Given this power to define and live our own Purpose is distressing to most of us. Ralph Waldo Emerson said, *The chief want of man is to have someone else tell us what it is we can do.* As children we enjoy this luxury since we can depend upon someone else to map out each day providing us comfort, stability and predictability. But as adults this luxury vanishes forcing us to make our own way into the world. We then too often find ourselves without a guiding Purpose, lacking focus and direction.

We, therefore, need to ask not only *What am I here for?* but more immediately *Why do I really want to get out of the bed this morning?* Without a Purpose to stimulate us, we will not act, or if we act at all, we will not act in a way that provides any deep satisfaction or fulfillment in our lives. Our actions must have energy and focus to be truly meaningful.

So what is it that will purposefully lead us forward? Aristotle said twenty-three hundred years ago, *What man seeks most is happiness.* But Aristotle gave us only part of the answer. While Purpose can provide happiness, happiness is not the sole result of having Purpose; it is merely a by-product. Ralph Waldo Emerson came closer to the truth of Purpose when he said, *The purpose of life is not to be happy. It is to be useful, to be honorable, to be compassionate, to have it make some difference that we have lived and lived well.*

Thus, a purposeful life is inspirational. It gives us something to stand for. By living our Purpose, we can overcome life's many barriers and rise to meet our highest hopes and aspirations. With Purpose, we will know what we want in life and we can stay the course to achieve it, with integrity and vision. Purpose gives us our roadmap through life. How we choose to manage our time, our business, our families, and our health all comes from having a clear sense of Purpose.

Therefore, our daily performance should always be Purpose-driven. What we do and how well we do it should be centered within our Purpose. Our physical and mental welfare, even our vitality, is determined by the Purpose we have established in our lives. Indeed, our very survival depends on us recognizing the importance of our Purpose. Victor Frankl, the psychiatrist and Holocaust survivor, found his rediscovery of Purpose in the concentration camps to be the key to his survival. He discovered that the worst crises and most difficult challenges encountered are easily managed when we renew our Purpose and hope in life. The philosopher Nietzsche aptly revealed the answer to our Purpose by stating, *He who has a why to live for can bear almost any how.* Therefore, if Purpose is the key to our happiness, our accomplishments, even our very survival…

…How can I be sure I've found it?

Discovering our Purpose is purely intuitive. It comes from our human yearning for fulfillment and promise. It emerges from our sense of hope and our quest to fulfill our greatest needs and expectations. Our individual Purpose is, therefore, of our own creation and design. It may be reasonable, but not necessarily rational. It may not always be condensed to a few words nor is it always explainable to others. Our Purpose is not dictated to us nor is it transferable to others. It is whatever compels us to live our own lives with personal integrity, honesty, dignity and great enthusiasm. It comes entirely from our thinking about our own meaning for our lives, that is, what truly compels us to take meaningful action.

Despite the challenge of discovering a Purpose that is uniquely ours, we must also recognize that it is continually emerging and evolving. Our Purpose will transform as our sense of *Self* changes over time. As a young person, we may feel that our Purpose is directed toward certain careers. As we get older, our Purpose may be found to exist in our family. As we age further, we may find our Purpose to be more spiritual in nature. Our Purpose never wishes to stand still; we only need to grasp and hold onto it at each stage of our lives.

It is also possible to have more than one Purpose working in our lives. Multiple influences may be directing us, requiring our Purpose to take on many faces of importance. But most importantly, we need to acknowledge our Purpose, to be conscious of what we believe to be the current driving force in our lives. And while our Purpose derives from our present feelings about ourselves, especially with regard to our family, talents, creative expression, spirituality and our value system, we should recognize that our feelings about these influences will likely change over time. Thus, our Purpose must be rediscovered and re-embraced as we encounter changes in our travel down life's pathways.

Discovering our Purpose will not be accomplished by simply pursuing happiness as a goal in itself. Nor will it be found solely through our behavior or actions. It will not be revealed through others or through any material possessions. It is not found through factual or logical analysis. It comes only from our own awareness of what is most important to us and what we expect from our lives. It is discovered by ourselves and only for ourselves.

The risk of not knowing what matters most to us is to risk life itself. As Thomas Caryle aptly warned us, *A man without a purpose is like a ship without a rudder.* The secret of a significant and satisfying life, therefore, is to know who we are, what we want, and where we are going.

Who am I?

When we discover our Purpose, we will know who we are. Conversely, when we know who we are, we will know our Purpose. Our minds and our hearts will be clear about where we are going and how we are going to get there. The challenge for each of us is to look within, at any stage of our lives, and find that yearning that wakes us up and gives us a reason to act and live with as much passion as humanly possible. When we totally experience a powerful will to live and are motivated to make every waking second count, we will know exactly who we are and what Purpose we have in life.

To achieve this personal enlightenment, we must spend time thinking about the key elements of our lives and what they really mean to us. We need to consider all dimensions of our *Self,* including our personality, our habits, our likes and dislikes and our most cherished values. It is important to not only think about what makes us happy, but what really drives us to live with enthusiasm and zeal.

The only means for this self-discovery is to have a serious, in-depth dialogue with ourselves. While we rarely have these deep internal conversations, looking within is the only way to open up our innermost feelings about life. By searching our own hearts and minds, we will discover who we really are and what we are expecting from life.

No one else can tell us this much about our Purpose. If we don't ask *Who am I?* we have no right to ask *What do I want from my life?* By not seeking the answer, we have essentially been given one: *We are nobody and we have no right to choose our own life!* Sounds harsh, but the truth is we are solely responsible for determining who we are and what our lives should be.

Josh Billings told us, *It is not only the most difficult thing to know oneself, but the most inconvenient, too!* Undoubtedly, it is a tremendous challenge to *Know Thyself.* But it is also such a wonderful opportunity. And in the words of George Herbert, *By all means we need some time to be alone. Salute thyself; see what thy soul doth wear.* We will learn that the *Who am I?* question is inextricably tied to the *What is my Purpose?* question. Together, they will tell us what is most important and what our lives should look and feel like.

What *Self* am I?

To discover our *Self,* we must first recognize that we are human beings with thoughts, desires, needs and dreams. Collectively, these feelings make up our concept of who we are. We acquire these feelings as we travel through life and interact with the world around us. We receive feedback from our total environment that tends to shape our self-concepts of self-worth and self-esteem. Through our successes and our failures, our victories and our disappointments, our praises and our punishments, we begin to understand what we want and what we want to avoid.

The world around us nurtures and teaches us, determining the way we feel about ourselves and those we interact with. This will be a lifelong process, with our formative years being the most important, especially in terms of our self-image and personality development. Unfortunately, we are often victims of this process since we do not initially choose the cultural, social or physical environment in which we learn about ourselves. But as we mature, we begin to develop more self-awareness and self-confidence, giving us the freedom to determine our own environment. As our knowledge of our *Self* becomes clear and more self-evident, we will tend to choose schools, jobs, neighborhoods and churches that conform to our self-images. In psychological terms, we become *looking glass selves*, that is, when we see our environment we see ourselves, and when we see ourselves, we see our environment.

We should remember, however, that we should never be too content as to who we think we are. We should not allow ourselves to become stagnated in an environment that does not encourage our natural needs for growth and change. Despite the adage that *a leopard never changes its spots*, our need to continually redefine ourselves is healthy and desirable. Our needs and expectations will change as we travel through life. The key is in knowing which *leopard spots*, which set of needs or expectations we will be wearing today.

Our *Self* then becomes an amalgamation of these needs and expectations. These are our feelings toward life. What do I want? What is missing? What moves me in certain directions? What fulfills me? What makes me feel like a whole person?

Collectively, our needs and expectations are essential to determining our definition of our *Selves*. When our *Self* is defined, we are closer to defining our Purpose. As we gain this enlightenment, our Purpose begins to take shape and will become the driving force in our lives. Also, we will continually evolve in that self-knowledge, moving toward whole and complete persons. Our satisfaction must come from knowing that we are always moving in that direction, constantly seeking, striving, moving toward Abraham Maslow's concept of *self-actualization*. Our objective then is to merge the essence of our *Self* with the essence of our Purpose. As they become one and the same, we become unified in thought, spirit and action.

So how do I get to know myself?

Our first step in knowing our true *Selves*, and ultimately our Purpose, is to conduct a *needs* analysis of our lives at this moment in time. Our essential needs and expectations for a meaningful and satisfying life reflect our self-beliefs and self-concepts. We can only determine this by asking the tough questions about each major area of our lives. Let's take sufficient time to reflect upon the following questions that are designed to get at the inner core of our true self-beliefs:

1. What would I do to change myself?
2. What would I do to change the world?
3. What thing am I most proud of about myself?
4. What would I rather be doing next week? Next year? 5-10 years from now?
5. What is the funniest (saddest) experience I ever had?
6. What is the dumbest (smartest) thing I ever did?
7. What do I like to do most in my free time?
8. What book affected me the most in my life?
9. What job do I like (dislike) most?
10. What type of game gives me the most pleasure?
11. What is the greatest success (failure) I've had in my life?
12. Who do I love (hate) the most (least)? Why?
13. When did my life feel the most hopeful (hopeless)?
14. Where do I want to live?
15. Who is my hero?
16. Who taught me the most about life? About myself?
17. What makes me laugh? Cry?
18. What is the best present I ever received?
19. Where did I come from?
20. What happens to me when I die?
21. What kind of vacation do I like to take?
22. What makes me most angry?
23. What am I best at?
24. What would I do if I had a million dollars?
25. What would I do if I knew I couldn't possibly fail?
26. Who is God to me?
27. What movie affected me the most?
28. What is my deepest secret?
29. What would I be willing to die for?
30. Would I let my best friend read my diary?

31. What personal motto do I live by?
32. On what issue would I never change my mind?
33. What do I want said about me at my funeral?
34. What was the biggest turning point in my life?
35. What one thing would I like to be better at?
36. What was my biggest disappointment in life?
37. What is my worst habit that I would like to break?
38. What do I want to do different, starting tomorrow?
39. What is the first thing I would do if I was the President?
40. How would I sum up my philosophy on life?

These questions are designed to flex our minds into thinking about ourselves. Our answers comprise a self-analysis of the belief systems and programming that we (and others) have done to our minds since we were born. As we answer them, we should determine which feelings really belong to us versus which were implanted by our environment and cannot be accepted or trusted as valid feelings.

Certain patterns will emerge as to what Purpose or meaning we really wish to ascribe to our lives. Collectively, our answers will make up our core identity, our true sense of *Self.* Our objective is to know who we really believe we are and what we are expecting from our life at this moment in time. Our ultimate goal is to translate this knowledge into a compelling reason to live with greater significance and enthusiasm.

As we answer the above questions, we begin to capture the essential elements of our belief system, and thus, our concept of our *Self* and our Purpose. We should write brief answers to these questions, preferably the first thing that pops into our minds. Then, we should return to each answer, identifying and underlining the key words or concepts that sum up our feelings. These key words, phrases, or concepts will weave a pattern of beliefs that we feel most strongly about.

We should make a list of these key thoughts, which, in turn, will form an inventory listing of our basic feelings and expectations toward life. Again, as we get to know ourselves better, we will also get to know our Purpose. With hope and the belief that our *Self* holds promise and meaning, we will discover our Purpose and how to live with Purpose.

As we continue to embark on our self-discovery we should continually ask questions of ourselves, writing down our answers so that we may review them at different stages in our life. Most likely, our answers to these questions will change over time as we develop new self-beliefs and expectations for our life. This explains why our Purpose can also change over time. Our concern should not be with changes in what life's meaning is to us. Rather, our concern should be in not knowing what life's meaning is to us at any point in time.

Those without Purpose generally have no understanding of their *Self*, their dreams and their strongest reasons to live. They merely go through the motions of life, leading a meaningless existence. Henry David Thoreau told us, *The mass of men lead lives of quiet desperation.* With Purpose, however, we are no longer desperate to find meaning in life. We will become deeply connected to our *Self* and then live with the deliberation and determination that our life deserves. Our Purpose will give us our motivation, our inspiration, and our meaning for life. Our Purpose is an undeniable force. Whatever we choose it to be, we should choose wisely.

I still don't see how my Purpose leads to a more meaningful life?

Defining and accepting our Purpose is just the beginning of life's journey. The task of living our Purpose is the greater challenge that awaits us. Fortunately, there is a process that will guide us to the results we are seeking. This process leads to our *Life Plan*, the roadmap that marks the course we need to follow. Life planning gives us a Vision of where we want to go, a destination that fully embraces our Purpose.

Once we have a clear direction in mind, we will be able to outline our Mission, the goals we will vigorously pursue as well as our total commitment to reach them. With a *Life Plan*, we will also know our key Values, the things which we most cherish and live for. Finally, after identifying that which matters most to us, we can actively govern our daily lives with resolute determination to ensure the results we seek become a reality. The ultimate satisfaction of life planning is to know that we have consciously lived our Purpose and that our lives were exactly what we wanted them to be.

We begin the process of life planning through self-reflection on what makes us feel right about ourselves. Whether we just close our eyes at our desk, sit under a tree and think, or lie on our backs and watch the clouds drift by, we should take the initiative to allow deep introspective thoughts to slowly enter our mind. Let's think about where we are along the path of life. What do we want most out of life? What will not only get us out of bed in the morning but also make us leap into the world with excitement and anticipation for the day ahead?

As we contemplate those needs and expectations that we must fulfill to achieve a rewarding life, our Purpose will begin to come into better focus. The clarity of our Purpose is at the core of our *Life Plan*. It is our understanding of what we want our lives to be. As the integral component of our *Life Plan,* our Purpose functions like the stabilizing influence of the gyroscope, bringing balance and meaning to our choices and decisions. Our Purpose will be carried with us as we travel through life and be put to work daily allowing us to make decisions and choices that will influence the rewards that we hope to ultimately receive.

Therefore, our Purpose cannot exist by itself; it must be converted into action. Our decisions to act, however, are predicated upon our Vision, the insight that tells us where we want our Purpose to be delivering us in life. Once we know this, we can define our Mission, the actual plan of action for getting us there. Along the way, we will identify which Values are most important to us. While our Purpose keeps us balanced like the gyroscope, our Values will serve us like a compass, giving us a direction and a course to follow. We can then make choices and decisions each day that will determine the exact Behavior we must follow to ultimately reap our Rewards - the consequences of everything that we have not only chosen to do but that we have actually done in reality.

As each of these events of life planning unfolds, our Purpose and our Values will have to stand up to the test. If all runs smoothly, our gyroscope of Purpose will continue in perfect balance and our compass of Values will keep us on the right track. However, if we change our view of where we want to be going, alter the importance of any of our Values, take a new course of action along the way or don't even like the results we are achieving, our Purpose and Values will begin to spin wildly out of control.

Continuous life planning is the tool that gets our Purpose gyroscope back on its steady spin and our Values compass pointing to true North.

To initiate the process of life planning, let's reflect upon the following questions:

PURPOSE: *What am I here for?*

This is the core set of needs and expectations that determine and define our *Self*? They become the motivating forces that compel us to live and achieve a harmonious state of *Being*, where we feel balance and control and a sense of inner peace and happiness. If we expect something is missing or we find needs that are not being met, we will adjust our Purpose to keep our life flowing forward in its chosen direction.

VISION: *Where am I going?*

This is our chosen direction in life. If we understand our Purpose, we will know where we want it to lead us. Our Purpose is not static and complete in itself; it needs fulfillment to survive. We only sense our Purpose being alive by continually discovering where it will take us along life's journey. Our Purpose needs passion, time, and a place to travel to for us to live whole and fully manifested lives.

MISSION: *How will I get there?*

Our Purpose needs an action plan. We cannot set our Purpose on a shelf and expect it to be realized. We must have goals and specific commitments to provide energy to our Purpose. When we state our Mission, our Purpose then has an objective. Our targets are chosen; we can clearly see the bull's eye, and we are focused in our efforts to make them happen.

VALUES: *What is most important to me?*

If our Purpose is our gyroscope, then our Values become the guidance system, the compass that leads us and keeps us on track. When we have a Purpose that centers and motivates our life, we will adopt the Value system that sustains our Purpose. When we have defined our Values, we will know how to define our Purpose. One cannot exist without the other. When we know what is most important to us, our highest wants and aspirations, we will know our Purpose.

BEHAVIOR: *What actions do I take? - How do I spend my time?*

Our behavior is where the rubber meets the road! Until we undertake specific actions to live our Purpose on an active basis, we are only dreaming about it. Through purposeful behavior, we become the master of our own mind, our attitude and our time. We can then take charge of our life and become not only the architect, but also the builder of our own destiny.

RESULTS: *What do I get for it?*

Fulfillment of Purpose is the end objective. While we will accomplish many interim goals along life's journey, our ultimate reward is to know that our hopes are fully realized and that we lived a life without regret of missed opportunities or wasted potential. The result of purposeful living is to reach our *Higher Self*, where we know that our life did, indeed, make a difference. We will find our rewards and know that we lived with the power of great Purpose.

With greater knowledge of these building blocks to a purposeful life, we can begin to understand the complete picture. Our *Life Plan* must be built around our response to all of these components of life planning. As we develop and continually update our *Life Plan* we will find that, yes, still other questions will need answers: What are my talents? What do I need to learn? What do I have to give up? What do I do first? What effect will I have on others? What compromises or tradeoffs do I need to make? How do I organize my priorities? What changes must I make? All of these questions will pop into our mind and require deep reflection and well-thought out answers. Then, from time to time, we will need to review them and see what revisions need to be made.

Why is planning my life so difficult?

This is not an easy process - much like life itself - but it is a vital requirement to truly understand how we can get the most out of our life. We tend to avoid the entire process of life planning because we don't welcome the difficulty of a forced analysis of our lives. But unfortunately, if we don't plan to live our own life, then somebody else or our external environment will do it for us. We should ask ourselves if our life is something we want to give up so easily. We must revere the sanctity of our life and vigorously protect the right to plan our future as we choose.

Most of us, however, don't fully understand the value of committing ourselves to make life as enriching as it could be. We tend to spend more time planning our vacations or our grocery list than we spend time in planning our life? We hesitate in life planning because we think life is too uncertain and unwieldy, simply too complex for us to get our arms around. Our *Life Plan*, however, creates certainty and order to our lives. It centers our thoughts and becomes the catalyst for the execution of our Purpose.

But unfortunately, it does not provide the complete answer. We need to be equally aware that our Purpose sets off a chain reaction where the other aspects of our lives can be better understood. It opens the door to our Vision, our Values, our Mission and our specific Behavior. An old inscription on a church in Sussex, England reminds us, *A vision without a task is but a dream. A task without a vision is drudgery. A vision with a task is the hope of the world.*

As we incorporate all of these elements into our *Life Plan*, we begin to better understand the full dimension of our lives, from beginning to end. Developing our *Life Plan* allows us to see new possibilities, even to the point that we may modify our original Purpose.

Doesn't my Purpose automatically create my Life Plan?

We often get bogged down with the clarification of our Purpose because we think it is a monolithic thing, a single element of truth that would explain everything we need to know about our lives. We believe that Purpose is a *cause* and that our life is the *effect*. If we simply knew our Purpose then we would simply know our life. This linear thinking is faulty in the process of life planning. Purpose is not linear, but circular. Like *time*, Purpose bends back on itself. As we gain a greater awareness of our Values, for instance, we may discover that our original Purpose needs an overhaul. Our Purpose shapes our Values, and our Values equally shape our Purpose.

Each component of life planning and life management – our Vision, Mission, Values, Behavior and Results – blend seamlessly into each other. They exist symbiotically, counterbalancing each other until their presence in our lives achieves a high degree of synergy. As we later discuss the *Wheel of Life,* growth management and life balancing, we will gain a total awareness of how this all works together. For now, we only need to realize that our thoughts must remain fluid and open to change as we embark on the life planning process.

Again, most of us avoid the task of life planning because we feel that it is either not in our control, that our environment has more control over us than we have over it, or that it may involve risks, risks that could lead to disappointment or failure. We don't want to ask, much less answer, the tough questions. We are simply not willing to take charge of the life we lead. But life is not a dress rehearsal. It will go on, with or without us. We have the choice to make it as meaningful and as purposeful as we choose it to be. Planning our lives and then living our lives according to that plan is not an option. We have no other choice if we want to realize the life that we deserve and expect.

But what life do I deserve and what life should I expect?

Again, that is up to each of us. To some, this may seem an unfair burden as it places tremendous responsibility on our capacity to make decisions and then live with our choices. To others, it presents an exciting opportunity and freedom to design our lives as we see fit. We are the architects and builders of our future. We should decide if we will gladly accept this role or if we prefer someone else to do it for us.

Despite the challenge of controlling ourselves, we also face the obstacle of managing the changes in our lives. We are continually evolving in our thoughts, desires and expectations while everything around us is also changing. Because of the imbalance of our needs with the changing nature of the world in which we interact, we are always chasing a moving target.

Therefore, our Purpose may change as we travel down life's path, but this is no way relieves us from the responsibility of knowing what our Purpose is at every bend in the path.

By accepting the changing nature of our Purpose, we must understand who we are at any point in time. We are not static beings and do not have the luxury of standing still. We are continuously transforming and growing throughout life. The process of fulfilling our Purpose is the process of managing this continual growth and change. Many of us will find the process too difficult, throw our hands in the air, give up and just *allow life to happen.* Consequently, we then choose to wander aimlessly without a plan. Too many of us will follow this course, allowing life to evolve without a great deal of thought or effort, and then wonder what happened when we are old and looking back at the years that have passed.

James Allen summed up the consequences of not knowing our Purpose when he wrote, *With the majority the ship of thought is allowed to drift upon the ocean of life. Aimlessness is a common vice, and such drifting must not continue for him who would steer clear of catastrophe and destruction.* The key point to remember is that spending ample time in knowing ourselves and then planning our life will pay immeasurable dividends in the quality of life that we hope to enjoy. Knowing our Purpose, our Values, our Mission and what Behavior we will follow puts us in charge.

Having this knowledge allows us to *make life happen* rather than *having life happen* to us. We can master the change process and perceive it to be an opportunity, not as a threat. We can grow with a Purpose-centered Vision, with renewed energy and excitement. We can develop our own hierarchy of Values and then manage our time to be congruent with those Values. We can make our life have meaning and then look back in our old age with the satisfaction of having lived a life that was planned well and lived well.

We have many roads to travel, but we must always know the overall direction in which we are heading. And while these diverging roads force us to make choices, our Purpose will act as a road map, giving us the confidence to take the right ones. To understand where we are heading, we must consciously apply our Purpose. It is paramount to always remember that it has to drive us to action. We should regard our Purpose as our most important tool for self-navigation through the complexities of life.

When we know *what we are here for* and *where we are going*, we won't allow the chance obstacles of life to get in our way. They will be reduced to mere bumps, and we will scarcely feel their effects as we pass over or steer around them. Once we state our Purpose and commit to it, we will possess our own navigational system, one that clearly points the way to our own self-directed destiny.

Do I have to declare my Purpose?

According to Samuel Smiles, *Life will always be to a large extent what we ourselves make it.* We alone are in charge of what life is and what it can be. Our life has to have a deep meaning that is important only to us and lived only by us. We cannot allow others to tell us what is most important or how we should live. If we respond and conform to them, we have allowed them to define our Purpose. We must create our own sense of *Self*, such that our unique Purpose compels us to achieve our own goals, the goals that are self-intended, self-designed and self-directed.

We alone decide what will give our life great meaning and satisfaction. By asking the question, *Who am I?* as we go through each stage of our life, we will gain the necessary insights to form our own answer as to our Purpose. We will have discovered our reason for life and we will know how to make it worth living. We should commit ourselves to our Purpose by writing down our own Purpose Statement. This will become our basic declaration of what we believe to be the greatest driving force that we have within ourselves.

When drafting our own unique Purpose Statement, we need to reflect upon the following affirmation:

> *This is my life! It is mine to live to the fullest? I need to wake up to the truth that I am in control of what my life will be. What Purpose will best define what I expect from it? What clearly reflects my greatest passion for living? I do not need to get opinions from anyone else. Only I determine what meaning I will give to my life. My life is precious; my time is priceless; and I am in control of my own destiny. My Purpose belongs only to me. It is up to me to decide… So what will it be?*

MY PURPOSE IN LIFE IS:

Don't be discouraged if you find this difficult at this time. Sleep on it for a few days or weeks and think of what compels you to live with a driving sense of who you are and what you really want from life. Just remember that your Purpose is not as much about *Doing* as about *Being*, that is, don't labor as much over what you want to do in your life… It is far more important to ponder who you believe you are as a person.

As you reflect on this, you will likely have moments when you become very emotionally connected to this process. If those moments are intense enough to make you want to shed some tears, then you are definitely on the right track. This is when you are truly connecting with your inner self… where you have the undeniable opportunity to discover your Purpose.

Gaining additional insights throughout this book will also make you more confident in defining what you want it to be. So believe in yourself… You can *make it happen!*

CHAPTER THREE

How Do I Get There From Here?

Renewal and Transformations

All that a man achieves and all that he fails to achieve is the direct result of his own thoughts. In a justly ordered universe, individual responsibility must be absolute. A man's weakness and his strength, purity and impurity, are his own and not another man's. They are brought about by himself, and not by another. They can only be altered by himself, never by another. His condition also is his own. His suffering and his happiness are evolved from within. As he thinks, so he is: as he continues to think, so he remains.

James Allen, As a Man Thinketh

A strange paradox of life is that the more we attempt to perfect it, the more imperfect it seems to become. At first, this paradox would seem to imply that life is hopeless. But it is precisely this imperfection that makes it so interesting and promising. From birth to death, life is a continuum of change - an ongoing series of events, happenings, and transitions. We are born as a bundle of potentiality. We grow and learn. We face challenges and obstacles. We experience the good and the bad, hope and despair, happiness and sadness. We mature from these experiences and develop a much richer understanding of our Purpose in life. William James gave us a clear *Wake-Up Call* when he said, *These then are my last words to you: Be not afraid of life. Believe that life is worth living and your belief will help create the fact.*

Having a clear Purpose and faith in ourselves will help us navigate the twists and turns of life. Life is never going to move in a straight line. It will never be predictable at any point in time. It spirals continuously, from some place we have been to some place we are going. To keep pace with these constant transitions we must always be aware of our Purpose as we confront the challenges of change and self-renewal. We can manage the effect of life's paradoxes by first recognizing and accepting their inevitability and then by making Purposeful choices to manage them. Since we have unlimited opportunities to do so we have an open invitation to make life more significant and worthwhile. The one thing we cannot do is stand still.

By examining our **Life Spiral**, we can see where our path will lead us:

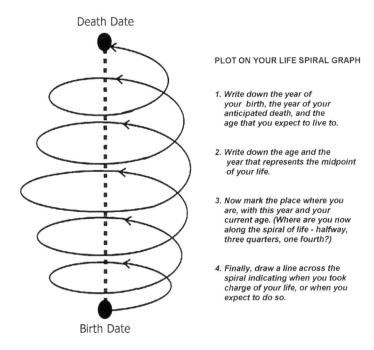

Death Date

Birth Date

PLOT ON YOUR LIFE SPIRAL GRAPH

1. Write down the year of your birth, the year of your anticipated death, and the age that you expect to live to.

2. Write down the age and the year that represents the midpoint of your life.

3. Now mark the place where you are, with this year and your current age. (Where are you now along the spiral of life - halfway, three quarters, one fourth?)

4. Finally, draw a line across the spiral indicating when you took charge of your life, or when you expect to do so.

At some point along our *Life Spiral*, we have the opportunity to take control of our Purpose. We usually decide to do this when there is a life-changing event that dramatically shakes us up to the reality of living. This is our *Wake-Up Call*. (Let's mark the points along our Life Spiral where we had our *Wake-Up Calls*): It could be a death, a divorce, a major illness, a spiritual awakening, an educational experience, a move to a new location, a financial disaster or windfall, a new relationship or the loss of something very important to us. It is rare, if not impossible, to pass through life without experiencing one or more of these *Wake-Up Calls*.

Since we cannot avoid the twists and turns of fate we also cannot avoid having to react in some way to them. Our reaction can, in fact, be one of the most positive things that will ever happen to us if we look at the life-changing event in a positive way. We can use it to grow and to renew our sense of Purpose going forward. When examining our *Life Spiral*, we also have the opportunity to look at our life in its entirety. While the management of daily events may seem to be our natural progression through life, it is very beneficial to step back and look at the whole picture. If we are too focused on the details of the trees, we may soon discover that we have become lost in the woods of life.

From time to time, let's use the *Life Spiral* as our *Purpose Indicator*, to assure ourselves that we are soundly navigating our lives from the beginning to the end. We may discover things about our past that are valuable lessons to repeat in the future. Or we may discover that our past actions and beliefs need major overhauls, such that the negative elements of our personal history won't tend to be repeated. We may wish to view our *Life Spiral* as a reprogramming tool. It may tell us that we have existed in a non-productive rut for years and that we are not where we want to be today. Let's ask why!

What self-image or set of beliefs detoured we? Why did we drift aimlessly for so long? Are those negative beliefs still valid for us today or can they now be discarded? What got in our way? Also let's critically examine our *Wake-Up Calls*. Were they really life changing events or just bumps in the road? We may possibly find that there was a significant opportunity for changes that we failed to take advantage of. Or we may find that our *Wake-Up Call* was highly significant, leading to a major self-renewal of our beliefs and our expectations for the future.

Either way, our task is to self-examine what has happened to us along the way so that we are better prepared to self-direct what happens the rest of the way. Most of us fail to learn from our past experiences. We just assumed they happened for some irrelevant reason and then ignore them as being nothing more than chance occurrences.

Let's examine a contrasting example:

Bob, an accountant, gets fired for his incompetence. He then blindly searches for another job as an accountant. Was his termination telling him something more about himself? Perhaps he really didn't want to be an accountant after all and his lack of desire showed up in his performance. If he had taken the time to learn this about himself, maybe he would have chosen another career and realized greater career success.

Mary, on the other hand, is bored and drops out of high school yet tests had shown that she possessed higher than average intelligence. After years of working in a minimum wage job she is diagnosed as having low self-esteem due to her parents' poor expectations for her. Upon accepting her real sense of value and self-worth, Mary gets her GED and enrolls in college. Ultimately, she regains her self-esteem and enjoys a prosperous and meaningful life.

These are two different people with two different concepts of *Self* through their self-beliefs. Bob didn't perceive any other future while Mary took charge and self-directed her future. Bob blindly traveled along his *Life Spiral* while Mary accepted her *Wake-Up Call* and found new Purpose in her life.

Daily life is a series of snapshots along our *Life Spiral*. Each day is a picture of where we are at any one point in time. Our *Life Spiral* is a collage of these pictures and pieced together they weave the fabric of our life. Our task is not to look at daily life as the summation of our Purpose; instead we must look at the twists and the turns, the *Wake-Up Calls*, the complete spiral from beginning to end. Then we can determine where our Purpose was off track or where it can be reinforced going forward.

We must be continuously growing, self-renewing and making decisions based on a clear sense of our Purpose. We will always be transforming throughout our lives. By knowing and accepting our responsibility to change, we will possess the secret to living a life that is significant and complete in its Purpose.

How do I manage major changes in my life?

Our personal growth is the process of transforming with change. As we receive *Wake-Up Calls* at several points in our lives, we will see that our challenge will be to convert to new ways of thinking. Having a strong Purpose to propel us forward will smooth the bumps and ease the pain of the process.

So why do we dread these *awakenings*? Is it because we prefer our comfort zone, the life that conforms to our existing habits and allows us to take the path of least resistance? No doubt, it is difficult to let go of what we are comfortable with, but it is this process of letting go that allows us to experience and enjoy new parts of ourselves. Without letting go, we remain in the rut. It is said that the only difference between a rut and a grave is the dimensions. And if we do not look above the edges of the rut, we will only see the walls of the grave that imprison us.

Therefore, managing change is the act of transforming by choice. This requires active decision making on our part, where we're always seeking new solutions to our life. Yet, these solutions don't always spring out at us. This leaves us frustrated and depletes our energy. It is at these stages that we are most inclined to give up. In its worst manifestations, we may turn to drugs, endure deep depression and even contemplate suicide.

Psychoanalysis was created for those of us who have no Purpose from which we can base our decisions. It is reality that we wish to avoid, but unfortunately reality does not avoid us. Reality is unrelenting; it comes at us with a vengeance; it is sometimes ugly and scary, but nevertheless, it is there and has to be dealt with. Reality begs for our decisions!

However, perfect decisions are often difficult to come by. We grow by trial and error, through experimentation. But all that is required of us is to make decisions that are strong and based on our Purpose and our convictions. They will move us over the edge of the rut and out in front of the new order of things. We must take a stand; we must put a stake in the ground; we must draw a line in the sand and dare the world to confront us again.

This process gives us strength and reinforces our Purpose. The process of searching for new ground to stand upon is the process of self-renewal. It requires introspection and critical self-analysis. If we take the time to search, we will always be developing a new Vision and a new Mission and then a new plan of action.

This process is what ultimately leads us to our *Higher Selves*, where we will have taken our minds to a new and higher level of operating. Our transformation to achieving our *Higher Self* requires us to make significant, intentional changes in our life. Our personal transformation is a creative process where we are continually clarifying what is most important and then acting upon this newly acquired knowledge. As we do this, we begin to see our reality much more clearly than we had in the past. And rather than letting events control us, we can then choose a new reality within the context of what we want it to be.

This disciplined approach allows us to literally create our own reality whereby we visualize the results we are seeking and then conform our behavior to match this new reality. It is essentially the process of resolving the tension between where we are and where we want to be. This tension - our feeling of frustration and dissatisfaction - signals us to make significant changes to effect a new reality.

All of life transformation and self-renewal is embodied in this process of relieving the tension between the reality we have and the reality we want. For instance, if we are overweight, we feel the tension between our current self-image and a projected self-image. If we are not happy in our job or career, our anxiety tells us that something needs to be done about it. If we are feeling tired and physically unfit, we sense the need to exercise, sleep more and improve our diet.

In virtually every aspect of our lives, there is a perceived gap between where we are and where we want to be. This gap is a void we must fill to make life more significant and meaningful. If we let the gap widen, we feel more tension and frustration. By not attempting to close the gap, we are passively allowing *life to happen to us.* But by taking action to bridge the realities of what we have versus what we want, we are taking charge and *making life happen.*

Write down the 5 most important reality gaps that you have at the present time:

CURRENT REALITY	FUTURE REALITY
What I Have Now	What I Want to Create
1.	1.
2.	2.
3.	3.
4.	4.
5.	5.

When answering the above think about the degree of tension that exists between the two sets of realities that we perceive. How strongly do we feel about bridging the gap? Are we willing at this time to seek some resolution between the two? If not, do we really want that future reality to happen? If so, are we prepared to outline the steps necessary to make our future reality happen? And finally, how committed are we to making our future reality happen?

This process of closing the gap brings our Behavior in alignment with our Purpose and our Values. By knowing what we are here for and what is most important to us we gain clarity of our current reality. We can see exactly what is missing, what expectations are not being met, and we will become compelled to take action and redraft our future reality. We can literally make our life what we want it to be!

How do I know where my life is heading?

Let's project forward and anticipate what this process of self-renewal will accomplish for us - the reality we wish to achieve by closing the gap on where we are now compared to where we want to be. As Oliver Wendell Holmes told us, *The great thing in the world is not so much where we stand, as in what direction we are moving.* Therefore, what void needs to be filled to make our life more meaningful? What negative thoughts, actions or bad habits do we need to break? If we perceive certain changes are needed to make our life more complete, what will our life look like after we make these changes? Where do we want to be, not this weekend, but one year from now? Five years from now? How do we want to spend the rest of our life?

Where Do I Want to Be Next Year?

Five Years From Now?

At the End of My Life?

Let's take a moment now to fill in the spaces above. We should answer these questions in terms of our highest wants and aspirations. In later sections, we will more fully understand our Values, Goals, Commitments and the Rewards we are seeking in life. After reading these sections, we should revisit our answers above and see what changes we wish to make. We may be very surprised at the results!

It is difficult to develop an immediate response as to where we are going because life's landscape is always shifting. Our stages of life keep changing which keeps us perpetually out of balance. We begin our journey in childhood and just as we become proficient at being children, we become adolescents. We enter this period thinking with the mind of a child and have difficulty adjusting to the demands of the new territory. We are forced to deal with our sexuality, our self-esteem and our new freedoms. As we gain experience at this stage and begin to believe we are firmly in control, we are then thrust into adulthood with the new challenges of careers, families and financial needs. And as soon as our eyes adjust to this reality, we reach old age and face our retirement and our own mortality. It seems we are always just one step out of sync in our journey, just one step behind where we really are.

This may sound despairing, but it should not be debilitating. We still have the freedom to adjust and grow into our new personas, with a heightened sense of self-worth. Psychologist C.J. Jung says we can make this journey in one of two ways, *We can walk through or we can be dragged through. The one thing we cannot do is stand still.* Or more succinctly, we can go through life with a clear Vision and a calm Purpose in mind. Or we can be pulled through it backwards, kicking and screaming. The choice is ours to make. The reason we resist these transitions at successive points in our journey is because we perceive or fear that we have to give up something. We feel that what we are giving up is a loss with nothing better to replace it. But each transition does not have to be a loss. Each stage we pass through is actually an expansion of our *Self* and our core identity. Even a serpent has to shed its skin to grow. We, as well, must shed our previous *skins* in order to progress in our Purpose. Thus, our mindset should not be focused on a loss in our life at each successive transition; rather, our focus should be on the fact that we are completing our life.

Can I transform into the life I want?

Absolutely! We alone determine what our needs are for a meaningful life. We are only required to spend some time with ourselves to determine what would constitute a life worth living. And then transform ourselves in that direction.

Each of the world's religious messiahs went through their own transformation in a quest for life meaning and fulfillment. Facing their own versions of life's *Wake-Up Calls*, they withdrew from the complexities of daily living to contemplate their Purpose. As John Dunne pointed out, Buddha, at age 29, relinquished his position of power as a prince and entered the forest as a monk. Jesus went into the desert when he was 30, and Mohammed at 40 withdrew to a cave outside Mecca to pray for his insights into the meaning of life. All returned from their self-exiles to teach us that we must let go of our previous beliefs and accept the revelations that will guide us through life.

This transformational process is referred to as a *conversion* in Western religions, and the Eastern belief is that we must attain *enlightenment*. While we may never achieve the powerful insights of these spiritual leaders, we still have numerous, smaller insights to gain along our own journey through life.

Charles DuBois summed up the realization of our Purpose when he wrote, *The important thing is this: to be able at any moment to sacrifice what we are for what we could become.* Transformations involve change and continually becoming the whole person that we can be. We must embrace this process of change and self-renewal for that governs our own *conversion* and *self-enlightenment*. The perfect culmination to a life of Purpose is in knowing that we gracefully anticipated and adjusted to all that life had to throw at us.

What if I regret my decisions in life?

We often discover that we never reached our destination in life when it is, unfortunately, too late to do anything about it. As we wistfully review our life in retrospect, we will discover all the missed opportunities that could have been. We lament if only we had been given a better roadmap in the beginning of our journey. With a clearer sense of Purpose and a more positive sense of *Self*, we would have done so many things differently as we traveled down life's many roads. Hindsight gives us that clear vision, yet we are always blind in our foresight. Looking back, we will discover that we will most regret what we failed to try. Over the long term, by not taking risks, we will experience far greater regrets than taking risks that may have led to failure.

Our fear of failing in life actually stems from our potential fear of regrets - not the regrets of short term consequences, but rather the regrets of our long term failure to act. We may briefly regret that we didn't fill the tank in our car before a long trip, but this only makes us upset at ourselves for the moment. We may regret not buying a great investment or for not asking for a raise when the boss was in a good mood, but these regrets pass in short order and will not have any lasting impact on us. Of greater consequence is the regret of inaction that leads to a lifetime of shortcomings and missed opportunities.

Our greatest regrets will be due to not living what we regarded to be a purposeful life. We may regret that we didn't take our education seriously enough; or that we took the wrong career path; or that we didn't spend enough time with our children; or that we married the wrong person. These regrets involve a longer-range perspective. Running out of gas may have been an inconvenience, but not spending more time with our children may affect how they turn out in their own lives. These regrets happen because we feel that there was something we could have done, should have done, but didn't. We find that we either made the wrong choice or we made no choice at all.

With the plethora of choices that are offered to us, we will not always choose wisely. The very opportunity of so many choices for our future also limits us in knowing the right choice to make. While our wisdom grows as we mature, we nevertheless will make choices that are wrong. We learn this after the fact when we see the consequences of our decisions. Seldom do we make a choice while knowing at that moment that it was the wrong choice to make. It, therefore, seems that since we cannot know in advance the right decision to make, why should we even try?

Can I even aspire to living a life of *no regrets*?

The answer is emphatically - *Yes!* Life is a contact sport; it is about trying, doing, going for it - not sitting on the sidelines. According to Helen Keller, *Security is mostly superstition. It does not exist in nature nor do the children of man as a whole experience it. Avoiding danger is no safer in the long run than outright exposure. Life is either a daring adventure, or nothing.* The goal is always worth more by pursuing it, rather than simply thinking about it.

The fact is that as of today we each have 100% of our life ahead of us. Will we choose to make it an adventure or a life of missed opportunities and regrets? According to William Arthur Ward, *To hope is to risk despair; To try it all is to risk failure; But risk we must because the greatest hazard in life is to risk nothing…*

But won't I risk making the wrong choices?

By living our Purpose and mapping our future as we go along, we steer ourselves toward a life of *no regrets.* We can have the satisfaction of knowing that the choices we made were the right ones at the time we made them. We will gain our wisdom as we mature, and with this wisdom, we can project more clearly our future. According to Jean Paul, *The more sand that has escaped from the hourglass of our life, the clearer we should see through it.* We need only ask ourselves if we were aware of the full range of choices that are available to us. Then, we should ask if these choices were congruent with our Purpose, *What am I here for?* our Vision, *Where am I going?* and finally our Mission, *How will I get there?*

If we know what is most important to us, we can then plot our direction and the actions we should take. Once we have our global perspective, our decisions will be clear. We will make them, live by them, and then have *no regrets* that we did the best we could. We may still look back and say, *What if… ?* or *I should have… !*and then feel remorse about the decisions we made, but this reasoning is faulty and unproductive. If our decisions were made on the basis of our Purpose and the best information we had available to us at the time we made that decision, we never have to spend one moment regretting anything!

With the benefit of hindsight, the decision may have been wrong, but that no longer matters as that *future knowledge* was not available to us at the time we made our decision. And since God does not give us the benefit of this prior knowledge, why should we burden ourselves with guilt and feel any regrets? We were never issued a crystal ball in the beginning of our life. It is total nonsense to criticize ourselves for not being able to predict the future nor the value of our decisions.

We can only be critical of our life if we just allowed the future to happen without taking some responsibility for the outcome. If we failed to ask the questions of our Purpose, our Vision, our Values, and our Mission and then made the wrong decisions, then we have every right to feel regrets. Taking risks and being wrong for the right reasons is far better than not taking risks and being right for the wrong reasons. As long as we endeavored to live a purposeful life, we can live with ourselves, even if our lives turned out less than we had hoped for.

Life is to be lived. It is to be lived with zeal and enthusiasm. We need to think of life as an exciting opportunity to experience all the feelings, emotions, events and happenings that are offered to us. If they don't come our way, we should seek them out. If we had our life to live over again would we do anything differently? Would we have lived with more Purpose?

The following passage from Nadine Stair on her 84th birthday, *If I Had My life to Live Over*, should become our credo for living a life of *no regrets*:

> **If I had my life to live over, I would start barefoot earlier in the spring and stay that waylater in the fall. I'd wade in more mud puddles. I would go to more dances. I would ride more merry-go-rounds. I would pick more daisies.**

If only we had this wisdom before we grew old and questioned how our time had been spent. Perhaps the best way for us to do this - to live a life of no regrets- is to project backwards. If we knew the outcome, we would be better prepared to shape the events that lead up to it. Thus, we should turn our *Life Spiral* upside down starting at the end with our death, and then write the script that precedes it. If we could write our own epitaph, what would it say? What do we want people to say about us at our funeral? What inscription on our tombstone would best sum up our life?

Our choices can then reflect what we wish the end result to be. Do we want people to say at our funeral that we lived a meaningless life or that we lived a life with great Purpose? That we squandered our opportunities or that we kept our integrity and resolve to succeed? That we were miserable and unhappy, or that we picked more flowers and waded in more mud puddles? That we wasted our potential or that we lived with great Purpose… and with *no regrets*?

Let's take a moment to reflect on the final outcome.

I would like my epitaph to say:

```



```

Our epitaph should reflect our highest Purpose. It should not reflect the fact that we earned a lot of money or that we never missed a day of work. It should reflect our uniqueness, that one thing which sets us apart from the masses. We would do well to have lived the words of Richard Bach: *Our only obligation in life is to be true to ourselves.*

Thus, a life without regrets states that we self-directed our own course from beginning to end. Our obligation to ourselves is to live as we intended, not as others intended us to live. Our *footprints* in life will then lead us to our own personal glory and legacy, to that inscription on our tombstone that says we lived a life with Purpose… A life with *no regrets*.

CHAPTER FOUR

What Is The Meaning Of My Life?

Destiny or Determination

"What should I be when I grow up?" quizzes the puzzled first grader of her father at the dinner table.

"So what am I going to do now?" asks the bewildered college senior while staring at the rejection letters piling up from her job search.

"What reason is there to live anymore?" implores the desperate young man precariously perched on the narrow ledge, blanking staring at the traffic eight stories below.

"What's the point of even trying to get ahead?" laments the laid off account executive, victim of the latest corporate merger.

"What kind of life is this?" asks the aspiring athlete from his wheelchair, paralyzed from an automobile accident.

For thousands of years, the central question of philosophy has been the meaning of life. From early eastern mystics to new age transcendentalists, great debate and thought has been undertaken to decipher and expound upon the meaning of life. However, the direction we should be taking on this issue is not determining *What is the meaning of life?* but rather *What gives life meaning!*

Understanding the meaning of our life is predicated upon our knowledge of that undeniable force which gives meaning to our life. And that force is the unique Purpose that we have chosen to guide us through life. As Madam Curie said, *Nothing in life is to be feared. It is only to be understood.* Thus, the meaning of our life is derived through our understanding of our Purpose. For our life to have meaning, we must decide what allows us to live with Purpose. When we understand one, we understand the other.

We, therefore, choose meaning in our life. It is not granted to us like a diploma nor do we receive a seal of approval for having lived a life of great meaning. We create meaning for ourselves on a daily basis through our own conscious acceptance and application of our Purpose. Finding meaning is simply a matter of living our Purpose, manifested through our conscious recognition and utilization of the most compelling forces that motivate us to live. And depending upon how deeply we are connected to our chosen Purpose, the more meaning we will find in our daily life. When we know that we lived in accordance to our Purpose, we will know that we have lived a life with meaning.

This sounds too simple. Surely, life's meaning is more complicated than that!

It was once said, *Anything, no matter how complicated, if looked at just the right way, will become even more complicated!* So let's attempt to un-complicate life's meaning by first looking at the *meaning of meaning,* which should be a sufficient life challenge in itself. To accomplish this, we need to connect the concept of Purpose to the concept of Meaning. For us to ascribe meaning to anything, including our own life, we need to first look at the requirements for something to have meaning:

1. **We have to be able to give a set of informative facts to represent the thing, an event, or a phenomenon. In other words, we must be able to describe it in concrete terms that we can understand.**
2. **We have to show that a causal relationship exists, that is, something can have meaning if it can be shown that it has an effect on something else. If nothing happens there is no meaning, but if something does happen, there is an implicit meaning in the fact that it happened. Also, if something can be experienced, it has meaning.**
3. **We have to show that it has an inherent reason to exist, that it has a Purpose in itself.**

Thus, the *meaning of meaning* is anything that can be described, that can be shown to *exist* through its *effects*, and that can be shown to have a *reason* or Purpose to exist. Not convinced yet? The paradox of Purpose (the meaning of life) will have more clarity by using the same analysis of the *meaning of meaning*. To demonstrate that our life has meaning, let's apply the following model:

1. **We can certainly describe life on a factual basis, as we could describe our perception of all aspects of reality.**
2. **We can clearly show that life exists through its effects, as there is a causal connection from one event to another over time.**
3. **We can demonstrate life to have meaning if we can show it to have a reason or a Purpose.**

While our first two definitions are relatively easy to grasp and accept, we still must agree that life has a reason or a Purpose to complete our analysis. If we can show that our life has this Purpose, then we will have completed all three conditions for our life to have meaning. Therefore, if our life has a Purpose, then our life by definition has reason and meaning. Purpose and meaning then become one and the same. If we can ascribe Purpose to our life, we can then ascribe meaning to our life.

As Paul Kordis and Dudley Lynch, authors of *Strategy of the Dolphin*, have written, *The most profound thing we can say about being on-purpose is that when that is our status, our condition, and our comfort, we find our lives have meaning, and when we are off-purpose, we are confused about meanings and motives.* We, therefore, only need to manifest our Purpose to put meaning in our life. As we sense and apply our most compelling reasons to live, our life will seek its own level of meaning. Thus, the higher our level of Purpose, the higher the level of meaning we will have in our life.

Okay, but I still don't know how to actually put meaning into my life!

We have learned that our Purpose is that motivating force which is intentional and drives us forward. Thus, our Purpose is anything that we choose life to be, as long as it is firmly held as our reason for living and motivates us in a clear direction to achieve the rewards that we are seeking. If we identify our Purpose, we have the potential for meaning in our life and, thus, a reason to live.

We should not confuse ourselves with the circular reasoning of, *If I had meaning in my life I would be able to discover my Purpose…* or *If I knew what my Purpose was, my life would have more meaning.* These are equivalent statements. Our problem is that we too often fail to discover our inner happiness because we over complicate it with our own definitions of what it should be. Let's keep it simple and remember that the true meaning of life is whatever Purpose we choose to give to it.

But it does not end with the notion that our Purpose is merely a definition for the meaning of life. We must also live our Purpose for life to have meaning. Thus, creating meaning in our life involves the transference of our Purpose into specific actions. Essentially, we will feel that we have significance in our life only if we are realizing our Purpose. We give meaning to life not by thinking about what we want, but by seeking our rewards through our actual life experiences. Our life will not have meaning unless we make the effort to achieve our Purpose.

Therefore, the meaning of life is not a static concept nor can we define our life's meaning by simply giving it a name or a definition. Needless to say, life would be much simpler if we could stand on a mountaintop and loudly proclaim, *The meaning of my life is…* but we wouldn't find that to be extremely rewarding. Just saying it is so is meaningless; we must also experience the meaning of our life on a daily basis.

Let's return for a moment to the earlier scenarios of different individuals seeking some Purpose in life. Remember our young athlete who was paralyzed from a football accident. At one moment, he was vital, healthy and enthusiastic, and his entire future held great promise. The next moment he is confined to a wheelchair and dependent on others for the rest of his life. What Purpose or meaning can he find in this tragedy? What hope is there for his future happiness?

As for all of us, this young man's Purpose must come from within as he contemplates his new situation. While knowing that his body will not allow him to do the things he did before, he must recognize that his disability is not the end of his life; rather it is a change in his life. He may not be able to catch touchdown passes on Friday night nor, for that matter, even be able to walk. And while these are significant setbacks, they do not preclude literally millions of other forms of expressions of his life. His Purpose will not end with his accident; it will only change to a new form or dimension. Rather than close the door on his possibilities, he must open the door to new ones.

Therefore, changes in our life, no matter how severe, are only changes. We cannot blame life for these changes. As George Bernard Shaw told us, *People are always blaming their circumstances for what they are. The people who get on in this world are the people who get up and look for the circumstances they want, and if they can't find them, they make them.* We are not always responsible for the changes that happen to us, but we are responsible for our reactions to these changes. How we respond will determine our future *circumstances.*

Our Purpose, therefore, is to grow into a new *Self* while letting go of our old *Self.* We must keep moving forward and find new approaches to life, while always knowing that we still possess great potential for happiness. Our life has meaning once we know our Purpose and then give it direction. The harmony of living comes from knowing our intent (our Purpose), striving toward our goals (our Vision), and having a plan to get there (our Mission).

Achieving the meaning that we ascribe to our life, however, is not the most important thing we can acquire. The greater reward is found in the act of achieving. Our resolution to achieve and our energy expended in the act of achieving is the challenge we face to make life have meaning. It is the chase, not the capture that fulfills our Purpose. If we are not finding our inner peace through the pursuit of our Purpose, we must reevaluate the forces that drive us to action. If our Purpose changes, then the meaning of our life changes.

By keeping our commitment to our Purpose, whatever it is at any point in time, signifies our continuous discovery of the meaning of our life. It is, therefore, not a place nor a thing, nor even an idea. The meaning of life is purely the process of rediscovery, a travel through time where we are continually seeking and living our Purpose.

Should I just accept my destiny?

We will discuss spiritual destiny in the next section, but at this point we need to recognize that we create our own destiny by creating what happens to us. The simple, universal *law of cause and effect* clearly indicates that whatever we do will determine a specific result. For that matter, whatever we *don't do* will also cause *no* specific result. While this seems overly simplistic at face value, it is remarkable how few of us put this law into effect in our life. Many of us literally believe that we will get what we want in life through chance, hope, miracles and good fortune rather than through applied effort. While we may, in fact, benefit from time to time through wishful thinking, we must still recognize that this benefit was an effect from some other cause.

As an example, we may get rich from Aunt Mary's inheritance, but our benefit (the effect) still had a cause - Aunt Mary's death. Although Aunt Mary's destiny certainly changed, ours did not. And while our bank account's destiny may have changed, we still must wake up the next morning and decide what to do with our new wealth. The money in itself will not have changed us. We are free to decide for ourselves what effect the money will have on our life. We still must determine what our Values are and what behavior will guide us in the future. We still have the free choice of being charitable or miserly. Or we can freely choose to start a business, travel, buy new toys or gamble it away. The point is that we are still in control of creating our own destiny. While our options may be greater than before, we are still responsible for how we will *make our life happen*!

The remarkable thing about the law of *cause and effect* is that events (effects) we don't feel we were responsible for are often traceable to our past behavior. For instance, if the neighbor runs off with our spouse, our dog bites the mailman, or our child is arrested for stealing, all of these events (effects) may actually be the direct result of something we did or said, or even due to some example we may have set in the distant past. The adage, *What goes around comes around* was born out of this basic law of *cause and effect*. The point is that we control more than we are even consciously aware of.

Arnold Patent, the author of *We Can Have it All*, stated, *What we have, or the result of what we achieve, in anything and everything, is exactly what we want. Everything that we experience is a direct reflection of what we ask for.* Thus, we should never discount the powerful effect that all of our choices and decisions will have upon us. We may not witness the effect of our decisions for quite some time but that does not mean that the effect will not eventually happen.

Our specific reaction to the events (effects) that we created (caused) is even more important in establishing our own destiny. Depending upon our reaction to these events (whether positive or negative), we may unknowingly be determining the future course of events (effects) in our life. For instance, we can either reject or accept our responsibility for how things turn out the way they do. We can choose to be angry, bitter or depressed about negative events (effects) or we can perceive them to be *Wake-Up Calls* for future growth and change. Thus, we can create our future destiny by self-determining these future cycles of events (effects).

Positive cycles tend to repeat themselves just as well as negative cycles; thus, we have the power to break negative cycles created by self-destructive behavior as well as the power to perpetuate positive cycles through self-constructive behavior. This is where the law of *inertia* directly affects our destiny. Good things tend to build more good things while bad things tend to build more bad things. The choice of which future we wish to build is entirely our responsibility and our obligation.

We must, therefore, understand that we do not reach a destiny in life. Rather, we unfold it as we travel along life's pathways. The trip itself is the destiny of our life, and the more Purpose we put into the trip, the more meaning and significance we will find along the way. The clearer our Vision, the more we can see the distant turns on the far horizons. The stronger our sense of Values, the more aware we are of the wonderful scenery along the road. The greater our Mission, the farther we will travel. And by aligning our Actions with our Purpose and Values, we will find our pathway to be one that we chose rather than one we were forced to choose. These are the pathways of our destiny; the key for us is to always be taking the right ones. Robert Frost, in *The Road Not Taken*, gave us our options most eloquently:

> *Two roads diverged in a yellow wood,*
> *And sorry I could not travel both*
> *And be one traveler, long as I stood*

I shall be telling this with a sigh
Somewhere ages and ages hence:
Two roads diverged in a wood, and I -
I took the one less traveled by,
And that has made all the difference.

Our destiny, and thus, the meaning of life emerges from our choices – those decisions that will *make all the difference*. To find fulfillment, we must master the law of cause and effect, whereby we are consciously *causing the effects* of our life. According to Bruce McArthur, a writer and lecturer on the readings of the great psychic Edgar Cayce, The *Law of Chance* is the corollary of the *Law of Cause and Effect*. He states that, *We cannot leave it up to chance, as nothing happens by chance. There is a purpose to everything that happens. As thought and purpose and aim and desire are set in motion by minds, their effect is as a condition that is.*

Thus, we create (cause) the events (effects) for our future through the purposeful application of our thoughts, aims and desires. As we create the conditions of our life, we are continuously creating our own destiny!

Where does my spiritual destiny fit into my Purpose?

We cannot look at the meaning of life and our life's Purpose without at least considering the importance of spiritual intervention. The question we must ask is whether or not our life is pre-ordained and pre-structured by a higher force, or if it is simply a series of random and meaningless incidents that we must continually react to. In other words, does God give us a destiny that we are to fulfill, or did He just set life in motion leaving us to determine the events that follow? Is life purposeful or is it in the words of William Shakespeare, *A tale told by an idiot, filled with sound and fury, signifying nothing?* Is our spiritual destiny the only basis for our Purpose that we should be considering? Or should we be determining our own unique destiny?

Let's immediately dispel a wishful notion about our Purpose. Trumpets will not blare, clouds will not part, and a golden scroll will not fall to our feet with our Purpose inscribed in God's own handwriting. We cannot expect God to tell us why we should leap out of bed in the morning and charge into the world with enthusiasm and great Purpose. Most assuredly there is a *Grand Plan*, but the divinely inspired reason for our existence belongs to God, not to us. God has chosen us to be here for *His* reasons, not ours. We may gain certain insights into God's Purpose for us (any priest or theologian would have a great deal to tell us about that subject), but we should not confuse *God's* Purpose for our life with *Our* Purpose to live.

Undoubtedly, *Our* Purpose exists within the realm of *God's* Purpose, but *Our* Purpose for living a purposeful life is not the same thing as *God's* Purpose for our life. God has given us the power to decide for ourselves how purposeful our life will be. And the Purpose that compels us to live is based upon our own choices and decisions. Our quandary in finding *Our* Purpose is that many of us are still standing on the mountaintop waiting for God to tell us what it is.

Assuredly there is a *Grand Plan*, and we should find deep Purpose from God's gift of life to us, but the Purpose we need to discover is the reason for utilizing God's gift of life to us to the fullest extent possible. We have been given the opportunity to find it for ourselves. Our commitment to live in accordance with a spiritual awareness of this gift is vital to a fulfilling life, but the answers we seek to daily living reside solely within each of us, in that place where we are in touch with our own hearts and minds. It must only reflect the rich meaning and value that God expects us to be giving to it. We may search for insights into the mind of God, but it is equally important to pursue our reasons to rationalize and enhance the life we were given.

For His reasons only, God has chosen for us to discover our own Purpose and make our own way in the world. The task He has given us is to explore our innermost convictions and expectations for a meaningful life as that is the only knowledge that will guide us to the destiny that we desire. God has empowered us to create our own peace and happiness; He has given us life, but He cannot be expected to live it for us. We are the masters of our own fate. The Purpose and the Value we give to our life is entirely upon our own shoulders. God has left our Purpose up to us!

Formalized religions will tell us God's Purpose is for us to be honoring, worshiping, loving and living God's word. But within that framework, they don't tell us what to put on our planning calendars for the upcoming week. The universal truths found in all religious doctrines open the window to our Purpose and allow us to frame our thoughts as to who we are, where we came from, and why we are living our earthly life. But this does not mean that our daily acts of living, breathing, doing and feeling are governed specifically by God.

God generally sits on the sidelines and lets us live our own lives. He does not say *Get out of bed! Go to this school! Marry this person! Buy this house! Choose this career!* Nor does God tell us, *Get drunk and drive your car! Beat your kids! Curse your neighbor! Deal drugs! Rob a bank!* We choose to do these things ourselves based on our own sense of Purpose in daily living. We are, therefore, relinquished to considering our life's Purpose on our own terms. While we may be guided by books, teachers, church leaders, friends and family, we can only decide for ourselves what we want from our life.

How much of my life is left up to chance?

Ancient beliefs held that humans were the playthings of many gods and cosmic powers that only toyed with our lives. This notion held for eons until the modern religions of the world surfaced. The monotheistic views of Christianity, Judaism and Islamic faiths in Western and Middle Eastern cultures, as well as the Taoism, Buddhism, Hinduism and Confucianism faiths of the Eastern world gave us a more orderly concept of our destiny. And while all of these faiths differ in their basic message, they each agree that our life is a spiritual journey, where our Purpose, the meaning of our life, is to be found among the chance events of everyday life.

Dr. Darrell Fasching, Professor of Religion at the University of South Florida wrote, *Discovering meaning in the interplay between chance and destiny is the spiritual task which we all face as we travel through life.* He concludes that the truth is probably somewhere in between living a life based on destiny and living a life without meaning, that chance events do happen but they are not always accidents. It is possible that while we have to live with the seemingly random nature of events in our life, these events may happen for a reason and that we can derive meaning from them.

We must, therefore, decide what significance we will ascribe to the chance events in our lives, and whether or not we deem them to be predetermined or merely happenstance. Our answer will depend on our interpretation of life's random events and how we wish to relate them to our Purpose. The meaning we give them will be based upon our own attitude and perception of their importance in our lives. Do we wish to accept them as our destiny or as opportunities for a self-directed path through life? Is everything that happens to us divinely derived and out of our direct control? Or do these events lead to an open field of infinite possibilities that we can react to and possibly have some influence over?

As humans in a largely indefinable universe, we must accept certain of life's events as being nothing more or less than chance occurrences that are outside of our explicit control. We will never be able to understand everything, nor perhaps should we even try. Modern science has great difficulty with this, believing that everything can eventually be explained through certain laws and experimental testing (excluding Chaos Theory which is gaining in popularity among certain scientists). But ultimately, we will be forced to deal with most of these random events on both a pragmatic and a spiritual basis.

Has God left my Purpose up to me?

We must each decide for ourselves what impact God's presence will have upon our Purpose and our destiny. That is, to what extent will we assume that God's divine providence will be guiding us and leading us? Many of us will put great faith in just that occurrence. But while our faith is important to our orderly concept of life, we cannot rely exclusively upon it. The world's religions hold that there are hidden purposes at work in our lives but this does not mean that everything that happens is divinely purposeful. A spiritual hand may guide us into our marriage or our careers, but that does not mean the same spiritual hand caused the deaths of six million Jews in the Holocaust or the death of a group of children on a school bus.

Our destiny is complex and unknown, yet we will discover that it is largely under our power to control. God has actually given us this option. He may know our ultimate destiny and may share His wisdom at various points in our life but God is not obligating Himself to make all of our decisions for us. He has, in fact, given us free choice to make our life as purposeful as we wish. William Jennings Bryan said, *Destiny is not a matter of chance, it is a matter of choice. It is not something to be waited for; but rather something to be achieved.* Therefore, *we* cannot wait for God to determine what our life will be; we must assume that responsibility for ourselves.

Without question, God has a Purpose for us. But while God is the only source of knowledge as to our ultimate Purpose, He keeps us somewhat in the dark. This effectively requires us to utilize our own faith and our own decisions to determine the path we take through life. He points us in the direction to finding our unique Purpose, but He does not tell us why He chose to create us nor does He answer our ultimate question, *What am I here for?* God gave us the resources to think and to act but then leaves it up to us to put great Purpose in our own life.

We often ask for His divine intervention through prayer and meditation, but we do not always receive His answer. Unless He decides to reveal His Purpose for us through visions, words on tablets, or the appearance of angels to specifically guide us, then our definition of our own Purpose must be deduced through our own hearts and minds. In the words of Arnold Toynbee, *As human beings, we are endowed with freedom of choice, and we cannot shuffle off our responsibility upon the shoulder of God or nature. We must shoulder it ourselves. It is up to us.*

Spiritual references like the scriptures of the Bible do offer us a moral code of guidance, but the actual divination of our Purpose is not revealed in these words of wisdom. We learn from the Bible, for instance, that God gave Adam and Eve the opportunity to make choices. It was the first opportunity given to us for discovering our own unique Purpose. The Bible has given us the basis for our earthly knowledge, the foundation upon which we think and act. It also has provided us with history, instruction, inspiration and prophecy, but it still leaves unanswered the basic question of how we should define our earthly Purpose.

Essentially, our eternal Purpose and our day to day mortal Purpose do not always align. The problem of waiting for our earthly Purpose to be delivered from God is well illustrated by a story from Kierkegaard. He tells us of a deeply religious Indian man who was on his way home in the mountains when a tremendous avalanche blocked his path. Because of this man's deep devoutness, he got down on his knees and prayed fervently to God to move the mountain. He waited there in faith and ten years later, still praying, the mountain never moved. Never losing faith, he died there beside the mountain. In the man's village, he is still referred to as the *man who waited for the mountain to move*. Kierkegaard's point is that God does not move mountains for us. He expects us to climb over them with His help. Our goal is to identify our own mountains, then to find the motivation to conquer them and put great Purpose in our lives.

What is my spiritual destiny?

Our spiritual destiny is of our own choosing. God has allowed us to determine our own spiritual awareness and the part it will play in our self-guided tour through life. While we normally interpret our destiny as something that happens to us, we should instead regard it as a product of self-determination. Essentially, pre-determination and self-determination are one and the same, as opposed to an either/or situation. While divine intervention has distinct possibilities in our life, we should not rely exclusively on God's hand to lead us through every daily action we take. Our destiny may have spiritual roots but we alone determine what specific course it will take.

Our destiny is, therefore, governed by the potential we were granted by God, but God expects us to uncover and use that potential with our own free will. Likewise, we should never discount the possibility of miracles actually occurring, but it would be a grave mistake for us to sit around waiting on a miracle to be the solution to our problems; Miracles cannot and should not be the basis of our decision-making. Our self-determination, our own decisions, must become the principal source of our destiny, spiritual or otherwise. Good things will happen to us, as well as bad things, but there is never any guarantee that what we want to happen will always occur.

Reinhold Niebuhr inspired us to self-determination, to make our own choices, when he wisely counseled, *God grant me the serenity to accept the things I cannot change, the courage to change the things I can, and the wisdom to know the difference.* Only God knows why we were created and we will perhaps not know the final answer to that until we die. His Divine Purpose, the ultimate reason for our existence, will be revealed to us after our spirit is reunited with Him in the eternal dimension. Our greatest Purpose should be to be reunited with God and the choices we make in our life will likely determine that possibility. We are the masters of our fate, the managers of our destiny, both here and in the hereafter.

As self-appointed spiritual masters, we will travel through life and at some point come to define our own spiritual destiny. We will, therefore, be ultimately responsible for developing our own concept of religion. While formalized religions can provide us a framework for spiritual consciousness, we should not rely only upon the church to tell us our Purpose or what spiritual meaning we should have in our life. We can find numerous examples of people who regularly attend church, who claim to be Christians, then live their daily lives with total unawareness of their Purpose. Conversely, we can find individuals who do not practice a formal religion but who have infinitely more spiritual awareness and Purpose in their daily lives than their Christian counterparts.

Spirituality should be a deeply personal thing for each of us. Our religion comes from our own understanding of the reality of the larger world than the one in which we live. It is essentially our view of this universal world and our place in it. By increasing our self-awareness and our Purpose in the context of a higher order, we can enhance our overall spiritual awareness and religious views. Thus, all of us will eventually possess some form of defined religion, and it should become much more than a simple belief in God. It must become our collective consciousness, our total set of beliefs upon which we choose to live for today. And once we have taken our Purpose to its ultimate conclusion, we will have prepared it for eternity.

Thus, our spiritual destiny is a process of continually seeking and searching for answers. Our quest for eternal truths can be facilitated by formal religions, but the true meaning of life and our unique Purpose must ultimately come from within. We are not merely evolutionary robots or machines that come and go, with little to show for our existence. Our life must be shaped by the spiritual persuasions that are within us, and we should regard our Purpose as a distinctively strong moral force. Our existence is eternally purposeful and we are endowed with a uniqueness that will never die. Our faith in our unique Purpose, whatever we choose it to be should never subside.

In Revelations 2:17, there is a passage that tells us, *To anyone who overcometh, saith the Spirit, I will give a white stone, on which a new name is written which no one will know except the one who receives it.* We have, therefore, been granted our own individual *Self* and it carries with it its own unique signature. God also told us that, *He knew us before He put us in the belly.* Thus, we have been endowed with our own unique and eternal Purpose, one that existed before and will exist beyond our brief tour on Earth. The Purpose we will carry throughout our life has descended from our heavenly origins and taken root in our earthly life. Having received this gift, we must elect from this moment forward how purposeful our life will continue to be.

The small white stone, the symbol of our unique Purpose and our commitment to it, is ours to carry as long as we live this promise to ourselves. Our promise needs to reflect an enduring self-belief that we have in the power of Purpose working in our life. As we master the principles of self-empowerment, we will know who we are, what we want and where we are going in life. It is our destiny to create our own destiny. Each of us should carry a small white stone on those days that we feel that we are creating life in accordance with our Purpose. It will then remind us that we are *making our life happen* and constructing our own wonderful possibilities for our own future.

CHAPTER FIVE

Who Am I Really?

Discovering My Higher Self

We know not of the future, and cannot plan for it much, but we can hold our spirits and our bodies so pure and so high, we may cherish such thoughts and such ideals, and dream such dreams of lofty purpose, that we can determine and know what manner of men we will be whenever and wherever the hour strikes that calls to noble action... No man becomes suddenly different from his habit and cherished thought.

**Joshua L. Chamberlain, General Commander,
20ᵗʰ Maine, Union Forces, Battle of Gettysburg**

Each of us possess the capacity to reach a *Higher Self,* the state of *Being* where we are consciously aware of our Purpose and are incorporating it into daily living. To achieve our *Higher Self,* we must find that force which individually defines us and becomes our singular source of inspiration. This will be a personal journey since our Purpose must be individually discovered, uniquely belonging to each of us and uniquely manifested.

Unfortunately, there is no universal Purpose that will serve all of us alike. Like snowflakes, no two of us are born alike nor pass through this world alike. We each come into this world with our own genetic code, created with rare and uncommon characteristics that serve our own individual needs for survival and happiness. We each begin our lives in different environments with different mentors to guide us, then subsequently face different daily challenges that determine our unique modes of thought and action. We are each distinctively atypical in our potential, our talents, our expectations and our beliefs. We, thus, are individually born on a different plane from everyone else, and then live from that moment forward on a plane that is significantly different from everyone else.

Our Purpose is shaped by who we start out to be but is further developed by understanding who we can become. By answering Plato's question, *To be or not to be?* we literally determine what our Purpose will be, that unique power that belongs only to us and to no one else. During our brief presence on earth, we will base our Purpose upon those feelings about our own *Self.* By knowing ourselves, we define ourselves. The more we connect to our own *Self,* the more we relate to our Purpose and ultimately transcend to our *Higher Self.* Through our highest consciousness and awareness of what brings meaning to our life, we become a living embodiment of our Purpose. We become one with our Purpose and one with our *Higher Self.*

How do I discover my *Higher Self*?

Realization of our *Higher Self* demands a lifelong commitment, a prolonged search for meaning in our life and a desire to actively live with great Purpose. To reach this level of *Being* requires us to live a contemplative life that is intensely dedicated to our Purpose. Few of us will reach our *Higher Self* and few will even try to attain this level of enlightenment. Most of us will be contented to just *get through life* with minimal discomfort or disruption, being satisfied with a basic, if unspectacular, existence. Many of us may feel that the attainment of one's *Higher Self* is the domain of Buddhists, mystics, mountain top gurus or new age transcendentalists, that it is not the concern of *normal* people. Thus, discovering our *Higher Self* will not be a worthy goal for many of us. But for those who perceive that life can be something more, that it is worth our effort, then the embodiment of our Purpose will take us on a marvelous journey.

If we wish to take the trip to our *Higher Self* we must first gain an understanding of our basic *Self.* It begins at birth, where we are granted ownership to the trilogy of: our Physical/Living *Self* which is made up of our bodies and our capacity for a healthy life; our Mental/Emotional *Self* which is our conscious awareness of our thoughts, feelings, knowledge and intellect; and our Spiritual/Eternal *Self* which is our desire to be connected to a higher power and achieve eternal grace.

These three components make up our potential *Self,* and as wonderful as these gifts are they are only the beginning of what we can become. We can choose to be satisfied with our basic endowments or we can endeavor to a higher realm, a dimension of *Being* where we realize our *Higher Self* by fully integrating these three potential *Selves* into our Purpose. As we live our Purpose, we will continually transform our *Selves* into a more complete *Being* where our Purpose becomes fully actualized.

Our Purpose is revealed by our continuing exploration and desire to achieve our *Higher Self*. As we are uniquely granted a physical, mental and spiritual form, we must seek ways to attain a state of great awareness as to what these gifts are and what we can do with them. We must observe the natural laws of our physical/living *Self* so that we maintain a robust body to carry us through life. We must become conscious of our mental/emotional *Self* so that we increase our knowledge and learn to rationally control our thoughts, thus, shaping our self-beliefs and attitudes toward life. And we must learn to appreciate and cultivate our spiritual/eternal *Self* to ensure our final rewards are manifested as eternal beings.

Discovering our *Higher Self* means that we must be continually in touch with ourselves, not through a cursory examination, but through an active, in-depth self-analysis that leads to our own version of self-enlightenment. Let's begin by trying to understand the most essential elements of our current *Self.*

Rate your current self-beliefs in on a scale of 1 to 5, with 1 being the <u>least</u> applicable and 5 being the <u>most</u> applicable:

My Mental/Emotional Self

- ☐ *I have a hopeful outlook on life.*
- ☐ *I seldom worry or feel stressed.*
- ☐ *I am contented with who I am.*
- ☐ *I feel that I am in control of my life.*
- ☐ *I am understanding and patient.*
- ☐ *I feel joyful most of the time.*
- ☐ *I enjoy a significant challenge.*
- ☐ *I am creative and seek knowledge.*
- ☐ *I am intelligent and make decisions easily.*
- ☐ *I have a good sense of humor.*
- ☐ *I enjoy loving relationships.*
- ☐ *I sense inner peace and harmony.*

_____ **Total Score**

My Physical/Living Self

☐ *I have the correct weight for my height.*
☐ *I have normal blood pressure.*
☐ *I have normal cholesterol levels.*
☐ *I am currently a non-smoker.*
☐ *I exercise on a regular basis.*
☐ *I obtain adequate rest and sleep.*
☐ *I meet current nutritional guidelines.*
☐ *I rarely become ill or injured.*
☐ *I consume alcohol in moderation.*
☐ *I feel contented with my present health.*
☐ *I am physically and aerobically strong.*
☐ *I make healthy living part of my life.*

_____ Total Score

My Spiritual/Eternal Self

☐ *I believe in God or a divine power.*
☐ *I trust and believe in the miracle of life.*
☐ *I pray or meditate on a regular basis.*
☐ *I feel a spiritual presence in my life.*
☐ *I am at peace with dying.*
☐ *I have faith in my goodness.*
☐ *I feel that I am an eternal being.*
☐ *I am accepting of other religious beliefs.*
☐ *I feel that I have a higher Purpose.*
☐ *I consider myself to be a spiritual person.*
☐ *I live by certain guiding principles.*
☐ *I sense a greater truth than myself.*

_____ Total Score

There is no correct score when we assess our current *Self.* The score we give ourselves is simply whatever the score is; we have to decide for ourselves if the score we received is acceptable to where we want our *Self* to be. By design, the foregoing sets of self-beliefs are very elementary. We could take a more complex questionnaire to assess our current *Self*, but when we make our self-concepts too complicated, we are unable to clearly see our strengths and weaknesses.

The objective here is to develop our own opinions of our *Self*. The physical/living, mental/emotional and spiritual/eternal *Selves* that we each possess can be diagnosed respectively by doctors, psychologists and spiritual leaders. Although their opinions would be helpful, we must be careful to conclude that their views are not necessarily the same as ours. It is our own conclusions that matter in terms of self-enlightenment.

As we get to know our *Selves* on a more intimate basis, we can refine our methodology to investigate very detailed and subtle variations of our self-concepts. By looking at the most basic statements that define our current *Self*, we are establishing a baseline for self-improvement. For instance, if we scored a 12 on our mental/emotional *Self*, we can see this as a benchmark to self-determine how far we want to go in pursuing a higher score. Or if we find that we scored very high in our physical/living *Self* but very low in our spiritual *Self*, we can decide what needs to be done to create a more balanced *Self*. All three components of our *Self* need to score as equally as possible. If not, we will find that we need a more holistic attention to all dimensions of our *Self*.

Again, our objective with this exercise is to establish a reference point from which we can see our needs for improvement. We also will have a score that can be used to compare our current *Self* to what we should perceive to be our *Higher Self*. Obviously, our *Higher Self*, by definition, would score very high. If we are not there yet, as evidenced by our score, we can see that we are not yet connected with our Purpose, our Values, our Vision and our Mission. As we put the power of these concepts to work, our scores will naturally improve.

How do I create more value to my *Self*?

The entire objective of reaching our *Higher Self* is to become more in control of life's significance and fulfillment. Most likely, there is a gap between where we are now and where we want to be. Our Mission is to close this gap through purposeful decision-making. If we evaluate our *Self* as a place where we are now versus a place where we want to be, we will see the gap that must be bridged to attain our *Higher Self*. Our three *Selves* are essentially our highest personal Values – the core needs for life fulfillment. The more we nurture these *Selves* or self-values, the more significance and meaning we will give to our lives.

Let's think of our three *Selves* as life accounts, much like a savings account at a bank. The more we deposit, the more value we create and the more we can withdraw at a later date. Making regular deposits to enjoy future withdrawals leads to greater life fulfillment. Our regular deposits (contributions of time, energy and focus to our *Self*) are like credits in the bank. Our regular withdrawals (personal satisfaction and fulfillment of our *Self*) are debits from the bank. We can only keep our life accounts in balance if we are continually depositing (crediting) enough to ourselves to make up for future withdrawals (debits) for ourselves.

Evaluate yourself below at the *Bank of Self-Fulfillment*:

Life Accounts (Self-Dimensions)	Credits (Contributions of Time, Energy & Focus)	Debits (Withdrawals of Self-Fulfillment)
Physical/Living	1 2 3 4 5	1 2 3 4 5
Mental/Emotional	1 2 3 4 5	1 2 3 4 5
Spiritual/Eternal	1 2 3 4 5	1 2 3 4 5
How I Rate My Life Accounts	_____	_____

Again, the score we give ourselves is not as important as our feelings about our score. Are we contributing enough to ourselves to gain greater benefits than what we are presently receiving? How much have we already deposited and how much have we already withdrawn? How much life success are we experiencing? What do we need to do differently going forward to reach a higher sense of self-fulfillment?

How do I know when I am successfully fulfilling my *Higher Self*?

The only enduring definition of life success is self-fulfillment, a state of being where we are connected to and living our Purpose. Although we tend to measure our life success with fulfillment words like money, prestige, power and position, these definitions will not hold up for the long term. Most of us spend our time, energy and focus to gain more material possessions or status in life only to discover later that their attainment was not as self-fulfilling as we had hoped. The world is full of rich and famous people who are miserable. We all know of individuals that have big names, positions or titles who are very lonely and depressed. There are numerous examples of people who appear to *have it all* yet became alcoholic or drug addicted as a means of coping with their reality.

Attainment of goals that exist outside of our Purpose and core Values will leave us feeling empty in the long run. Until we recognize what truly motivates us and then live congruently within a purposeful reality, we will always come up short in meeting our life's expectations. Successfully fulfilling our *Higher Self* means that we have attained a true sense of *Self*, consciously pursuing what matters most and manifesting these ideals in daily life. In essence, we are self-aware and self-actualized, *making life happen* in all aspects of our lives within the context of our Purpose.

Having a self-awareness of our Purpose means we are fully cognizant of our *Selves* and know how to create the life we want. We feel self-empowered, having learned to recognize our potential for life success and fulfillment. *Self-Actualization* of our Purpose means we are fully utilizing our skills, talents, resources and abilities, pro-actively *making life happen* every day of our lives. Henry David Thoreau captured this concept well:

> *If one advances confidently in the direction of his dreams, and endeavors to live the life which he has imagined, he will meet with a success unexpected in common hours. He will put some things behind, will pass an invisible boundary; new, universal, and more liberal laws will begin to establish themselves and within him; or old laws will be expanded and interpreted in his favor in a more liberal sense, and will live with a license of a higher order of beings.*

The following chart shows us the realm of the *Higher Self.* When we find ourselves in the top-right box, we are *self-actualized* and *making life happen* with choices and decisions based upon positive self-beliefs about out true potential. We know who we are, what we want and how we will attain it. To do anything less with our life will leave us with feelings of emptiness, confusion and wasted effort. Let's review the diagram and determine where we are now in our life. The realization of our *Higher Self* is within our grasp through adopting the right attitude and belief in its possibility. Let's ask ourselves where we want to be…

Realm of the Higher Self

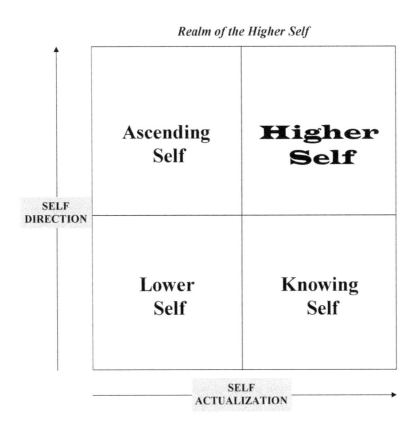

As we think of how we will reach our *Higher Self,* we must reflect upon our most compelling reasons to live with great *passion*! The more passionate we feel about our life, the more compelled we will be to act in accordance with our Purpose. Thus, our Purpose becomes synonymous with our *passion.* In fact, what other Purpose should we have than one that totally absorbs, involves and enthralls us? If we have any inkling of what truly motivates us, then that very motivation must, by definition, be inspiring and stimulating. There is really no other way to live. If our Purpose, our Vision, our Values and our Mission are not extremely motivating to us, then of what value are they?

Life is not meant to be mundane, ordinary nor boring. In order for it to be significant and meaningful, it must be relished and deeply savored. We cannot live on the sidelines unsure of our strongest convictions and desires. We have to believe so strongly in our Purpose that we literally live it in everything we do, from our life at home, to our work and to our community. When our Purpose is activated with *passion*, we will discover infinite opportunities to enjoy an intensely exciting life. Let's think back to those moments when our Purpose seemed as if it was *on-fire*, when we had that burning desire to do something and nothing could get in our way. Did we not feel profoundly immersed in our own happiness? Were we not sensing the greatest joy ever in being alive?

The human brain has an infinite capacity for this self-induced *passion*. It is a pinkish-gray, almond shaped organ weighing approximately 3-4 pounds. It consists of 100 billion neurons each capable of firing at a rate of about 80 times per second. There will never be any computer capable of producing the range of feelings, emotions and thought processes that we already possess - resting quietly between our ears. Within our brain's structure are myriad receptors for opiates such as heroin, morphine and even marijuana. The incredible thing is that we already produce these chemicals (known as endorphins) naturally within our own bodies. We already know about the *runner's high* or feats of strength from mothers lifting automobiles off of their children. These intense emotions are actually produced through our own will.

Imagine what life would be like if we could call forth these naturally *passionate* feelings whenever we wanted to? The fact is that self-induced euphoria is within our capacity to achieve whenever we desire these feelings. Ordinary people accomplish this every day of their lives by tuning into their own *passionate* attitudes toward life. They know how to achieve the *fire-in-the-belly* feelings by becoming fully engaged in their Purpose, their Values and their Mission in life. They literally become lost in their pursuit of what is most important to them. Nothing stands in their way as their *passion* fuels their brain with euphoric chemicals and intense nerve impulses. Their energy level soars, their actions are powerfully self-directed, and their passion for achievement is unstoppable!

We will find that our *passion* is most always evident in our life's work, or at least it certainly should be. As the late George Burns reminded us, *I would rather be a failure doing something I love than be a success doing something I hate.* At some point, we have all felt this *passion* to succeed and accomplish something with our life. When we passionately pursue a career or a task that is vital to us, we are certain that our Purpose is at the root of our feelings and our actions. For in knowing our Purpose, we know exactly what it is that we will do with our lives, career or otherwise. It is not difficult to find those people who are passionately pursuing what they love. These people seem to possess a certain vitality and an ability to accomplish extraordinary achievements.

Imagine for a moment we are so excited about going to work that we actually arise from bed at 5:00 AM while a blinding snowstorm rages outside; we are humming the tune from *Rocky* while making a pot of coffee; then pound our chest and let go at the top of our lungs, *I love my life!* Not something we do every morning? Sound a little strange? While rare, there are people who actually think and act like this. They believe that anything is possible with the right attitude and the right effort.

And these people are not just motivational speakers. They are everyday people who are in touch with themselves and their Purpose. They *make life happen* because they have chosen to be self-directors of their own destiny. They have realized their highest sense of *Self* by developing a positive self-image and are continually in pursuit of happiness in everything they do. They are at the peak of the hierarchy of their human needs, continuously striving to reach Abraham Maslow's concept of *self-actualization*.

Let's suppose for a moment that we really do love our job, our family, our financial situation, our health, and our future. Suppose also that we love breathing, smelling, seeing, hearing, feeling and learning. Let's assume that we think we are important, worthwhile and valuable to ourselves and to the world in which we live. We are self-confident and proud of our accomplishments. We believe that we are unstoppable in our quest. We know ourselves, what we want and expect to get what we want… and we believe that tomorrow will be an even better day.

Does this sound like a script for a Walt Disney, happy-ending movie? Perhaps, but this scenario is not as unrealistic as it may first appear. We actually can create that script for ourselves. It is purely a matter of holding self-beliefs and creating a powerful self-image based on a strong sense of Purpose. If, as we have repeatedly stated, Purpose is the meaning that we give to our life, then whatever meaning we choose will be the meaning that we live by.

If we choose our life to have little meaning, then that is exactly what we will receive. If we command a greater meaning for our lives, that belief will also make it so. William Shakespeare said, *There is nothing good or bad, but thinking makes it so.* Virtually every aspect of our lives can be controlled through our thought processes. Our attitude is paramount. We can become the person we wish through adopting a passionate attitude of great expectations.

We would do well to follow the advice in the following passage:

> **The longer I live, the more I realize the impact of attitude on life. Attitude, to me, is more important that facts. The remarkable thing is that we have a choice everyday regarding the attitude we will embrace for that day. We cannot change our past. We cannot change the inevitable. The only thing that we can do is play upon the one string we have, and that is our attitude. I am convinced that life is ten percent what happens to me and ninety percent how I react to it.**
>
> **- Charles Swindoll**

Self-realization and the attainment of our *Higher Self* is the direct result of *self-actualizing* our Purpose. We reach our highest human potential not through what happens to us but through what we allow to happen to us. If we take life's events at face value, assume that they are our destiny and agonize over their presence, then we will have succumbed to a future that we no longer control. If, however, we adopt the attitude that life's events are merely occurrences, that they deserve no more importance than what we ascribe to them, then we can become the master and life becomes our servant.

Thus, self-realization is not just the identification of our most inner needs and expectations but rather their reflection in the way we feel about ourselves and in how we choose to approach life. Essentially, our *Self* becomes *actualized* through our thoughts, our self-beliefs and our actions, all of which are based upon a passionate purpose-driven attitude.

We must acknowledge that we are not simply a *Self*, some amorphous thing that sits on a shelf in a dark corner of the room, complete in its own essence. Our *Self* is a living, breathing, learning, acting, doing, thinking human being. Our *Self* moves through life, facing continuous stimulation that requires continuous responses. It survives and prospers by coming out of the dark, out of its basic shell, and then charging into the brightness of each day, participating with great Purpose and Vision. The choice we must make is whether to let our *Self* turn into Shaw's *tired, selfish clod with grievances that the world is not making us happy*, or a *Self* that passionately realizes what it is, what it wants and what it is going to do. Taking the higher road ultimately leads us to our *Higher Self*, where we never have to regret the choices that we made - because they were the choices we meant to make.

We can only believe in our Purpose after first believing in our Self!

Discovering our true *Self* comes not only from answering the hard questions about who we think we are, but rather by molding the self-image of who we want to be. Self-imagining is a powerful tool for determining our feelings about success and what we want our lives to actually look and feel like. It is well documented that if we hold ourselves in low esteem, this self-concept will generally lead to a series of life-long failures, whereas an attitude of supreme self-confidence and self-worth will generally lead to greater life success and happiness. Whether we choose to feel inferior or superior is a matter of personal choice.

This is not to imply that we can just flip a few switches and then radiate supreme confidence, but we can with practiced effort over time develop a mental picture of ourselves as achieving, purposeful individuals. As we carry a higher sense of self-confidence around with us and act as if we are unstoppable, we will find that our string of small victories will build upon themselves, creating even more momentum for success. When Dwight Eisenhower was asked how he would feel if his invasion forces had been turned back in Normandy, he said, *I don't know. I never let that thought enter my mind.* We, as well, can develop mental pictures of ourselves as always winning, gaining, enjoying, succeeding, and those powerful suggestions will more often than not produce those exact results.

Conversely, we can take a self-defeated attitude. That self-suggestion will lead to failure in itself, as that is exactly what we will have imagined for ourselves. Again, the choice is ours: We can either feel that we have a strong Purpose and a passionate life force within us, or we can feel that we are merely victims and our lives serve little meaning or Purpose. Either set of feelings will determine the results we are seeking.

The concept of developing a positive self-image was well-documented by Dr. Maxwell Maltz in his renowned study of *psycho-cybernetics.* As a plastic surgeon, he had ample opportunity to study the effects of self-images through changing the appearance of his patients. He found that making people beautiful did not necessarily make them feel beautiful unless they also acquired a psychological face-lift. Changing one's appearance did little to change the person unless there was a concomitant change in self-image.

He further discovered that *positive thinking* only works if we develop a self-image that is affirmative and then carry that perception or attitude over a period of time (usually a minimum of twenty one days). That is, we must *experience* our positive self-image before it becomes part of us. For the same reason that we develop negative perceptions of ourselves due to past experiences, we can just as easily develop positive perceptions of ourselves through future experiences that support this self-image. That is, we can unlearn our feelings of inferiority, replacing them with positive concepts of ourselves.

Having a powerful and passionate self-image based upon a clear sense of Purpose and then living that Purpose over time will ensure the higher results we are seeking. We literally have a built-in success mechanism that is powered by our sense of Purpose. We were born with the natural capacity for achieving happiness and success. If we derail ourselves along the way, it is purely a consequence of our learning a negative self-image that we have used to guide us through life. If, however, we choose to rediscover our

Purpose, renew our faith in ourselves and restart our lives with a positive self-image, we will be unstoppable.

Will we take the path to our Higher Self?

To decide if the path to our *Higher Self* is worth the effort, we must learn to accept the truth about our *Selves* and our God-given potential. We need to recognize that our past has little bearing on who we can become in the future. If we truly accept the fact that the future course of our lives is within our power to change, we can develop a conception of ourselves that is continually renewing for successful results. We will have nothing to lose by passionately believing in ourselves. Our only regret will be in not trying.

As we read the remainder of this book, we will guide ourselves toward a discovery of our *Higher Self*, the ultimate result of self-enlightenment. We will discover our real *Self* by gaining an acute awareness of our Purpose, our Vision, our Values and our life's Mission. We will design a life of great Purpose by making decisions and choices that are clear and controlled only by us. We will understand and apply the principles of mental mastery, time and goal management, and techniques for living a focused and balanced life. Most importantly, we will learn how to recognize our true *Selves* and then how to grow and transform into our *Higher Selves*.

In the next chapter, we will learn the process for closing the gap between our *Essential Self* and our *Potential Self.* We will learn how to climb our growth curve and make self-renewal part of daily living. We will begin to understand the most important things to us, how to prioritize our Values and make them the basis for all of our choices and decisions. We will also learn why we so often fail to reach our true potential and discover how to overcome the barriers that are thrown in our way. The path to our *Higher Self* puts us in charge of our life again, where we are aware of our Purpose and are consciously putting it into action.

To do this, we must travel on a path that puts to work the power of the *Purpose Principle*, where the realization of our *Higher Self* is gained through the knowledge and application of Purpose in our life. Discovering and living our Purpose is an exciting and valuable process, an endeavor that we should not take lightly. While we may decide that life is simply easier to comprehend or to *just get through* by not focusing on these higher concepts, we may one day find that we gave up too much.

For us to live without any conscious Purpose is to live without self-worth and self-esteem, where we will have allowed our personal *Self* to wallow in its own untapped potential. It would be tragic to let our lives simply waste into oblivion where our fate was dictated by forces outside of our control and outside the parameters of our chosen Purpose. Our lives are far too valuable to be relegated to the vagaries of chance and aimless wandering. If we look back and wonder what could have been, we will have lost in the game of life.

But if we look back and realize the path we took was ours, that our decisions where based on our Purpose, we will never have to regret the outcome. Our reward will be to know that we have lived our life the best way we knew how, that we were in control and that we alone decided our Purpose and our ultimate fate.

CHAPTER SIX

What Is My True Potential?
Realizing My Higher Self

All of the significant battles are waged within the self.
Sheldon Kopp

The process of self-renewal or self-change is one of life's greatest ironies. We demand the right to change but resist our entitlement to do so. The compelling reason for this is that change requires choices. While this opportunity provides us unlimited freedom, it also tends to paralyze us. We don't wish to be limited by the options in front of us but we also fear the risk of exercising them. We fight self-change because it removes us from our comfort zone of predictability, opening us up to the risk of failure. Our commonly held belief is that since change involves risk, we can just avoid the change and, thus, avoid the risk. This attitude, however, results in the self-limitation of remaining who we presently are rather than opening the door to who we can become.

Intellectually, we know that we must change in order to grow. It is the natural order of the universe. We tend to accept the change of seasons, changes in the weather, and even accept, albeit reluctantly, the changes in our bodies as we age. We know that we have little power over these types of changes. But the changes that we do control require some action on our part, and it is our fear to act that limits us. Yet, this same fear limits our potential for personal growth and our opportunity for realizing our *Higher Self*.

Moreover, reaching our *Higher Self* means we must let go of parts of our existing *Self*, consciously accept change, and be willing to *grow forward*. We must recognize that by not accepting this process we can, in fact, actually *grow backwards*. Resisting these changes is senselessly self-destructive. We receive absolutely no value nor personal benefit in living a risk-free existence.

Our vain attempt to avoid all risks atrophies our *Self*, relegating it to an empty shell of wasted energy. Taking risks, however, is a liberating experience. It fuels the passions of our *Self,* giving us the joyful experience of being totally alive. Most significantly, risk taking lets us discover and enjoy the benefits of growth and the new opportunities that await us.

Without question, much of the change that we will face in our lives may not give us many options to consider. For that reason alone, we could not map out our lives with changeless predictability even if we wanted to. The world is continually changing around us and sweeping us along with it. We cannot resist this dynamic change simply because it doesn't fit our comfortable conception of what we wish reality to be. Reality does not care a great deal about what we want it to be. Thus, we are literally forced at times to *Wake-Up* to new dimensions of our *Self.*

The important thing is to be embracing change while reshaping our *Self* in terms of what is most important to us. As George Bernard Shaw told us, *the reasonable man adapts himself to the world. The unreasonable man persists in trying to adapt the world to himself. Therefore, all progress depends on the unreasonable man.* Our only valid option is to demand our right to choose, to change, and to grow with a clear sense of Purpose. The world in which we live then becomes an adaptation to our own sense of *Self,* conforming to us rather than us conforming to the world.

How do I accept change in my life?

We must first recognize that change is unavoidable. It is also accelerating in our lives at a tremendous pace, creating intense pressure on us to adapt quickly. Mankind has now been on earth for approximately 800 lifetimes, and for the first 794 of these lifetimes nothing much happened in terms of our need to adapt. By the 795th lifetime, however, the explosion of knowledge and technological innovation has forced us to rethink all of our assumptions about daily life - culturally, socially, politically and economically. The cybernetic revolution of computers and the Internet has occurred in our 800th lifetime and has completely thrown us into a tailspin of new realities. Even more important, the time intervals in which we must react to change have shortened dramatically, forcing us into constant re-evaluations of what is most important in our lives.

Our current scenario is more difficult to manage than anything we have encountered before, undoubtedly creating for us more tension and stress than our forefathers had to deal with. But we cannot exist in isolation of the continual state of flux that surrounds us; rather, we must decide the manner in which we will adapt, respond, relate and cope with this change. We must decide and settle upon the level of meaning our life will take despite what is happening around us.

The key for us is not to focus upon the change that we cannot control but rather to focus upon the expectations and needs of the *Self*. Our *Self* is where stability should reside while the world around us remains unstable. This does not imply that we become *selfish* and never accept responsibility for the world in which we live. Instead, we must adapt the world to our *Self*. We must become the *unreasonable man,* the agent for changing our perception of the world to conform to our own sense of *Self*.

We accomplish this by not permitting the world to dictate our life; rather, we modify our world-views so that it is becomes adapted to us. If we do not set the pace for change, we will continually be forced to adapt to changes that we do not control. Change, in fact, should not even be our concern. We should welcome it as the opportunity presented to us for growth and renewal. Our only concern is to manage it relative to our own Purpose and Values. We are the *change-agents* and we determine what matters most. Sustaining our self-discovery is a process of change, one in which we must be making courageous, yet difficult, choices and decisions.

Our process for change is threefold: First, we must engage ourselves in thorough self-reflection on the needs and expectations that define our *Self*. We must identify those feelings that are most important to us (our highest wants and aspirations); Second, we must consider the design of our *Life Plan* for achieving our life goals (where we want to go and how are we going to get there); and Third, we must actualize our plan into specific commitments and behavior (the consciously applied effort of putting Purpose into our daily life). Again, our choices reflect the Purpose Statement we earlier adopted for ourselves. Our Purpose drives our Vision, our Vision drives our Values, and our Values drive the Choices we will make in our daily behavior and how we choose to spend our time.

Our decisions will be clear once we have a clear Purpose and know what we most desire in our lives. We will not fear change, but rather welcome it, especially if we feel that our life is not being lived in accordance with our Purpose. Once we accept change we have the opportunity to grow into our *Higher Self* and will eagerly seek every opportunity to become who we want to be.

But aren't their risks to changing my life?

All of life is change, and all change can and should be self-change. Our process of self-renewal means we must accept this mandate in our lives, in the same way we accept the change of seasons. We sense the need to change, either through a *Wake-Up Call* in our lives or through a more subtle dissatisfaction with our current situation. We then can begin the process by rationally analyzing our choices from which we can act upon.

Risk-taking is difficult for us because it is tied to our emotional self-image. If we accept the risk of change with negative emotions, we feel self-defeated, yet if we accept the same change with positive emotions, we will feel that we have grown and matured into our *Higher Self*. By accepting our responsibility to grow, we embrace a reflective and expressive view of ourselves.

Again, our greatest enemies to this process are self-doubt and fear. Together, they destroy our courage to grow. But as Franklin D. Roosevelt warned us, *The only limit to our realization of tomorrow will be our doubts of today.* These doubts are, in fact, the greatest threat to our lives today, even greater than heart disease and cancer. When we don't grow, we wither and die. Richard J. Leider (The Inventure Group) in his book *Life Skills*, refers to this self-limitation as *Inner Kill*. He describes it as *the art of dying without knowing it.*

Thus, we experience *Inner Kill* when we avoid decisions and let *life just happen* without any thought as to where we are going. This occurs when we talk about what we are going to do and then do nothing about it. *Inner Kill* is just the opposite of self-renewal. It is allowing circumstances to control us rather than us controlling them. It is due to staying in our comfort zone and not taking risks. It is being afraid to live. It is being afraid to die.

Death, however, can be life's greatest teacher as it demands that we live in the now. Although our greatest fear is death, once we accept its inevitability, we should no longer fear it. Death is only to be feared by those who are afraid to live. In fact, the mere reality of death should make us want to live with even more Purpose. Our greatest mistake is to realize too late that every day we have to live, the time we are allowed to possess, is the most precious commodity we own. This very moment in time, the moment that you are reading these words, is the most important thing you own in this life. Death, therefore, is not be feared if we live each moment with great Purpose. The only thing we should ever fear is a life without meaning.

Our fear of living is with us subconsciously, but pervasively. We fear living because we fear our *Selves* and the consequences of our decisions. When we fail to act, we are saying that we don't trust ourselves with the responsibility to act, that we lack the self-confidence to make decisions that we will have to live by. But it is our failure to act today that means we must live with the consequences of tomorrow. We must realize that our time to live is a finite commodity, much like a product to be consumed. Unfortunately, once it has been consumed, we cannot go to the store and buy more of it. It must always be consumed with Purpose!

We, therefore, should approach our life much differently, with greater intensity for living and making decisions - today! To avoid our own *Inner Kill*, we must realize that by our failure to act, we will limit our opportunity to get another chance. We should not take for granted every moment we have to live, to learn, to share, to love, to grow. Our time is ours; it should never be used unwisely or squandered on things that do not matter. Our greatest tragedy would be to look back at our life, saying to ourselves, *If only I had…*

Living with *no regrets* places the responsibility upon us, not just to decide what we want out of life but to then go and achieve it. Since we have a finite timetable for life, why not decide today what risks we are willing to take and then begin the process of taking them. Why not decide today if we are going to allow *life to just happen to us* or if we are going to take charge and *make us happen to life*? Will we answer this question for ourselves or will we let others answer it for us? Will we act out of fear or out of courage? If we decide to *go for it*, what will *It* be? What will the rest of our life look and feel like?

How do I decide what that should be?

A solution would be to take our Purpose Statement and translate it into an action plan. If our strongest motivation is our family, then what can we do to enhance our relationship with them? If our highest motivation for living is our spiritual quest, then why not map out an action plan of ministry? If our Purpose is to live with thrilling excitement, then why not take up a more adventurous lifestyle? Or if our Purpose is centered around knowledge and enlightenment, then why not return to school and initiate a career as a professor or a researcher? There are perhaps hundreds of things we may wish to do with our life before we die.

Whatever we decide to do, however, nothing will happen unless we consciously decide to actually *make it happen*. Whether our desire is to go to the moon or just to make a better pot of chili, we need to assign a high degree of significance to its undertaking, enough importance so that we will not be deterred from our efforts. Nike has said it best in their advertising, *Just do it!* We may come up short in some of our desires, but we should never come up short in our efforts.

Undoubtedly, there will be tradeoffs or compromises that we will need to make, but if we believe firmly enough in our Purpose, we will never miss what we have to give up. The important thing is to not look back if we firmly believe in our Purpose and what will bring new meaning to our lives. As Ralph Waldo Emerson told us, *Unless you try to do something beyond what you have already mastered, you will never grow.* The one thing we cannot do is fear trying.

The first step in our path to self-renewal and growth is to decide what we want our future life to look like. As life literally consists of our actual experiences, we should map out those experiences that we wish to enjoy as we go down the path of life. Based upon the conviction of our Purpose, let's decide what would bring more enthusiasm and excitement to our future. From this day forward, let's forget the fears that have led to our inaction in the past.

What is it that we have always wanted to do? To try? To experience? Let's make a Master Wish or "Bucket" List of everything we want to do with the rest of our life:

My Master Wish List

1.	11.	21.	31.
2.	12.	22.	32.
3.	13.	23.	33.
4.	14.	24.	34.
5.	15.	25.	35.
6.	16.	26.	36.
7.	17.	27.	37.
8.	18.	28.	38.
9.	19.	29.	39.
10.	20.	30.	40.

List and number everything that you always wanted to do, even if the list needs extra pages. Let your creativity run wild for a moment. Nothing is too ridiculous or impossible, e.g. ride a camel, climb Mount Everest, work with a charitable organization in Calcutta, earn a Ph.D., solve a murder, meet the President, etc. You should place a check mark next to each item so that you can note every time you actually did something on your list. While you most likely won't realize every wish on your list, the fact that you wrote them down and endeavored to make them happen will surprisingly make many of them come true.

We are born on this earth without any fear of failure. Every aspect of an infant's being is geared toward accomplishment and achievement. They literally demand success in their quest for food, comfort, love and warmth. Just try to stop them in their pursuits and watch what happens! They are created with the genetic program that tells them to learn, grow, challenge, change and evolve into complete human beings. Thus, we all begin our human lives knowing no other way to exist. But somewhere along the way, we are advised by wise and caring parents to be afraid of certain things. This advice established our initial fear response, and with too much of this programming we ultimately become afraid of our own shadow. Eventually, we *unlearn* our natural tendencies toward successful achieving and, in some extreme cases begin to question our ability to do almost anything.

Babies are not afraid of airplanes, bridges, snakes, spiders or other phobias. They are taught to be afraid. Nor are they afraid of public speaking, telling their boss what they want, or of putting strange things into their mouth. They are conditioned to not take chances only after some trial and error experimentation and some negative programming from their environment. The point is not to try foolish things, but rather to realize that we are naturally inclined to achieve and only fear trying because of our reprogrammed attitudes. We must not let these acquired negative programs inhibit us from accepting the mandates of growth and change.

How do I know when I need to change?

If change is inevitable, then growth is inevitable. We learn; we change; we grow. It is an immutable fact of life, something we are powerless to stop. The best way to understand the process is to look at the growth curve that is governing our lives, a simple S-curve that demonstrates the waxing and waning of change and how we should control it, respond to it, and learn from it.

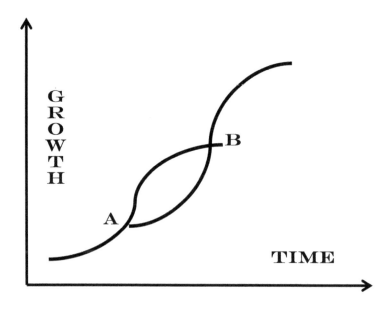

We begin on the curve with the potential for growth, and then travel upward as we experiment and learn about life. The pace accelerates as we move up the steep edge of the curve and just before it declines downward we start a new curve, **at point A**, and renew the learning and growing process.

Our second growth curve needs to begin at **point A** because at this precise moment in time we have the energy and resources to start anew, fresh and ready for a new challenge. If we hesitate, we stagnate and our growth stops, turning us downward into the non-productive backside of the first curve. At **point B** on the first curve, we face hopelessness, where our emotional energy is so depleted it is difficult to start a new growth curve. The key is to start the second growth curve at **point A** to keep our future bright and promising.

Often times, we get stuck in the overlapped area because we are confused about our choices and what actions we should take. We receive conflicting information or we are unsure of our Purpose and Values, at which point our minds are muddled about what to do next. This is a critical moment for us. If we don't take risks to move ahead, we soon leave the overlapped area of indecision and begin the trek downward to **point B** where it is more difficult to jump-start a new growth curve.

If we have clarity in our Purpose, Vision and Values, we are always self-renewing new growth at **point A**. We must continually be **point A** (second curve) thinkers to keep us moving forward and upward through life and in a positive direction. This requires discipline and possibility thinking at all times but the payoff is great. We gain our own lives back and enjoy the rewards of greater success in everything we do. And most importantly, instead of *Inner Kill*, we gain *Inner Peace*.

Can I improve my life at any time?

Being human, we always seem to learn more from our failures than from our successes. By taking risks in life, we will expose ourselves to making mistakes, but those very same mistakes are what teach us the most. Growth is a learning process and it continues throughout every stage of life. If we stop the growth process, we succumb to *Inner Kill*. We must learn to play the opposite card of *Inner Kill* which, according to Richard

Leider, is *Living at risk, on one's growth edge… Life is seen as an error-making and an error-correcting process. We learn over time; our problems become our teachers.*

The Japanese refer to this process of continuous self-improvement as *Kaizen*. Their assumption for success is to be forever searching. They take the long view and are never complacent about where they are. They always strive to be on the second growth curve in their approach to life and business. If we can learn anything from the *Kaizen* concept, it is to question the established way of doing things and keep searching for a better way.

We usually don't perceive the need for this curvilinear logic when everything is going well in our lives. As we are ascending up the curve, life is good and we see no need for change. The paradox we face is that what got us where we are today won't necessarily keep us there tomorrow. This point was well defined by Oliver Wendell Holmes when he said, *The greatest thing in this world is not so much where we are, but in what direction we are moving.*

In order to continuously grow and succeed, we have to start our second curve before the first one ends. In essence, we have to keep starting over before we reach an ending. This gets more difficult as we get older, but as soon as we quit practicing our *Kaizen*, our lives begin to whither and head into a long decline. Understanding the growth curve will help us understand the endings, the beginnings, and the transitions that make up our lives. Innovating new solutions and risk taking is the hallmark of growth. Continuous improvement lets us be in charge of the outcomes we are seeking. We must be attentive and receptive to every opportunity to remove our uncertainty.

How do I know if I am living up to my potential?

In order to realize our full potential, we must consider the balance between who we are versus who we could become. There is an *Essential Self* in all of us that is basically our genetic makeup, our talents and our potential to become a complete person. Outside of our *Essential Self* resides the world and the environment in which we interact. This is where our *Essential Self* operates. It is the place of possibilities where our mind and our actions go to work every day. It is where we can expand our limits and grow into our *Higher Self*. Jean Paul Sartre, the existentialist, told us, *Man is not the sum of what he has but the totality of what he does not yet have, of what he might have.* We are, therefore, defined by our innate abilities combined with our willingness to develop and maximize their full potential.

This is best understood by visualizing the *inside-out doughnut*, a concept from Charles Handy in *The Age of Paradox*. He described this conceptual doughnut as having the hole on the outside and the dough in the middle. To extrapolate from this, we can understand our potential for growth by looking at the relationship between the core of the doughnut and the bounded space on the outside. This doughnut image embodies our *Essential Self* as the core that is surrounded by the open flexible space of opportunity for change and growth. The key is to balance the relationship between the two areas of our lives. If we are only core and no space, we are not tapping into our potential. If our open space is too large, meaning we make our realm of possibilities too difficult to handle, we will just drift without any initiative in life. We need to take a critical look at what our core looks like and decide how large we wish our outer space to be. And we must then decide to what extent we wish to be involved in our larger space of opportunity.

To realize our full potential, we must continuously measure the size of these two spaces and keep them in harmonious balance. It is easy to imagine the conflict and the implications by choosing to ignore this balance. For example, if Albert Einstein, whose core was filled with great intelligence, decided to live his life as a street sweeper, he would have contributed little to himself or to others. Conversely, a man of feeble mind who wanted to pursue quantum physics as a career might find his goals coming up a little short. Common sense tells us that if we can't sing, we shouldn't audition at the Met or if we are only five feet tall, we shouldn't try out for an NBA basketball team. And a woman of great spirit and creativity will not find fulfillment working on an assembly line. Although these examples seems obvious, it is surprising how few of us really put the doughnut principle to work in our lives. In our careers, we often find ourselves with jobs that are nearly all space with little core or no boundary. Or we may find ourselves in jobs that are just core and no boundary in which to expand. In other words, we could find ourselves in the position of working in a job with little discretion to make decisions while we are capable of handling more responsibility. Or we could be tremendously empowered to take charge, yet we have not equipped ourselves with the necessary skills to make any impact.

We need boundaries in order to feel secure that our capabilities are matched with our responsibilities. But as importantly, we must decide if they are in balance. Too large of a boundary will have us floundering in too many directions, while too small a boundary will frustrate us because our talents are not being utilized. A sensible approach is to strive for a balanced doughnut. More space in the outer circle gives us more choice, but too much choice confuses us and causes us to make the wrong decisions. Too little space relative to the core of our *Essential Self* stymies our growth because of the lack of opportunity for us to grow. We need to keep pushing out the boundaries of the outer space but only to the extent that we can continually fill our inner doughnut.

This becomes the ongoing challenge for us. Make our outer doughnut keep growing but keep filling it with the inner doughnut. As we take risks and move in new directions, both the inner and outer doughnut will keep inflating. If stress or incongruence occurs, we need to let out a little air. If we feel like we are stagnating, then we must pump some more air into it. If the outer doughnut gets to large relative to the inner doughnut, then we need to adjust the pressure in each accordingly.

The doughnut concept works by knowing our talents as well as our Purpose, our Vision, our talents and our Mission. We fill the outer doughnut by knowing our limitations, by taking risks, and by making decisions that are congruent with the contents of the inner doughnut. We have the freedom to design our own doughnut, to define the space where our limits can be expanded. But most importantly, we should never let it be empty.

Why do I fail at realizing my true potential?

Realizing our true potential involves self-knowledge, self-acceptance and self-guidance. As we gain greater awareness of ourselves and take positive, purposeful action we begin to validate our potential. This validation of our potential creates a *success-reality* for us that in turn will carry us toward higher achievements. The key is to convince our *Selves* of this possibility. Our failure to do this is usually because we are not convinced enough. We simply don't believe that we can do it!

Essentially, we fail to produce positive results due to the self-sabotage taking place in our sub-conscious minds. There are powerful *mind-triggers* that hold us back just as their equally powerful *mind-triggers* that tell us to go for it. We listen to our negative sub-consciousness because of imbedded commands that have been programmed into us, i.e. little voices that we have heard for many years from parents, teachers, spouses, bosses and even our best friends. We don't receive nearly as much positive reinforcement from others as we get reasons why it can't be done: We are told that we need more experience! We have never done it before! We don't have enough education! We can't afford it! We have to take care of this or that problem first! We should be content with who we are! We need to take care of other responsibilities! For some bizarre reason, people just don't like to encourage us to succeed. But the far greater problem is that we tend to listen to them. And believe them!

Positive programming must, therefore, come from our inner *Selves*. Our imbedded commands, if negative, need to be overruled and replaced by new affirmative commands. Since we know our capabilities and our talents better than anyone else, we should know what we want from life. We are in charge of our own destiny and cannot allow others, our circumstances or our environment to determine it for us. Regardless of the negative programming we receive, we must not allow these undermining messages to take hold in our subconscious minds.

We need to trust and believe in ourselves. As our actions are dictated by our thoughts, we must diligently and relentlessly pursue a positive, can-do attitude. If we find ourselves accepting anything less, we are holding nobody back but ourselves. To sustain positive self-beliefs, we should only use strong action statements when describing ourselves: I AM ENERGETIC! I AM POWERFUL! I AM A GENIUS! I AM SUCCESSFUL! I AM UNSTOPPABLE! We should never let negative verbiage enter our self-vocabulary when we can just as easily use more assertive words to define who we are.

It is a complete waste of time for us to not believe in ourselves. If we are not going for more in life, then we will always be going for less. For us to get what we want from life, we must first want it; then we must go for it. In fact, we should never say that we want something and not go for it.

Some time ago, a young man was observing the golfing legend Gary Player hitting perfect golf shots, one after another, on a practice range before a tournament. After Gary was through, the young man walked up to him and commented how he would give anything to hit a golf ball like that. Gary looked at the young man, quickly sized him up and said he didn't believe him. To the young man's surprised and puzzled face, Gary said, *If you really wanted to hit a golf ball like me, you would be out here first thing every morning and hit balls until your hands bleed, then you would go inside the clubhouse, wrap your hands in gauze and tape, then come back out and hit another thousand balls. When you are prepared to do that every day for many years, then I'll believe you want to hit a golf ball like me.* The young man then realized the difference between wanting something and making the sacrifice to attain it.

To realize our potential, we must first master ourselves. Real self-mastery is accepting what we believe in as being true. We must then attain the proper tools to make it happen, that is, the skills required to take action. Finally, we must leave the comfort zone of wishful thinking and then take action. Our most dominant thoughts will move us in the direction of what is most important to us. The key for us is to have these dominant thoughts. What we think about the most will expand the power of that thought. What we think about the least will diminish the power of that thought. Thus, our minds give power to those thoughts that we choose for ourselves. We are what we think; our actions are what we do. The choices we make will determine the results we seek. This is the only secret to realizing our true potential and our personal success.

CHAPTER SEVEN

What Is The Value Of My Life?
Going Forward with Purpose

Affirmation of life is the spiritual act by which man ceases to live unreflectively and begins to devote himself to his life with reverence in order to raise it to its true value. To affirm life is to deepen, to make it more inward, and to exalt the will to live.
Albert Schweitzer

We are a composite of what we believe to be worth pursuing; that is, our *Self* is literally defined by its highest Values – *our greatest aspirations and expectations*. If we do not aspire to nor value anything, our *Self* has no validity or reason to exist. If, however, we have great expectations and are passionately pursuing them, we will have created vast significance and meaning to our life.

Indeed, the value of life itself is predicated upon the intensity of the Values we are in pursuit of. The more intensely we target our highest aspirations, the more Value we bestow to life. As Walter Lippman told us, *Ignore what a man desires and you ignore the very source of his power.* By knowing what we most desire - *the Values that are most important to us* - we will know who we are and possess the power to act with conviction and Purpose, to self-determine our own meaning of life.

By actively living in accordance with our Values, we actually create the value of our life. In fact, we are comfortable with our choices and decisions once we are in touch with them. While we may not be consciously aware of their general presence in our daily activities, they are always there - behind the scenes, guiding us in all that we do. And as we knowingly and deliberately make decisions based upon our highest Values we will be experiencing the full value of life.

How do my Values specifically guide me?

With our Values governing virtually everything in our life, we know how to respond appropriately to any situation we encounter. We will act from *the inner to the outer*, meaning that our Values - the aspiring forces within us - will always determine our external behavior. And as we face our many challenges, we will have the satisfaction of knowing that we are always acting in harmony with the Values that support our Purpose. Our Values, therefore, become our code of conduct since any violation of our Values is literally a repudiation of the beliefs we have chosen to live by.

As a combined set of rules, our Values then become our instruction manual for life. We may choose them based on criteria unique to us, but once they are internalized we tend to honor and hold them sacred. If we ever change a Value or the relative importance of one to another, we should do so only after great soul-searching and introspection. From time to time, we may actually question how important they are to us, but unless we can rationalize a change, we will experience enough internal turmoil that we will quickly return to them.

The feeling of doing what is most important to us is not necessarily governed by what we perceive as right or moral, although morality may play a large part in our Values. Rather, our doing the right thing depends upon the feeling that our actions are congruent to what we hold to be the most important things to us. This creates the feeling that what we do is always the right thing. When our behavior conflicts with our Values, we create stress and dissatisfaction within ourselves. And when our daily behavior doesn't support our deepest needs and desires, we will lack a sense of fulfillment in our lives. We may even achieve a goal that we desire, but if we have to give up a set of beliefs in doing so we are never truly happy with our accomplishment.

Our Values then become the ultimate predictors of our behavior. As the governing influence in our lives, they determine who our friends are, whom we marry, what careers we choose, and even the clothes we wear and the food we eat. Our ability to reason with clarity and Purpose, and the judgment we employ in handling life's complex situations is based upon the Values we choose to live by. We must, therefore, be clear as to what they are as they tell us who we really are.

Our key to reaching our personal goals and ultimate happiness is from knowing our Values, where they came from, how they influence our decisions, whether or not they are in balance with each other, and if they are congruent with our behavior. Carl Jung, the eminent psychologist, stated, *Your vision will become clear only when you can look into your own heart. Who looks outside, dreams; who looks inside, awakens.* Thus, we gain the freedom to act with a conscious Purpose once we have the insights of what is really most important to us. Our Values will guide us in the direction we wish to go, providing us inner peace and the confidence of knowing we are creating a valuable life.

So where do my Values come from?

The Values we live by are shaped by many forces. They are sometimes chosen consciously, but more often they are absorbed through subliminal messages from our environment. In order for a society or a civilization to survive, it must have a basic set of rules or ideals that promote harmony and peaceful coexistence amongst its members. Thus, we are continually influenced by our parents, spiritual leaders, politicians, educators, and those we work with. We also pick up our Values through the influences of television or from role models that we admire. And we are continually influenced with rules, regulations, explanations, symbols, slogans, lessons, and numerous rewards and punishments, all of which set the stage for our Value-system.

Most of our Values were actually established early in life. Our parents played the largest role through a punishment - reward process. If we did as we were told, we received praise; if we rebelled, we were disciplined. Essentially, our parents were programming our first Value-system into us. As we aged, we received Values from our peer groups - friends, neighbors, schoolmates - who gave us positive reinforcement for thinking like them or rejected us if we thought differently from them. Since acceptance had its own emotional reward, we adjusted our Values to the peer group we associated with. Our peer group could be a sports team, a church group or for that matter a gang of car thieves, depending on the Values we held at the time we interacted with this new group.

Throughout life, we will continually meet new peer groups with Values different from ours. We will choose to blend, adjust, change or adopt new Values depending upon the circumstances. We may even find ourselves changing the Values of these groups because of the strength and conviction of our Values as perceived by them.

We are also greatly affected by the Values of our country, the company we work for, or even the neighborhood we live in. These are all groups that we live with and seek support from. We will tend to share the same Values of the people in these groups or we will soon find ourselves changing our groups. If we sense enough internal conflict, we may even move to another neighborhood, to another company and even to another country. If our life in any community conflicts with our Values, we will address this incongruity by either changing or mediating our Values within that community or we will seek out another community where this conflict doesn't exist.

Which Values should I chose?

The dilemma we face, however, is sorting through the complex and competing diversity of Values that are presented to us every day. Our parents will present us with ideals that may conflict with our peer groups. Our churches will preach one set of Values to live by while Hollywood entices and tempts us to choose another set of Values. Our long standing historical and cultural Values will conflict with New Age, counter-cultural, alternative Values. We also have conservative versus liberal political Values; Protestant versus Catholic Values and even geographical Values, such as the northern versus southern way of doing things.

As teenagers, our most vulnerable age for value creation, we are expected to make decisions on becoming part of a group: prep, grunge, skater, jock, druggie, nerd, metal head, rapper, etc. The pressure of clothing styles, music groups, cults and competing cliques leave the young set in a constant state of imbalance regarding their clarification of Values. And as adults, we will continue to have many options for choosing our source of Values. We will model ourselves after different types of people, including those we find to be successful or rich, funny or popular, educated or wise, and caring or compassionate. The smorgasbord of Values will always be demanding our attention, providing us plenty of competing choices to consider.

Our own self-image also determines our tendency to change or adopt new Values. Therefore, we will choose those Values that raise our highest sense of self-worth and self-esteem. Often times, we will see others who possess qualities that we feel we don't have, forcing us to change our own *Self* to fit a new image. For instance, we may see ourselves as wanting to have a greater, more heroic sense of who we can be. Thus, we will model ourselves after certain heroes and role models, that in turn, will better shape our feelings toward ourselves. These can be movie stars, world leaders, a priest, a sports star, a professor, our boss at work, or our own parents. These mentors come from all walks in life and will continually influence our choice of Values.

But despite our free choice in Value creation, we seldom adopt a Value to live by through our conscious decision-making. We may reflect upon the things we do based on subconscious emotions, but rarely do we add or delete a Value deliberately. Our Value system more or less seeps into our subconscious flow of thinking. We may know that we Value honesty, but that is not because we woke up one morning and said, *Starting today I'm going to be an honest person.* Rather, we adopt Values over a period of time because of the benefits or rewards that seem to result from that Value. It is possible that we may decide to live honestly after a life of lying but this usually occurs after some life-changing event. For instance, some of us may actually place a high Value on theft and stealing, but after being arrested for it, we may decide while sitting in jail that this Value won't be as important to us after we get out.

Usually though, our assimilation of Values comes to us in a more subtle, less obvious manner. Thus, we unconsciously absorb our Values as we walk through life. In our daily activities, we either feel comfortable with our self-identification or we feel that something is missing in ourselves. We may value an image of being frugal and then fret that our car is too ostentatious or we may value the appearance of success and then worry that our car is beneath our image. We won't always know why we do the things we do or why we feel the things that we feel. We will know, however, that if something is out of sync between our Values and our behavior we will have to make a change.

Regardless of our confusing array of choices, we are ultimately responsible for the set of Values that we choose to live by. And we must act congruently with what we believe to be our greatest needs and expectations. For example, if our highest Value is our family and our job requires constant travel away from home, we will feel the pressure to secure a job that doesn't require as much travel. Or if we value integrity and our boss expects us to conclude deceitful deals with our clients, we will know that we cannot continue to work in that type of environment. If we value wealth and prestige, yet feel that we are stuck in a dead end career path, we will know that we must develop new skills, make new contacts, and seek new opportunities. Thus, we will always be adjusting our life to be lived in accordance with our Values.

How valuable is my life?

When we think about the value of our life, we should think about our Values, both quantitatively and qualitatively. If we have any Values at all (and few of us would admit that we don't), then we can measure the meaningfulness of our life by our specific expression of these Values. It would be ludicrous for us to claim that our life has no value and also claim to have certain wants and aspirations. If we desire anything at all, then our life has value.

The problem with those who feel that life has no value is their failure to realize what is really important to them. When we focus on what we do have, cherish or expect in life, we will immediately begin to recognize the value these things bring to our life. If we wallow in self-pity about our meaningless life, we are actually saying that we are too blind or stubborn to see what is right in front of us.

Thus, our inability to see the value of our life is due to our incorrectly focusing on what we don't have rather than focusing on what we do have. Assuredly, problems will occur in our life that distracts us from what is most important. Events like a serious illness, a broken relationship or financial troubles will tend to command our attention and focus our thoughts in the negative areas of our life. But while these events may require a definite measure of our attention, they certainly don't mean that the rest of our life went down the drain with them.

We have no right to say that our life has no value simply because we are getting a divorce, losing our job or even getting a terminal illness. While something of value may have been painfully lost, we must still focus on those redeeming Values that we do have. For example, we may lose a loved one, but if we still value the beauty of nature and are given a beautiful sunset to watch this evening, then by all means our life still has value. We must recognize the full perspective of a valuable life, not concentrating only on the negative at the expense of the positive.

Feelings of depression are a severe manifestation of the belief that life has no value. It seems that we witness this psychological malady with increasing frequency in today's complex and demanding world. But the root of most depressive illnesses stems from losing sight of our Purpose and the Values that we cherish. The ultimate solution to depression is to re-channel our thought processes into a more holistic view of our existence. The key is to elevate the importance of new Values in our life to replace the ones that may be temporarily or even permanently lost or misplaced.

It was once said, *If we really do put a small value upon our self, rest assured that the world will not raise the price.* Even the dispirited character of Scrooge was eventually able to perceive that there was more to his life than his small world of contempt and greed. It is simply a matter of changing our perspective. Therefore, to determine the real Value of our life, we should always maintain a running inventory of what we do have to offset the loss of what we don't have. Let's take a moment to focus on those Values that we perceive to be affecting our outlook on life. List below what you sincerely feel that you **do have** versus what you **don't have**:

What wonderful things do I really possess in this life:	What is missing from my life that I really want, need or expect:
1.	1.
2.	2.
3.	3.
4.	4.
5.	5.
6.	6.
7.	7.
8.	8.
9.	9.
10.	10.

The Purpose of this exercise is to visually show a balance of our *have's* and *have not's*. When we feel that life has little value, we are focusing on the right hand column and forgetting that the left had hand column even exists. By ignoring the left hand column, we set ourselves up for worry, anxiety and depression. While the pain of loss is often more intense than the pleasure of possession, we do not have to be psychologically victimized by this for any extended period of time. The following example demonstrates how we often fail to see the true value of our life:

Robert had just lost his family through divorce, was terminated as a sales manager for his resultantly poor attitude and performance and then faced personal bankruptcy for his financial problems - all within the span of three months. He saw no future value for his life as he hopelessly put the gun to the side of his head and pulled the trigger.

The eulogies at Robert's funeral went on for hours and countless people praised him for his wonderful contributions to this world. Robert left behind three adoring children and a sandlot football team whose kids saw him as a hero and a role model. The day he died, he actually had a voice mail on his answering machine from a new company that wanted to hire him at a higher salary than his last job. Robert was an aspiring writer and would have discovered, after countless rejections, a publisher's acceptance letter a week after his suicide. Co-workers at his previous company recounted his effect on their lives as a mentor and teacher.

On the day that Robert gave up his *valueless life,* he was completely oblivious to his educational accomplishments, his striking good looks and his overall great health. He could not see the possibilities of his future with all the blessings and good fortunes that had been bestowed upon him. Robert had given up his *valueless life* when there were many years of laughter, friendships, and beautiful sunsets still ahead of him. He only saw what he didn't have and never gave himself the opportunity to see what he did have - most importantly, his *Self*!

The life that Robert abandoned was due to his inability to value himself. Self-love is the act of self-acceptance, the belief that we have value regardless of what we feel we do not have. Our self-love will always determine the level of meaning we have for our life. If we do not value nor love our *Self,* we are incapable of loving others or even life itself.

This was evidenced by a group of Army psychiatrists who conducted a personality survey of a group of successful soldiers, asking them to state what was most important in their lives. While these soldiers did not agree on all their priorities, it was surprising to find that each of them stated their *Self* to be the most important thing to them. They were not selfish men, as each were highly compassionate and loving family members, but they all recognized that the value of life came from making the most of it - through placing the highest Value on the *Self*.

When we love our *Self*, we appreciate the value of life and will always want to live it to its fullest. Again, this is not a selfish attitude but rather a feeling that the value of life is predicated upon the sanctity of our *Self*. A fourteenth century monk defined self-love as having a sense of humility, that it is, *a true knowledge of oneself as one is*. By knowing who we are and what is most important to us, we have the true knowledge of our *Self*. We, therefore, value life because we value our *Self*. As we review all of our Values, let's put self-love at the top of our list, the one Value that allows us to place a high value on everything else in life.

Besides my *Self*, which Values should be most important to me?

Some of our Values will always be more important to us than others, allowing us to prioritize them. Although our Values are generally shaped over time with little conscious intervention, it is possible to develop a clearer understanding of the Values we most cherish and choose to live by. However, if asked to quickly list our top ten Values, most of us would likely stumble for an answer. The reason is that we seldom actively think about our Values and their relative importance to each other. We may know that we value love, health and money, but unless we really think about them, we usually have difficulty deciding which is most important and how they actually affect our lives and our behavior.

And it is not a matter of knowing which Values are right and which are wrong as that is entirely subjective to each of us. It is far more important that we learn our deepest Values, the relative priorities of each to the other and how we will put them into practice in our life. Through introspection, we will also find that we have a supreme Value, the one desire that is more important to us than anything else - the one Value that best supports the

Value of our *Self.* Examples might be love, security, freedom or our health. And while most of us want all those things, there is that one Value that will always surface as being the most predominant to us.

For instance, if we chose health as our supreme Value, we need to understand why we made that choice. Was it because we value longevity or was it because we value a great looking body? Or that we value health for having more energy in our daily lives? What if we chose financial security as our supreme Value? Was that because we really value early retirement? And if so, was that because we really value an opportunity to travel? Or did we want financial security because we really want a beautiful home? Maybe we want the beautiful home because we value prestige. If it is prestige that we value, is it really because we value social acceptance? Thus, by working through this process of values elicitation, we may discover that it was not really financial security that we valued in the first place, but rather social acceptance - our new supreme Value.

We can work this process on all of our Values. It takes a little effort and a lot of honesty but the benefits are immeasurable. We not only will be able to determine our supreme Value, but just as importantly, we will be able to determine our real reason for having that Value. We are then able to choose our second most important Value, third, fourth, and so on. By ranking our Values, we can develop a hierarchy of our most important needs.

This process is paramount to our self-awareness, especially since most of us don't really know what it is we want out of life. We may have vague notions of what we are seeking but few of us ever really zero in on what motivates us the most. We may insist that love is our supreme Value but upon closer inspection find that what we really value is a sense of security. And while that might be initially accepted as our highest need, an honest assessment tells us that it actually ranks second behind creativity or challenge as our supreme motivator. Knowing how all of these subliminal pieces fit together is absolutely critical. Until we are totally aware and conscious of our true Values, we will not understand how to deal with conflicting Values nor how we should translate them into our daily behavior such that our real needs are being met.

Eliciting our Values hierarchy is done through questioning our real intent. First, we need to list or compartmentalize what we think is most important to us. Our list can be as detailed or as long as we wish to make it. The chart below lists a small sampling of commonly held Values. It is not all-inclusive, but rather a list to get us thinking in the right direction, to help each of us to start our own list.

In no particular order of importance:

1. Family/Relatives/Children
2. Financial Security/Independence
3. Health/Energy/Longevity
4. Community Involvement/Citizenship
5. Physical Security/Safety/Protection
6. Sharing/Giving/Helping/Teaching
7. Career Satisfaction/Accomplishment
8. Recreation/Leisure/Sport
9. Time Alone/Solitude/Reflection
10. Freedom/Autonomy/Travel
11. Creativity/Inventiveness/Artistic Expression
12. Spiritual Awareness/Fulfillment/Enlightenment
13. Educational/Intellectual Pursuit/Knowledge
14. Recognition/Prestige/Fame/Respect
15. Power/Strength/Force/Domination
16. Wealth/Materialism/Entrepreneurism
17. Adventure/Challenge/Quests
18. Salvation/Redemption/Church
19. Peace/Goodwill/Reconciliation
20. Love/Companionship/Friendships

Again, the foregoing list is not all-inclusive but rather designed to help us think about the broad concept of Values. Each of us should develop our own list. It may include many of the Values listed above, and we may come up with many more commonly held Values. We will likely say that all of these Values are good or important. They are if they guide us to happiness and the fulfillment of our Purpose and if they are used as tools to provide a framework for our daily actions.

Considering this, we need to remember that our Values emerge ever time and are unconsciously assimilated into our belief system. We usually change our core Values only after a monumental *Wake-Up Call* challenges us to rethink what is most important to us. We should, therefore, be very careful in attempting to clarify what we hold as our highest wants and aspirations.

So how do I really know what is most important to me?

There is considerable debate as to whether we choose our Values or our Values choose us. There is an element of truth to both sides of the argument, but one thing is certain: We must know what our Values are at any point in time and then live in accordance with them. This is the secret power of Values - They are much more than a statement of what we believe; they define the way we choose to live.

According to Louis Raths, author of *Values and Teaching*, Value creation is accomplished not by simply eliciting our self-beliefs but by establishing the behavioral patterns that will support them. He found from his research that our Values are extremely vital to us; that we can clearly state or express what they are; and that we will actively live them in a predictable fashion. In other words, our Values are much more than the simple feelings and opinions that we have about life. We can readily identify and segregate them as the most critical components of our life, clearly stating not only what they are but also why they are so vital to us.

Thus, we can become so convinced of our highest needs and aspirations that we will actively lead our lives in directions that specifically support these self-beliefs. We can fully integrate these supreme Values into our behavior patterns such that we have optimized our possibilities for seeing that our Values are fulfilled. By having this high confidence of what is most important to us, we will have an equally high sense of our Purpose. Therefore, we will know our most compelling reasons to act and achieve what we consider to be a significant and meaningful life.

There are numerous Values elicitation exercises that walk us through the process of identifying what is most important to us. The following exercise should get us headed in the right direction:

MAKE A WRITTEN LIST OF THE FOLLOWING:

- *TEN THINGS YOU MOST LIKE TO DO*
- *TEN THINGS IN YOUR LIFE YOU COULDN'T LIVE WITHOUT*
- *TEN PEOPLE YOU MOST ADMIRE, RESPECT OR WOULD LIKE TO BE LIKE*
- *TEN IDEALS THAT BEST REPRESENT YOUR PHILOSOPHY IN LIFE*
- *TEN OCCUPATIONS THAT YOU WOULD LIKE TO DO IF PROPERLY TRAINED*
- *TEN PLACES WHERE YOU WOULD MOST LIKE TO LIVE*
- *TEN PERSONALITY TRAITS THAT BEST DESCRIBE YOU*
- *TEN REASONS THAT MAKE LIFE WONDERFUL TO YOU*

If possible, list your ten answers to each question on a large piece of grid paper where you can see the whole picture at one time. Underline the key words, phrases, concepts and ideas that bear similarity to each other. Use the list of commonly held Values that are listed above and try to link them with your most common set of responses.

As an example, if you want to live in Maui, work as a marine biologist, think water is wonderful and believe that life is an adventure, you may find that some of your key Values are Career Satisfaction, Travel, and Recreation. While this exercise is not precise, it is an entertaining way to discover the linkage between things you deem to be very important, thus, making bridges to The Values that encompass a number of your recurring wants and aspirations.

Now let's take these key Values and rank them in order of their importance.

DEVELOPING YOUR OWN VALUES HIERARCHY

Choose 10 of the top Values you listed for yourself. Are they congruent with the Purpose Statement you wrote earlier? Are they congruent with your dreams and your Vision? Are they congruent with your present location on the Growth Curve that we discussed earlier? Are they congruent with the epitaph you adopted for yourself? Will they lead to a life of *"no regrets"*? Will they hold up against the daily decisions you will make and the actions you will take going forward?

Challenge yourself and your choice of Values. Challenge the underlying meaning behind each Value that you selected for yourself. Did you discover that a higher Value existed behind one that you chose, e.g. if you chose career satisfaction were you really seeking the Value of financial security or were you seeking the Value of enjoying what you do for a living? Be honest with yourself.

Go back and list your top ten Values again after answering the above questions. Did they change?

Now let's rank them in order of importance. The best way to do this is to let your Values have a tournament against each other. Number your Values in no particular order, from 1 to 10. Test Value 1 against Value 10. If you were forced to choose one over the other, which one would it be? Write down that Value and number as the winner. Now, test Value number 2 against Value number 9. Force yourself to select one and write down the number and Value as the winner. Go through the whole list, 3 against 8, 4 against 7, and five against 6. Now match your 5 winners against each other, using the same process, pitting the last one against your first one.

You should end up with your supreme Value as the one that beat all the others. Your other 9 Values can be rank ordered by the same process with each tournament revealing the highest set of Values. More sophisticated models exist for ranking a number of choices but this simple method should give you a general idea about the relative importance of one Value over another. Now list your top ten values below in the final order of their importance to you.

MY NEW TOP TEN VALUES

1.
2.
3.
4.
5.
6.
7.
8.
9.
10.

A complete understanding of our Values and their relative importance is critical to our self-understanding. Our goal is to develop a Values hierarchy that will steer us in the right direction for managing our priorities. Once we know the relative importance of each of our key Values, we are better equipped to make the right choices in our daily lives. They will then become a roadmap for us so that we can balance our decisions against the things we hold most important.

However, we should not be extremist in our adherence to our Values as we make our choices. We should use them as guideposts, not as absolutes. We should feel free to question them. We should be flexible in our application of them. Most time management systems ask us to plan all of our daily activities around our Values. This leads to a great deal of pressure and consequent guilt when we are not living one hundred percent in accordance with our Values. Yes, our Values should guide our time and our actions but we cannot be slaves to the process.

Also, our Values should not be confused with our goals. Rather, our goals emanate from the Values we choose to hold. We decide what we will accomplish in life after we know what we believe to be most important to us. Some of us may aspire to lofty goals while others may choose a simpler, more basic path through life. Some of us take huge risks to match our Values while others may be content to *just let life happen*. The higher our goals, the stronger we will believe in the importance of our Values.

Our Values also set the foundation for our ideals. They determine the causes we adopt as they shape our idealistic view of how the world should be. We may become missionaries, consumer crusaders or political protesters based upon our deepest Values. Some of us tend to be more idealistic than others, even to the point of being unrealistic, but anything great that has ever happened required an individual who followed his or her deepest Values and most dedicated principles.

Due to the complexities of our lives, we cannot always predict every result. It was once said that life is what happens when we are planning something else. We live in a world with other people who are continually exerting influences on us. We are in a constant state of adjustment with our relationships, our careers and our families. If we must review our Value list each time we face choices, we will be too paralyzed to act. As every action has a consequence, we need to be in tune to our Values most of the time, but we need not be prisoners of ourselves.

As we walk the tightrope of life, our Values will give us balance and security… Nothing more, and nothing less. Our Values will not determine if we fall or not. But they will give us stability on the tightrope, and should we fall they will help us get back up. Through practice, we will all become more proficient at walking life's tightropes.

PART TWO

The Power of Purposeful Living

There's no thrill in easy sailing when the skies are clear and blue There's no joy in merely doing things which anyone can do. But there is some satisfaction that is mighty sweet to take, when you reach a destination that you thought you'd never make.

Spirella

PROLOGUE

He is great who can do what he wishes;
He is wise who wishes to do what he can.

Our journey toward our *Higher Self* must now take some personal motivation and self-direction. To this point, we have focused upon the critical elements of a purposeful life, but we have not yet translated our new knowledge into specific action. We are certainly more familiar now with our true *Self*, and undoubtedly we have a clearer understanding of *who we are, where we are going and what is most important* to us for self-fulfillment. But we have still not taken that leap of faith into applying this self-awareness to our daily life. Specifically, we have not yet answered the question: *How am I going to get there?*

While Part One answered our questions about *what we want from life*, Part Two answers the question: *How do I make it happen?* Specifically, we will now be guided toward greater self-awareness and self-empowerment to manage the following areas of our life:

Regulating Life's Difficulties & Complexities
Balancing our Greatest Needs & Expectations
Finding Inner Strength through Self-Empowerment
Designing and Planning a Purposeful Life
Goal Focusing, Targeting & Attainment
Avoiding Failure & Obstacles through Self-Choice
Mental Mastery and Rational Thinking
Time Management through Self-Management
Stress Control through Focusing, Flowing & Centering
The Unifying Principles of Purposeful Living
Self-Guided Happiness and Contentment
Making a Difference with Our Life

We should possess by now a newly found perception of what constitutes a meaningful and significant life. But unless we are committed to achieving it, to making it part of our new reality, it will always remain an illusion for us. The ultimate achievement for each of us is to know that we lived with great Purpose, that our life was significant and meaningful and that we truly made a difference. With a firm and appropriate base of self-knowledge, we now possess the potential to create the life we hope for.

Part Two will move us in that direction - where we finally take charge and *make life happen!* But we must remember that if we are not pursuing what is most important we are not engaged in what life is all about. Life is about doing, striving, achieving and *going for it* with great passion! And *Today* is the best time for us to begin!

Obviously, we are reading these words *Today.* And we are most likely eating, sleeping, breathing, working and thinking *Today.* We could even be facing some serious challenges and dealing with some level of crisis *Today.* But are we in control and taking charge of the life we want to live *Today?*

Part Two will empower us to finally take action. We must recognize that our *Self* can only be actualized through specific, purposeful behavior. Our *Self* is not an amorphous, inert object that sits on a shelf waiting for life to make it happy. Our *Self* must leap into the world with great passion and excitement for it to become fully realized. It must grow, transform, challenge and focus itself to reach its complete potential. We are in control of our *Self,* and we alone determine whether it will become fully manifested or wastefully squandered. And this challenge is what makes life so interesting and worthwhile for each of us.

In Part Two, we will explore the secrets to *Self-Success* by taking our *Self* to its highest form of existence - the self-empowerment of our Purpose. We will gain practical knowledge of purposeful living, where we become the master and life becomes our servant. Becoming more self-empowered, we will put our enlightened *Self* to work - where we plan and design the life we wish to live; where we establish and attain our goals; where we manage our time, our stress and the difficulties of daily living; where we live a balanced and contented life; and where we make a difference to those around us.

Part Two will challenge our *Self* to make a stand, to put a stake in the ground and dare the world to make us unhappy again. Gaining *Self-Mastery* means we must not accept anything but a passionate, meaningful existence based upon our highest expectations. Our new *Self* will find contentment and inner peace by controlling its own reality, rather than allowing the world to dictate what that reality should be. The end result will be to achieve our *Higher Self,* to know that our life was lived the way we meant it to be and that we did *make it happen*! And that in the end, we did make a difference!

CHAPTER EIGHT

How Can I Manage It All?
The Great Balancing Act

Fortunate, indeed is the man who takes exactly the right measure of himself, and holds a just balance between what he can acquire and what he can use, be it great or be it small!
Peter Latham
1789 - 1875

How can we do it all? The burden of modern civilization is that we are bombarded with choices, over loaded with expectations, confounded by change and stymied by time. Alvin Toffler's *Future Shock* has arrived and given us *Imminent Shock*. We are now faced with a world that is coming at us with blinding speed. Thus, we will often find it difficult to keep our internal balance when our external world seems so chaotic and perpetually out-of-balance. But therein rests the secret: Keeping the balance within ourselves while everything around us appears to be out of control.

By focusing within, we gain clarity of Purpose. As turbulent as the outside world appears on the surface, we have the capacity to internally remain calm and balanced. Our Purpose, assisted by our Values, becomes our gyroscope and steadies us even as our landscape is continually moving. By remaining attentive to what is most important to us, we can sort through the clutter in our lives and focus only upon that which really matters. While many things will compete for our attention, our only concern should be the key priorities that are congruent with our Purpose and our Values, i.e. only that which is most important needs to be managed and controlled. By recognizing this, we can set our own pace. And we can then control ourselves rather than allowing our external world to be in control of us.

The great German philosopher, Max Scheler, expressed this aspect of our lives: *In the ten thousand years of history, we are the first age in which man has become utterly and unconditionally problematic to himself, in which he no longer knows who he is, but at the same time knows that he does not know.* We, therefore, must get back in touch with ourselves - focusing on what is most critical... and nothing more.

Thus, we can construct a meaningful world for ourselves by clearly defining the way in which we will interact with it. It is vital that we consciously interpret our role relative to the events that surround us and then act according to that interpretation. We cannot allow extraneous and unimportant events to alter our views and actions. We must become *conscious actors* on the world stage rather than *rubber-stamp reactors* to those events that are not important or beyond our control.

Therefore, the art of a balanced life is sorting between those things that are perceived to be critical and those things that are perceived to be urgent or expedient. Rarely are they one and the same, although we often have difficulty in recognizing the difference between them.

Unfortunately, it has always been man's natural instinct to be reactive rather than proactive. We prefer, whether consciously or not, to respond to daily events rather than leading or controlling these events in our lives. This approach, however, puts us in a constant state of stimulus/ response where we are bouncing off of walls, going in circles, and getting absolutely nowhere. We become agitated, frustrated and feel guilty that we are wasting our lives dealing with all of these insignificant battles.

From time to time, we feel these pressures are too overwhelming and attempt to gain some control. But our actions are usually very cursory and expedient. We buy daily organizers and planners, make checklists with priority codes and set new goals to achieve. Our hope is that if we run faster and work harder, we can cram more into each day and collapse each evening with a feeling of great accomplishment. The next morning we start the race again and the cycle repeats itself. At some point we submit to stress and burnout, then take a hurried vacation and come back more exhausted than before we left. Our vain attempt to gain on the race leaves us at the finish line with little to show for our efforts. We may have made more money or achieved a bigger title in the process, but it is often at the expense of our family, our health and our peace of mind.

Thus, by responding to the urgent, we will lose sight of the important. And by allowing the turbulence of daily living to set our agenda our Purpose then languishes in the background. This constant sense of urgency overwhelms us and we eventually lose our focus. Having organized our lives around these fragmented events we then fail to see the whole picture. And by responding to the myriad number of daily urgencies, we ultimately fail to respond to the deeper sense of Purpose that should be guiding us and shaping our daily behavior.

The essence of balance, therefore, is to determine and act only upon the issues that reflect our deepest commitment to ourselves. By letting our daily lives run out of control, we fail ourselves. By taking charge of our daily lives, we will live our Purpose and shape our own destiny.

How then do I restore balance in my life?

In the previous chapter, we spent time in determining our Values – our greatest aspirations and expectations, that is, *what is most important to us*. Balance is achieved through: First, identifying *what is most important*; Second, by determining and avoiding events or situations that are keeping us from *what is most important*; and Third, by managing our time and actions to be congruent with *what is most important*. These are our highest wants and needs in our life – the most critical necessities that we must be pursuing to feel that our life has inherent balance.

If one of our Values is not being met, we will sense that something is missing, a void that must be filled to keep us in a proper state of balance. Equally importantly, our Values must be balanced around our physical, spiritual and mental needs, as they are they are the most significant objectives to fulfilling our *Essential Self*. We cannot reach our *Higher Self* until these basic needs or components of our *Self* are being met and working in balanced harmony.

We lose our sense of balance when we lose focus on any one essential need or Value, that is, we allow one to suffer at the expense of another. If we sacrifice our needs to the demands of the external world, we will have lost control of what is most important to us. And if we are constantly responding to these daily *urgencies*, we will have little time or psychic energy left to ourselves. The world will quickly consume us if we allow it to operate within our universe, our own sphere of influence.

We, therefore, must become the center of our own universe, whereby all that happens is a function of what we will allow to happen. This does not mean that events, situations or demands will not continue to affect us. It does mean, however, that we can choose to bring them into our own universe or let them go find another universe to rotate around.

Let's think of ourselves as an atomic particle with our *Essential Self* serving as the nucleus. Consider the electrons and neutrons that spin around us as being our most important Values, our highest wants and needs that keep us functioning as a balanced particle of energy. Our atomic *Self* exists as its own self-contained universe within a larger universe filled with competing particles of energy. From time to time, these other particles of energy will attempt to collide with us. If we are not vigilant, their electrons and neutrons will invade our space and completely alter our entire atomic structure.

By co-mingling the urgent needs of other sources of energy with our own internal energy, we lose the power of our *Essential Self*, having given it up to forces that previously existed outside of us. In fact, by giving up our *Essential Self*, we no longer would be able to even recognize what had been most important to us.

The following diagram demonstrates these relationships:

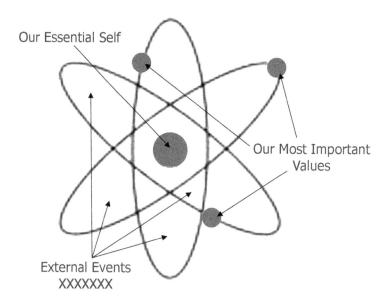

This is not to suggest that balance is achieved without some responsibility to interact with the world at large. It was once said, *No man*

is an island, thus, we should not be lured into thinking that we can exist in isolation of external demands and situations that wish to invade our *Essential Self.* Rather, we need to take control of the *urgencies* that invade our time and space, such that we let in what we deem to be most important and let everything else go elsewhere, to seek another universe to invade.

Let's take a moment to note the key sources of interference to what is most important to us. In a typical day, we have lots of activities. Some of these activities are where we are *acting out the things* that are most important. All other activities are where we are *reacting to the things* that keep us from doing what is most important.

Make a list of as many activities that you can think of that occupy a substantial amount of your time and energy in a typical day (or week). Try to refrain from listing basic life sustaining activities like cooking, eating, bathing, exercising, sleeping, etc. Just list those activities unique to you and your situation in life, e.g. Picking up the children's clothes, driving to school events, volunteering at the church, writing memos to keep your boss informed, balancing budgets, gardening, going to the movies, doing crossword puzzles, repairing things in the house, writing a book, job searching, etc. Look at your planning calendar to help you list as many activities as you can think of.

1.	11.	21.	31.
2.	12.	22.	32.
3.	13.	23.	33.
4.	14.	24.	34.
5.	15.	25.	35.
6.	16.	26.	36.
7.	17.	27.	37.
8.	18.	28.	38.
9.	19.	29.	39.
10.	20.	30.	40.

Now, go back through your list and place a "V" next to every activity that supports one of the Top 10 Values that you created for yourself in the previous chapter. How many "V's" did you collect? How do you feel you are supporting that which is most important to you through your actual

activities? In how many of these activities are you consciously pursuing your Values versus those activities that are interfering with your Values? Do you see any patterns emerging? Is there anything that you would like to change about yourself or start doing differently tomorrow (next week)?

As we said earlier, balance is the art of sorting between those things that we perceive to be important and those that are not. Creating value in our life is the process of moving our time and energy toward our most important Values while moving away from that which does not support those Values. Thus, we have *move toward* activities and *move away from* activities. All of our daily choices and decisions should be made in terms of *move toward* and *move away from* behavior patterns. If we know what is most important to us (our key Values), we must spend our time and energy *moving toward* the realization of their importance.

As we become more consciously aware and adept at practicing this, we will automatically *move toward* that which is most important and *move away from* that which is not as important. Practicing this over time, we will be able to accomplish this without even having to think about it.

We should now revisit our activities list above and determine which actions we will *move toward* and which we will *move away from* in the future. Once we have eliminated all future activities that don't support our key Values, we will find that what we have left to do can be managed more easily, thus, restoring more balance to our life.

So how do I do stay focused on what's most important?

Our problem is in how we see the problem. We tend to compartmentalize ourselves into separate lives. We have our work life, our family life, our financial life, our social life, etc. We try to take one hat off and put another hat on as the day progresses. This segmentation of our lives into different boxes of activity creates tremendous pressure on us to shift our roles continuously. We become much like that old Ed Sullivan act where the harried performer is balancing multiple plates on long poles. As each begins to fall, he has to run frantically back and forth to keep all of them spinning at the same time.

Doing too many separate things at once keeps us in constant agitation and turmoil. We do a poor job in each role because we are trying to do all the roles at the same time, with each role requiring a different and often conflicting allotment of ourselves and of our time. The solution is to perceive the entire landscape, as a single body of choice, not little bites of activity all occurring at the same time. Gandhi once observed, *One man cannot do right in one department of life whilst he is occupied in doing wrong in any other department. Life is one indivisible whole.* We need to act as if all of our roles are one and the same, that we are only spinning one large plate at the top of one pole.

This is the essence of balanced Purpose. Instead of thinking **either/ or**, we must think **of one and the same**. As we view and interact with multiple and competing events, we should not treat them as being distinct and separate parts, but rather as a single part woven into the whole of our lives. An ancient Sufi teacher once said, *You think because you understand* **one** *you must understand* **two**, *because one* **and** *one makes two. But you must also understand* **and.** This holistic concept is the basis for most Eastern religious thought. Everything is viewed as being in balance. We cannot see the individual parts of a picture without seeing the whole picture.

Even opposites cannot be viewed separately; they must be addressed together. The Yin and the Yang is essentially a balance between two forces that are opposite each other. One cannot exist without the other. There can be no good without evil, no light without darkness, no joy without sorrow, no positive without a negative. The Eastern view is that to treat a patient with an illness, you must treat the whole person. A person's life is not balanced until all aspects of his life are considered, working together holistically and in harmony.

Therefore, our Purpose, our Values, and our Behavior must all mesh together in balance, congruently with each other. Applying this paradigm requires us to view the total picture, that is, we cannot focus only on one component of life while forsaking another. Our Behavior must be congruent with our Values, but our Values must be congruent with each other. They are all interdependent, each working synergistically with the other. It's not **either/or**, it's **and.**

The universal nature of balance works in our life mysteriously and subliminally. Because of natural laws, equilibrium will always find itself, whether we are talking about the planets, the weather or even the forces that work within our minds and bodies. If we do not approach our life's balance from a holistic perspective, then our life will ultimately seek its own balance, sometimes with serious and negative consequences.

Fortunately, we are giving ample opportunities to live a balanced life before nature does it for us. We receive numerous warning signs when we ignore the laws of balance. We will know when our life is out of kilter because of the stress and anxiety we generate within ourselves. We will feel the effects on our health, our relationships and even our careers when we are overemphasizing one aspect of our life at the expense of another. The key for us is to recognize these incongruities and correct them before they have to correct themselves. Our opportunity is to be in charge, fixing the problem before natural laws do it for us. As they always will!

How is life made easier if I have to make everything work together?

The best way to visualize how life is more easily managed is to plot our Values on the ***Wheel of Life***. The ***Wheel of Life*** is a composite of our lives, representing the entirety of what is most important to us. It is shaped with a hub, a rim and spokes emanating from the center. The hub is our Purpose, the spokes represent our Values and the rim reflects our Mission. The wheel is in constant motion, turning everyday in the direction we wish to be heading.

Our Purpose Wheel

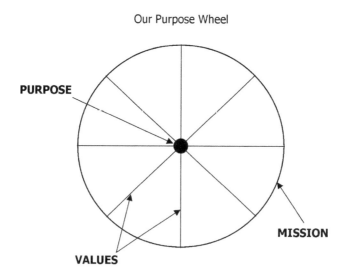

Along each spoke we should place one of the Values from the list we generated in the last chapter. If we are working with eight key Values, then we have eight spokes emerging from the center (Our Purpose) to the rim (Our Mission). The following wheel represents a hypothetical set of Values (yours should be unique to yourself).

Wheel of Life

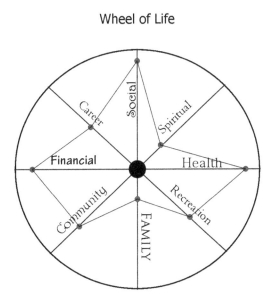

Once you have identified your highest Values along the spokes (your greatest priorities), consider where you are in meeting that Value in your daily life. Each spoke has a degree of fulfillment, from 1 to 10, with 1 being closest to the hub and 10 being closest to the rim. If you do not feel that a Value is congruent with your daily behavior, place a dot on the spoke closer to the hub; if that Value is part of your daily behavior, then place a dot on the spoke closer to the rim. If you are not sure, place the dot somewhere near the middle of the spoke. Do this for each Value and spoke on your wheel. Now connect the dots on your ***Wheel of Life.***

We need to determine how balanced our ***Wheel of Life*** is in our daily lives. First, we need to review the shape of our inner wheel of *connected dots*. Is it round, oblong or bumpy? Obviously, if we scored all *"10's"* on each spoke, we would be experiencing a totally balanced life where all of our Values are exercised everyday day through our Behavior and are subsequently congruent with our Purpose and our Mission.

It is doubtful that this is being achieved if we are honest with ourselves. More likely, our wheel looks like our hypothetical one, a little out of balance. In our example, the individual that this life represents is highly in tune with his *Social Value*, feels that his *Health Value* is somewhat congruent with his behavior, yet knows that he is severely lacking in meeting the *Spiritual* and *Family Values* that he believes are important. In other words, his wheel is not turning smoothly and real inner satisfaction is not being achieved.

We should look critically at our own **Wheel of Life**. Are we being tremendously congruent with our Career Values, yet sacrificing our Family Values to achieve this success? Are we in sync with our Financial Values yet losing our spiritual quest as a result? Is our wheel balanced and spinning smoothly, or is it out-of-round and bouncing and bumping down life's highway?

It is important to note that few of us will ever experience a smoothly balanced wheel that is spinning merrily down life's highway. More likely we will encounter potholes along the way. Our wheel will speed up, then slow down, sometimes spin wildly out of control, and then settle down again. As our Values shift in importance and as our actions become more or less congruent with our Values, our inner wheel will take on more odd shapes. The perfect **Wheel of Life** may never exist in our lives. We will lose jobs, have illnesses, experience family squabbles, have financial setbacks, etc. Life is just too complex for our **Wheel of Life** to be balanced with any regularity.

But with our wheel concept in mind, we can see where our priorities are and if they are playing a major part in our lives. We can determine if we are the source of the imbalance through our decision-making, or if external forces are affecting our balance. By envisioning our **Wheel of Life** as we go down the road, we can know where we stand with our Values and how well they are being applied in our lives. If we notice that we are placing too much effort in our Career Values, such that our Family Values are suffering, we can back off our work activities a little and get more involved in our family activities. This will move our dots on the spokes to a closer level with each other, making our wheel spin with a little better balance.

Our principal task should be to evaluate how well our Values are being met by our Behavior. If we are consciously aware of this process and keep a mental picture of the ***Wheel of Life*** with us, we can continually improve the balance in our lives. Each Value spoke in the wheel must be synergistically in tune with the others. Our challenge is to strive for a round, balanced inner wheel that gets closer in size to the outer wheel.

It is also helpful to think of each spoke as a role we play in life. We cannot continually play one role without sacrificing another role. We may gain deep satisfaction by playing one role exceedingly well, but this satisfaction will be short-lived if we discover that another role was shortchanged in the process. Also, if we don't miss the Value or role that we are avoiding or paying little attention to, then it was really not important to us after all. We should discard it and consider if another Value or role is not more important. Only Values and roles that are vitally important to us deserve a place on our spokes. Essentially, if they deserve to be on our ***Wheel of Life*** then that Value is a key to our happiness, and the role reflecting that Value must be played to the best of our ability.

Without question, this will be difficult since our Values will often compete with each other. But this doesn't mean that solutions can't be found. For instance, we may Value our family but at the same time we may also Value our Health. The choice is not which Value to give up, but rather how will we manage the fulfillment of both Values in our lives. For example, we plan to pick up the children after school, feed them, read them a story and then tuck them into bed, but this also leaves us no time to drive across town to work out at the gym. This does not mean that we should give up Health as a Value. Rather we need to explore putting a gym in our garage or a spare bedroom and then working out after the kids are asleep or early in the morning before we wake them. Or we could consider combining two Values together as witnessed by mothers or fathers exercising behind a jogging stroller.

Managing our Values is never easy, but it is important. If we truly value anything enough, we will search for the solutions or opportunities to make it part of our lives. But at the same time, we must not be enslaved to this process. It is not critical, nor even desirable, to be scoring a"10" in each stated value. Studies have shown that living with mostly "8's" is actually more satisfying than trying to achieve "10's" in every important area of life. Likewise, we should never allow the over-used phrase *work-life balance* to become a source of frustration. That term conjures images of see-saws, pogo sticks and balance beams, all of which require great effort and dexterity. If we substitute the term *synergy* for *balance,* we are much more likely to see how each Value works together instead of against each other.

To summarize, we must look deep within ourselves to determine what is really important to us. Only our highest Values deserve to be positioned on our **Wheel of Life**. Those Values create the roles that we play, thus, affecting the decisions we make. Each role or Value is obviously important and each must work synergistically with the other. We must be prepared to abandon a Value or role if it ceases to be an integral part of our Values-wheel. We must strive to keep the wheel as round as possible and rolling in a direction that is both positive and congruent with our Purpose and our Mission. This is the key to living a holistic and balanced life.

How exactly is my Purpose related to living a balanced life?

Our ability to realize our opportunities comes from seeing the big picture of life, from beginning to end. We need to design a clear path to follow, a self-directed journey that starts with our Purpose and ends with the Rewards that we seek. Our Rewards, whether short-term goal achievements or a lifelong feeling of satisfaction and inner peace, will require the conscious pursuit of our *Higher Self.* In the religious vernacular, this level of *Being* is a close cousin to being *born again* or reaching *Nirvana*. In essence, we will have found ourselves and know that our lives have great meaning.

Pursuing this means we must stay continually attuned to the natural rhythms found within our *Physical, Mental and Spiritual Selves.* The balance of these elements does not necessarily mean that we have to give equal time to them, but we must always be giving them equal emphasis. We now know that our Values are interspersed between these three components of our life. If we trade off one Value through our specific behavior, then we must make an equal tradeoff of emphasis on another Value to keep the total balance intact. These continuous *interchanges of emphasis* on our key Values is known as *Karma* in certain Eastern religions. We have good *Karma* when we are living a balanced, productive life and we have bad *Karma* when we are inefficiently pursuing too much of the wrong aspects of life.

As life is replete with paradoxes, we must find our balance within these incongruities. It seems that even our best choices will still have elements of discord and disharmony. The paradoxes of life force us continuously into compromises and tradeoffs. Good *Karma* or perfect balance is achieved when we let our highest principals dictate our decisions. When our Values compete with each other, forcing us to choose between them, we may even have to rely on Values that are higher than us to break the stalemate. For instance, we may need to sacrifice something we earnestly believe in because we know a greater good will come from our sacrifice. We may find that we must give up part of our wealth to fund a worthy charity or in the most extreme case sacrifice our life to gain freedom for our country or to save a child from a fire.

These higher Values are known as our *Unifying Principles,* which we will cover in detail in *Chapter Fourteen.* Their significance is that they achieve ultimate balance, always overruling the difficult decisions we must sometimes face. When life seems out of control and we see no easy solution, we can always turn to our *Unifying Principles* to restore balance and congruity to our lives. These principles can be found in the Ten Commandments, the Declaration of Independence, the Constitution, and the by-laws of our church or community. These laws, duties and obligations have been adopted by many of us as a critical tool for life management. They, in turn, guide us through the paradoxes and difficult decisions which we are sometimes forced to make. Ultimately, we must draft our own set of commandments to govern our life when the world around us seems so out of balance.

Let's now review the flow of thought and action that takes us from our original Purpose Statement all the way through to the Rewards we ultimately seek. The following illustration will complete the picture, pointing the way to a fulfilled and balanced life that we purposely managed and controlled:

Pyramid to the Higher Self

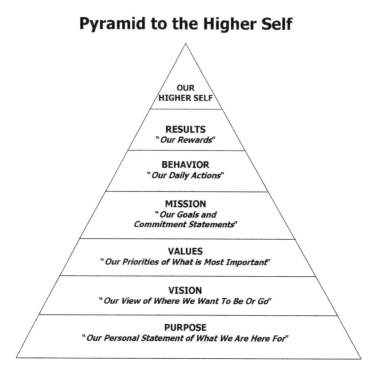

The pyramid path is clear and points in a single direction. Our first step in the journey is found within ourselves - our Purpose. Knowing *what we are here for* gives us a clear Vision all the way to the far horizon. As we begin our journey, we pick up our Values, like flowers along the side of the path. We bundle these Values into a set of goals or destinations in the far off distance. These destinations allow us to make our own roadmap to follow, our unique Mission in life. Then, as we journey forward, we make our own decisions along the way, decisions that will govern our daily actions. And at the end of our journey, we get our Rewards, the principle reward being the knowledge that we lived our lives well, that we plotted our own course and that it led to happiness along the way and to our final conclusion - where our Purpose comes full circle and we are again at the beginning.

CHAPTER NINE

What Is The Real Secret To Success?

Committing to the Vital

What this power is I cannot say; all I know is that it exists and it becomes available only when a man is in that state of mind in which he knows exactly what he wants and is fully determined not to quit until he finds it.

Alexander Graham Bell

We previously learned how to identify our greatest priorities and how to gauge their importance in living a balanced life. We asked about our Purpose, *What am I here for?* our Vision, *Where am I going?* and our Values, *What is most important to me?* We have clarified our dreams, our hopes and even wrote our epitaph for how we want to say our life was lived. But we have still not uncovered the method for making it all a reality, that is, what is it that drives us to *make life happen?* The hurdle we often face is that we don't trust or commit ourselves to the effort. We fear making any commitments because we haven't yet convinced ourselves as to what we should be doing or the right way to proceed.

Basically, what we have lacked is an action plan for incorporating our Purpose, our Vision, and our Values into our daily life. After clarifying our Values we began to understand the right things, but that was not the same as doing the right things, the right way and at the right time. By translating our highest aspirations into an action plan and into our daily decision making, we will then have our ***Mission***, the answer to what we asked ourselves earlier, *How will I get there?*

This is self-trust at its highest level; our Mission in life. By defining our Mission, we become deeply connected to our Purpose, our Vision and our Values. Our Mission gives us the energy to live and to grow. Our Mission gives passion to our life. Napoleon Hill told us, *Cherish your visions and your dreams as they are the children of your soul; the blueprints of your ultimate achievements.* Thus, our Mission will become our blueprint - the force that turns on the switch that makes our highest needs and wants come alive. It will tell us how to get to where we want to go. It will drive us to meet our goals and ensure the end-results we are seeking.

But to accept our Mission, we must first know what it is. Our Mission is our commitment to our *Self.* It takes our Values and places a demand on us to actually live them. It shapes the intentional acts of our Behavior, which says we are living congruently with our Values. Our Mission, therefore, becomes our reality, the bond between our Values and their manifestation in the real world. Our Mission determines our personal business plan, the plan of action that not only defines our goals but also how to achieve them.

While our Vision may tell us where we want to go, we still need arrows or signposts to point us in the right direction. Our Mission serves that purpose by telling us what our Behavior must be to ensure the results we are seeking. Our Behavior is governed by the goals we set for ourselves and the commitments we make to achieve them. Goals and commitments are tied together. An objective has no reason to exist without a corresponding obligation to achieve it.

We must *walk the talk,* or our promises to ourselves are hollow and meaningless. Our Mission requires us to take responsibility for our decisions and actions. Forsaking this duty cheats only us, for decisions without direction are simply motions without Purpose. We would only take up space on the planet and drift like tumbleweeds with the wind. To avoid this fate, we must take a stand on how we want our life to be lived. We must start with our original Purpose Statement, know our Vision for where we want to go, clarify our Values as to what is most important, and then accept responsibility for the Mission that will *make life happen* the way we most desire.

Therefore, our Mission is the engine that drives it all. It sets our goals, makes us committed to reach them and sets in motion the daily Behavior that turns it into reality. With this being understood, how do we each define our Mission?

Our Mission is a recipe made up of three parts:

1. **The Values we placed on our *Wheel of Life*. They become the chief ingredient that determines what is most important for us to achieve.**
2. **The Goals we set for ourselves which are the manifestations of our Values actually being achieved.**
3. **Our Commitment Statements which are the pledges we make to ourselves to realize our Goals.**

This recipe is a three-step process, with each of the three ingredients being added one at a time, then blended together to make our Mission:

VALUES + GOALS + COMMITMENTS = OUR MISSION.

Our Mission then becomes the statement that validates our responsibility to ourselves to achieve success in each important area of our lives. Let's review an example:

Step 1: Know your Values

Assume you have established *Physical Health* as a key Value in your life, one of your highest aspirations to achieve. Let's first evaluate what is important to you about this Value. You should list the aspects of *Physical Health* that you are seeking. For example, you may choose:

1. **Longevity**
2. **Endurance and Stamina**
3. **Daily Energy in My Life**
4. **Aerobic Conditioning**
5. **Freedom from Illness**
6. **Great Looking Body**
7. **Athletic Achievement**
8. **Lower Medical Costs**

Now run the same tournament that you did earlier in your Values Elicitation Exercise: Compare 1 to 8, pick a winner; Compare 2 to 7, pick a winner, and so on. Then rank in order from your most important to your least important aspects of *Physical Health*. Now that you have identified your real beliefs about this Value, you can move on to the next step.

Step 2: Set Your Goals

Your Goals should be the real-life manifestations of this Value of *Physical Health*, i.e. if you achieve it, what will it look like? If you realize this Value, it will have to take on a definitive quality, appearance or feeling. If it can be measured, that is even better. For instance, to say you have achieved *Physical Health* by saying you feel good is not as valuable as saying that a recent physical exam by your doctor showed all your bodily functions are in perfect working order or that you just completed your first Iron Man Triathlon. This is not to imply that you must put impossible standards on yourselves. Feeling good may be all that you want out of *Physical Health* but it is a greater reward to set and achieve some measurable goal even if it is only to lower your blood pressure by ten points.

Assume you chose your goals for *Physical Health* to be able to work energetically without being as tired at the end of the day; to have fewer bouts of colds, flues and viruses this coming winter; to be able to compete in your town's 15k run next spring; and to have 10% body fat before next summer's swim suit season arrives. You have determined these goals represent your definition of achieving *Physical Health*. If you could achieve these things, you will have seen this key Value or area of your life manifested into reality. These goals are achievable in your mind, and because they are measurable you will know when they have been accomplished.

Step 3. Write Your Commitment Statements

This is the final step in developing your Mission for this one key Value of your life. It is not sufficient to simply state what your Values are or to just set goals that you wish to achieve. You also have to confirm your Mission by committing to them. This is where the rubber meets the road, where you not only say what you want but turn it into a sacred promise that will drive you to action. Thus, to meet the goals you established in Step 2, you need to write down your *Commitment Statement* for achieving those goals.

As an example, for the Value of *Physical Health* and the goals you set to achieve it, your *Commitment Statement* might look like this:

VALUE: PHYSICAL HEALTH
GOALS: WORK MORE ENERGETICALLY WITH LESS FATIGUE
IN EVENING
LESS FLUS, COLDS AND VIRUSES THIS WINTER
COMPETE IN LOCAL 15 K RUN NEXT APRIL
HAVE 10% BODY FAT BY NEXT JUNE

MY WRITTEN COMMITMENT STATEMENT:

I will respect my body and physical health through a conscious daily effort to improve my overall state of physical well-being. Through an applied program of healthy habits and physical training, I will meet my stated goals that support this key area of my life. To support my mission, I will learn through self-education and from my doctor what is required to achieve my goals. I will establish a daily program of proper nutrition, rest and exercise to maximize my energy level and to minimize my opportunities for getting sick. I will lower my daily fat gram intake to less than 30 grams, take vitamins, eat more fiber and less carbohydrates, increase my jogging routine to 20 miles per week and get eight hours of sleep per night. I will evaluate my progress with a daily calendar and adjust my program as needed to ensure that I am staying on track to meet my goals.

Your *Commitment Statement* is highly personal and unique to you. You should take each key Value on your **Wheel of Life** and go through the three step process of Value analysis, goal setting to support that Value, and finally your *Commitment Statement*, the written vow that pledges you to the fulfillment of that Value or area of your life. If you also value *Financial Freedom* or *Spiritual Awareness*, determine what you want from each, how you will know when you have achieved it, and what you are going to do about it. If you have eight Values on your **Wheel of Life**, you should develop eight separate *Commitment Statements*.

THE FOLLOWING *MISSION CHART* SHOULD BE CARRIED WITH YOU ALONG WITH A COPY OF YOUR *WHEEL OF LIFE*. THIS SHORT FORM DISPLAY WILL SERVE AS A CONSTANT REMAINDER OF YOUR GOAL PROGRESSION AND TELL YOU HOW WELL YOU ARE SUPPORTING EACH OF YOUR KEY PERSONAL VALUES.

MISSION CHART

VALUE VALUE VALUE VALUE VALUE VALUE VALUE VALUE
_____ _____ _____ _____ _____ _____ _____ _____

GOALS:

**COMMITMENT
STATEMENTS:**

Our commitment statements will dictate our daily behavior, the decisions we need to make and tell us how to best utilize our time. We should carry them with us or put them on our bathroom mirror or refrigerator door to serve as a constant reminder of our commitments to ourselves. They are our mandates for goal achievement in the most valuable and important areas of our life. With a constant visual awareness of where we are heading, we will optimize our faith and resolution to determine the outcome we are seeking. The key is to remember the words of Socrates, *To thine own self, be true.*

Why do I fail so often in realizing my goals?

Without defining our goals and developing our statements of commitment to them, we are dealing with little more than vague wishes in our lives. Through the process of Values elicitation, goal setting and developing our commitment pledges, we are taking our formless wishes and transforming them into solid targets for our focused attention. Earl Nightingale put this succinctly when he said, *People with goals know where they are going.* Conversely, without goals we are doomed to keep repeating the past. Another popular sage once stated, *If we keep doing what we've always done, we'll keep getting what we've always gotten.* We can only make our Purpose take shape if we recognize that it must be realized through positive direction and positive intentions.

While clear goals are critical, just knowing them is not enough. If having goals alone got us to where we want to be, we could be smugly content that everything would run smoothly on automatic pilot from this moment forward. But we still have a virtual minefield of obstacles ahead of us. Even with our goals and the sacred promises we make to ourselves, we can still get sidetracked, lose interest, bog down with other commitments, run out of time, etc.

Does it still seem impossible to us? Why do we still run afoul of our best-laid plans? Maybe if we knew the reasons, we might be able to overcome them. Paul G. Thomas once observed, *Until input (thought) is linked to a goal (purpose) there can be no intelligent accomplishment.* If we think through the process of goal realization and develop a logical methodology for accomplishing it, we at least have the opportunity to succeed.

Again, just wishing it to happen will never make it so. There are numerous culprits lurking in our psyches to prevent us from realizing our goals. Following are the major barriers we will face and the required tools for conquering them:

HAZY GOAL SETTING

Most of us fail to reach our true goals because we haven't clearly defined them. We must spend sufficient and quality time going through the preceding exercises of goal setting and making our *Commitment Statements.* Ben Stein wrote, *The indispensable first step to getting the things you want out of this life is this: decide what you want.* If we are truly introspective, honest enough to determine our highest wants and make commitments that are absolute covenants to ourselves, we will have goals that are unambiguous and reachable.

How often have we said that we would like to be rich, to be in great physical shape, to continue our education, to be better parents, to start a new business, etc. These are not goals; these are fantasies! Not fantasies in the sense that they are unrealistic or not worth pursuing - rather they are fantasies in that they are merely items on a wish list. They are simply illusions until they are precisely sketched out in specific terms of achievement. For a goal to be worth pursuing, we must know the details of exactly what it is we are pursuing.

Part of our difficulty in crystallizing our goals is found in our ambiguous usage of the word itself. When we think of the word *Goal*, we immediately get an ambivalent feeling about it. The word *Goal* has been so misused and overused that we really employ it as a synonym for the words *Desire, Hope and Dream*. When we say, *My goal is to be rich someday* we are actually expressing our *dream, hope* or *desire* to be rich someday.

Child psychiatrist Leon Tec states that *goals* are really just *intentions*. He prefers to replace the word *target* for *goal* because a *target* is not an *intention;* rather a *target* is something in which we take specific aim. A *target* forces us to focus ourselves and to project a specific action in its direction. We must not think of our ambiguous goals and only see the dartboard. Rather, we should be thinking of our goals and see the bull's eye!

UNACHIEVABLE GOALS

We must have goals that are within our capacity to achieve. Motivational speakers tell us to shoot for the stars; that *if our mind can conceive it, we can achieve it*. This is very inspirational but highly unrealistic. We cannot reach certain goals that are beyond our limitations or capabilities. Reaching is important, but we should reach for that which is within our grasp. As we learned in the earlier section on the *Invisible Doughnut*, we must know what we can accomplish relative to our *Essential Self*. We have certain core talents, physical attributes, personality characteristics and genetically bred intelligence. While we are not suggesting that we should not test our limitations, we must not feel defeated if we cannot achieve goals that are irrational or even foolish.

While we make decisions relative to our Purpose, we must not force our Purpose to operate outside the boundaries of our *Essential Self.* For example, choosing goals that put stress on us because we are incapable of altering our *Essential Self* will undermine our Purpose in life. If we become extremist in our pursuit of unachievable goals, we may question or even abandon our Purpose when we fail. Let's set targets that inspire and challenge us, but let's also give ourselves reasonable opportunity for succeeding. Our self-esteem and self-worth are enhanced only if we pursue and achieve realistic goals. Setting goals that ensure our failure are designed for our egos, not for our Purpose.

LACK OF COMMITMENT

While we may state that a particular goal is important to us, we may lose the drive or the personal inspiration to achieve it. That is, we may simply not want it badly enough to make the necessary sacrifices to work toward its fulfillment. We may move toward the goal but at the first sign of resistance, we abandon the effort. If this happens, we need to go back to our original *Commitment Statement* and review how we said we would make it happen. If we rediscover that we can't support our Values underlying that goal or the steps we chose to take, then it should be abandoned as a false goal. Dale Carnegie told us, *The successful man will profit from his mistakes and try again in a different way.* If we still feel the burning desire for achieving the goal, then we must redirect and rewrite our *Commitment Statement* to a new set of personal instructions for follow through. The old adage, *If at first we don't succeed, then try again,* may sound simplistic, but it works.

Knowing our Purpose is the foundation that supports our commitment to everything we want from life. This leads us to be rock-solid in our commitment to goal achievement because we know the Rewards we are seeking and which Behavior or actions will be required of us to realize them. John McDonald once said, *The intensity of our desire governs the power with which the force is directed.* Commitment to our goals is easy once we know the whole playing field, the position we are going to play, and possess the passion to succeed. If we are deeply committed to our goals, we won't even conceive of any path to follow except the one that takes us to our destination. This is the true miracle of Purpose. Once we know what we are living for, we cannot imagine living for anything else!

LACK OF TIME

Perhaps our primary and worse excuse for failing to reach our goals is that we don't have the time. It is far easier to rationalize our failures by placing blame on something that all of us can understand and relate to - the element of time. But our excuse falls short when we look around us and find others who are realizing their goals. Why do some people seem to have time to accomplish more than others when time is the only thing that all of us have exactly the same amount of? It is simply a matter of scheduling and prioritizing that which is really important to us and eliminating time spent on that which is not really important.

This is a difficult, but learnable skill, which will be covered in more detail in *Chapter Twelve*, but let it suffice here to say that we all have ample time to realize significantly more than we normally choose too. Time is that limited and most important commodity in our lives. Efficient and productive time utilization should perhaps be our number one Value, for time wasted is equivalent to flushing our lives into a toilet! It is never recaptured nor recreated in our lives. Once it is gone, it is gone! Life doesn't care one bit how we use our time; it is indifferent to whether we choose to watch talk shows or volunteer at a charitable organization. And like our Purpose, our time utilization is ours alone to determine. In fact, our Purpose and our time may be one and the same, for to squander our time is to squander our Purpose. Let's use both as wisely as we can.

LACK OF DETAILS/TOO MANY DETAILS

We either haven't defined the detailed aspects of our personal action plan, or we made it so complicated that we overwhelmed ourselves. This is the classic forest versus the trees dilemma. We are either so focused on the broad landscape of goal achievement that we missed the interim steps, or we are so bogged down with every little step to take we never looked up to see the horizon. This is essentially a planning problem. Our original plan was flawed or we failed to revise it as we went along. Let's remember that our *Commitment Statement* became our personal action plan. When we are perplexed, we need to review that original plan. More effort in initial organization and preparation will get us off to the right start and keep us from getting sidetracked. If we plan our work correctly, then we can work our plan properly.

It is equally vital to not only keep our goal in perspective but also the necessary steps to achieve it. We may find ourselves too wrapped up in the enormity of the project or in the apparent complexity of our task. This may require us to take a step back and get away from it for a while to clear our minds. We may then discover that our entire approach was wrong or that we were pursuing the wrong goals. The new insights we gain will open up new possibilities or allow us to see more relevant dimensions of the goal that we are pursuing. It is said that the only way to eat an elephant is one bite at a time. By getting a clearer perspective on this task, we may even decide that we don't like eating an elephant as much as we thought we might!

LACK OF SCHEDULING/SEQUENCING

There is a right way and a right time to work on goal achievement. Without an awareness of the time sequences to make our goals a reality, we usually get sidetracked, spin our wheels in the wrong direction or deplete our energy trying to over-achieve. Goal achievement is not just doing the right things; it is doing the *right things right and at the right time.* There is a logical sequence of priority events that must take place on the road to goal achievement. They must be done in proper order without jumping ahead of ourselves, i.e. for certain things to happen, something else may have to happen before it.

Also, some of our actions can be combined to meet multiple goals at the same time rather than wasting energy in different directions. And we must recognize that there are certain times of the day that we can perform more optimally than in other parts of the day. Sequencing our actions in the proper order, scheduling our days to accomplish more and having an organized routine will keep us on track. As we move toward a targeted goal, we will learn that if our small, successive steps are successful, we will actually be creating more energy to keep ourselves moving in the same general direction.

Our successes will tend to build on each other and eventually we will find ourselves almost consumed with maintaining our great momentum. The key is for us to continuously receive feedback on our progress. If we aspire to run a marathon, we will have greater likelihood of success if we keep a training log that reveals the incremental progress we are making. Goals can only be achieved by pursuing them logically. When we build a house, we must first lay the foundation, then raise the walls, and finally attach our roof. Every goal has a similar order or sequence to follow. As we accomplish each interim step, we will receive the positive feedback that is necessary to keep us motivated and on track.

LACK OF SKILLS/TALENTS

Some of our most ambitious goals will not be achievable without a great amount of personal preparation. If we aspire to being a concert pianist or a bestselling novelist, we may have to spend years in the rudimentary acts of practicing and polishing our craft. Unfortunately, we often feel the enormous time and commitment required is just too much to comprehend or not worth the effort. We must decide if are willing to pay the price. This is not an easy choice for many of us, but it is the only choice. To cut down a large tree, we must first sharpen our ax. If our dedication to our Vision, our Values and our Mission is strong enough, we will sharpen our ax through more education, preparation and practice. Whatever talent we possess, we must adhere to the words of Zig Ziglar, *Success is the maximum utilization of the ability that we have.*

We must endeavor to enhance our skills and then intensely apply our acquired knowledge. To achieve our greatest goals, we will have difficult roads to navigate, bumpy roads that must be traversed to reach our destination. It was once said that, *There are no shortcuts to anyplace worth going.* Thus, our plans must incorporate an honest assessment of our aptitude for achievement, not only of our innate abilities but also of our capacity for improvement. And we must consider not only our innate intelligence but also our desire to make the necessary sacrifices.

But regardless of our level of basic talent, our dedication and unflinching efforts will do more to determine the results that we are seeking.

LACK OF CONFIDENCE/COURAGE/PERSEVERANCE

To achieve most, if not all of our goals, we must make giant leaps of faith in ourselves. This requires confidence in our beliefs and the courage to take the first step. Eugene Ware, the lawyer and poet once said, *All glory comes from daring to begin.* Courage combined with enthusiasm and self-confidence makes us virtually unstoppable. These qualities must be lived not only for the moment, but must be lived for a lifetime. The scientist Edward Butler once wrote, *One man has enthusiasm for thirty minutes, another for thirty days, but it is the man who has it for thirty years who makes a success of his life.* We can learn that our obstacles are illusions if we never give up. If we fail along the way, we will treat it as our sustenance for continual growth. Our goals will be ours if we are determined to go boldly and steadfastly. No challenge can withstand this onslaught.

Knowing our Purpose is the foundation for courage, perseverance and self-confidence. When we have a clear Purpose we never doubt our willingness to stay the course in goal achievement. Our Vision of where we want to go in life gives us the strength to never give up when the going gets difficult. Our Values, being our highest wants and aspirations, helps us establish our goals throughout life. In fact, our goal achievement is the embodiment of our Values being achieved. When we are aware of these pieces of life's puzzle, we have the blueprint for making everything we want in life a reality. It is our choice as to what we want and it is also our choice as to whether or not we will have the courage to realize it.

LACK OF A MENTOR, COACH OR PARTNER

All good intentions need a supporting cast. Whether a professional coach or a family member, seek out someone who will share your vision and dreams and be willing to help you achieve them. Too often, we make excuses or lose sight of the objective by having to travel the course alone. We may become despaired at a difficult moment or lose perspective on our goals by becoming bored or frustrated with the routine. For this reason, we have personal trainers to guide us to physical fitness, financial planners to keep us on track with our investment goals, and even life coaches to help us with personal challenges and staying true to our life purpose.

Another ear or voice will do wonders for our self-discipline and our personal accountability. By knowing that someone else is sharing in the responsibility for our achievement, we are less likely to give up on ourselves. We may be willing to personally throw in the towel, but we seldom wish to disappoint someone else. When choosing our partners, let's look for role models who have accomplished similar goals. Modeling our actions after someone who has already achieved the same objectives is not only highly motivating but it allows us to follow the same steps that created their success.

Following is a short list of common hints of wisdom for goal (target) achievement:

- *Write down your goals (along with your Purpose Statement) and carry them with you.*
- *Be precise in setting your goals; know exactly what you want and how you will get there.*
- *Don't allow the difficulty of the task to prevent you from beginning; just get started, see where you are and keep your perspectives clear.*
- *Break up your long-term goals into shorter ones; this will keep you motivated as you progress.*
- *Keep your eye on the bull's eye of your target, not the wall behind it.*
- *Learn to delegate; elicit the help of others to assist you along the way.*
- *Set your priorities; there is a logical sequence to getting anything accomplished.*
- *Keep attentive and focused; don't let distractions send you into new directions.*
- *Practice mentally rehearsing what it will feel like when you have accomplished your tasks.*
- *When encountering difficult obstacles, back off and consider other avenues to your destination.*
- *Analyze the feedback of your interim progress toward a goal; Learn from your achievements.*

- *Keep an inventory of your skills, talents and resources; Upgrade them continuously.*
- *Congratulate and reward yourself for incremental successes along the way.*
- *Become a master list maker; Keep organized and enjoy checking off things you have done.*
- *Understand the mechanics of planning and the proper execution of your plans.*
- *Combine tasks whenever possible; Try to kill two birds with one stone to economize your efforts.*
- *Recognize your biorhythms for efficiency; know your best time of the day to be productive.*
- *Work smart, not hard; don't think of quantity of effort, think of quality of effort.*
- *Never procrastinate without a valid and unavoidable reason.*
- *Secure a mentor, partner or coach to support your progress and to be accountable to.*
- *Keep a sense of humor; Laugh at yourself when you stumble and quickly get on your feet again.*
- *Remember that your Purpose is behind everything that you do.*

Before we leave our specific discussion on goals, we need to keep an important idea in mind. Most of us are taught throughout our lives that goal achievement is the measure of success for life. Without question, having goals and attaining them is our best yardstick of progress. But to think of goal realization as our motivation for living misses the main point. Goals emanate from our Purpose. Goals, in themselves, are only manifestations of our life, not the reason for our life.

In fact, the reason we have such difficulty with goal setting is that we tend to develop them in a vacuum of understanding as to what we really want from our life. Goals are merely by-products of our Purpose. We cannot know what our goals are nor have the motivation to realize them without first having a clear and conscious understanding of our Purpose.

When we are asked to respond to our parents, our teachers and our bosses who want to know which goals we are going to set for ourselves, we must turn the question back on them. We need to ask them what they have given us to better understand our Purpose for goal achievement. We cannot criticize our children for being lazy and directionless when we have done so little to help them think about their Purpose or inspire them to have any Vision. We cannot ask our students which courses they want to take or motivate them to do their homework without first helping them define a reason for doing so. We cannot ask our employees to be motivated and productive without first getting them to buy into the Vision of the company and its Mission Statement.

We spend far too much time and energy wondering about our goals in life when we haven't first laid the foundation for even having goals. Our preoccupation with goal achievement is futile without first defining our Purpose and establishing the Values we will embrace. It is pointless for our homes, schools and businesses to expect any goal achievement without a concurrent reason for their achievement. Without Purpose, Vision and Values, we will always be ambiguous about the goals we want to pursue. Finding our passion to succeed and then attaining our rewards in life always begins with knowing our Purpose.

CHAPTER TEN

How Do I Avoid Failure?

Mastering the Difficult

Little minds attain and are subdued by misfortunes; but great minds rise above them.

Washington Irving

When did you last feel that you were the master - that time in your life when you felt the world was serving you rather than you serving it? Can you recall when you last felt that any obstacle you encountered could be easily managed and put in its proper place? How long has it been since you truly believed that you were in charge and nothing in life seemed too difficult? And when did you last sense an entire day had passed with you in control, acting with a clear sense of Purpose and resolve?

If each of us were honest, we probably cannot remember the last perfect day in our lives. Regrettably, many of us feel that life is simply the burden of managing the turmoil and confusion that confronts us. We are, in fact, continually confronted with the stresses and pressures of daily living, staying in a state of imbalance just trying to keep on top of things.

Unfortunately, this is life. Rarely will we be asked to not respond to the trials and tribulations of daily living. We forget the umbrella. The cat rips holes in our new curtains. We are laid off from our job. We learn we have cancer. Or just as probable, we get a promotion and a large raise. We have a new baby. Or we may even win the lottery. Whether negative or positive, life's events will always come at us with reckless abandon. Many of these situations will not be our fault while others will be of our own creation. Nevertheless, one thing is certain - we cannot escape having to deal with them.

These events create turmoil if we are not accepting of them, confusion if we have not prepared for them, and imbalance if we are not able to program and assimilate them into our sense of Purpose and Value-system. Our greatest desire, of course, is to live without unexpected changes - to live without worry of our basic needs being met, to be free from pain, to not have to make the difficult decisions, and to be certain of our future happiness and well-being. This is our dream, but this is not our reality.

The conflict occurs when we are unable to manage the change or the unexpected effect of life's daily events. This discord is labeled *Stress,* which by definition is any event that we must adapt to. If we do not adapt, we create more turmoil and confusion which, in turn, creates even more stress. This continuing cycle of conflict adaptation is perhaps the most insidious feature of the human condition.

As the world becomes increasingly complex, the pace of managing change and uncertainty will undoubtedly accelerate. Unlike modern day man, the prehistoric caveman who was about to be devoured by the sable tooth tiger had only one of two choices to make: fight or flight. And as stressful as that decision may have seemed to him, his options were clear and simple. In today's world, however, we are faced with infinite choices, forcing decisions which usually fall somewhere between having to fight or flight.

For example, when confronted with an abusive spouse, we must think of multiple scenarios: our health, children, financial situation, reputation, and even our wedding vows that must be worked out. Or when facing a serious illness, we must consider treatment options, insurance claims, job security and family matters. Unfortunately, fight or flight is too simple a choice to make in today's complex environment.

Every lifestyle is filled with these stressful events, from the mundane to the traumatic. If, however, we are committed to what we believe, know who we are and what we want, we are better prepared to cope with life's inevitable conflicts. By knowing ourselves, these conflicts will then cease to be conflicts or at the very least can be reduced to something manageable.

Having a clear, purposeful perspective on life is the key, the tool that gives us the strength to deal with these crises as they arise. By having a strong belief system, we can confront these unavoidable conflicts with greater power to control them. By taking responsibility and committing ourselves to purposeful solutions, we have a better opportunity to be in charge. And with time, practice and the right attitude, we can even learn to master life's inevitable challenges.

Why do we want to avoid stress?

We often hear how bad stress is for us. It causes heart attacks, ulcers and migraines. Stress has been physiologically proven to be the root of most of our ills as it wears down our natural immune system and bodily defenses against disease. Stress breaks up our marriages, turns us to drugs and alcohol and makes us yell at our children. With all of the bad press that stress seems to receive, it would seem to be a difficult thing to appreciate.

Yet stress is not the real villain that we make it out to be. Its real desirability depends upon our perception of how it is influencing our life. Stress has given us the tools to survive. In fact, stress can also be highly motivating and inspirational. Without stress forcing us to adapt to change we would have all been eaten by those saber tooth tigers and not be around today to deal with traffic jams and telephone solicitors. But before we agree that stress can be a good thing, we must first understand what it is, how it affects our life, and what we can do about it.

There are basically two types of stress: *distress and eustress.* The former causes our ulcers while the latter is what gets us out of bed in the morning. When stress turns into *distress*, we become anxious and confused and have those nasty physical reactions that we would rather avoid. Yet, if stress is of the *eustress* variety, we are compelled to change our lives for the better, to take on new challenges and seek out rewarding opportunities.

Distress acts upon us. *Eustress* lets us act upon it. Negative stress (*distress*) preys on those of us who are valueless. Positive stress (*eustress*) creates a situation where we exercise our right to live the way we want to. Which one we allow to govern our lives depends entirely on how we choose to react to life's events.

If that prehistoric beast were to pounce on us today, we could look at the event in one of two ways: we could either see it as a very bad day in the making, or we could see it as an opportunity to try out that sharp, new spear we got for our birthday. Likewise, if our boss harasses us at work, we could either go into hiding to avoid his wrath, or we could polish up our resume and seek out a better work environment.

Distress is allowing the event to put us into a corner without a way out. *Eustress* provides us an opening for finding a solution or response, acting upon the event in a positive, controlling manner. The choice we make depends upon our feelings of self-worth, self-preservation and self-confidence. If we embrace the stressful situation as a positive *change-maker*, we are saying that we know who we are, what our Purpose is, and how we want our life to be lived.

Perhaps the concept of loving stress is a little to bold of an idea for most of us. While some people actually get an adrenaline high from addressing a large audience without notes, most of us would find this paralyzing. Some of us like to bungee jump while others believe this to be sheer lunacy. It all depends on how we perceive these events, as fun and exciting or as traumatic and painful. Even the act of getting married or taking a new job can elicit vastly different emotions in different people, from exhilaration to terror and every emotion in between. Thus, our perception of the stressors in our life is entirely dependent upon how we have programmed our minds to think.

Fortunately, we can re-program our minds to think differently. If an event is perceived as stressful, we currently have three choices in dealing with it:

Accept it (Fight). Accepting the situation is the choice of self-confidence. It says that we can handle the situation and deal with it in a mature manner. While we really don't want to make that tough choice, we know that by taking positive action we can usually eliminate or diminish the stressor. The bold solution for us is to kill the beast and not worry about it in the future.

Avoid it (Flight). Avoiding the stressful situation may sometimes be our only answer, but it is usually a short-term action that postpones the stressor without entirely eliminating it. Avoidance is our expression of self-doubt, which will only lead to further anxiety. Our problem is that if we don't kill the beast, we will have to worry about it returning to devour us another day.

Alter it (Change). We may see an opportunity to alter the event that is causing us stress. This requires judgment and logical reasoning, but it always gives us the opportunity to see all sides of the problem and possibly discover new solutions. Also, if we find that neither facing it head on nor running from it works, we may be able to navigate around it. We can choose to tame the beast, feed it something else or climb a tree and yell for help.

Again, whichever choice we make, or any combination thereof, depends upon how we perceive the situation that is causing us stress. As we stated earlier, most of the events that we face in our complex society do not permit a simple flight or fight response. Acceptance or avoidance of our stressors is sometimes possible but more likely we will be forced to deal with them in some creative or logical fashion. We may think this is more difficult at first, but the benefit is that we can possibly discover more about ourselves and the best way to deal with similar stressors in the future. If, however, we see our only choice as either killing or running from the beast, we will not see any better solutions to managing a similar beast the next time around.

We should look at every stressful situation as an opportunity for us to be in control of the event, or if not the event, at least in how it should be responded to. It was once said that, *We cannot direct the wind, but we can adjust the sails.* Therefore, if the event doesn't fit our perspective on how things should be, we should attempt to modify it, making it conform to us rather than us being forced to conform to it.

Take for instance a traffic jam that occurs every day on the freeway to our office. We can respond to it as a *Type A - Hot Reactor* by pounding our fist on the steering wheel and cursing the drivers in front of us. This may release some pent-up anger, but the traffic jam will still be there. We could avoid the problem by staying home but the same traffic jam will be there tomorrow. Or we could perceive the event as an opportunity for change and for us to take control. Our options might then include going home that evening and studying our roadmap for alternate routes to the office. Or perhaps we could leave earlier or later the next morning to mitigate the time we spend in the traffic jam. Or possibly we could use the extra time *granted* to us to listen to motivational tapes while we sit in our car. Our first two responses of fighting or avoiding would not have solved anything. Our last set of responses will at least allow us the satisfaction of managing the situation and feeling more in charge.

Turmoil and confusion in our lives is the by-product of helplessness; the feeling that we are out of control. When events control us, they rule us, leaving us as mere puppets on short strings. The feeling of not being in charge of our lives, our destinies, even our daily actions, is the sole cause of stress. Having to adapt to this feeling of helplessness, to events that we don't control is the root cause of all stress-related maladies. This is primarily because we don't know how to adapt, to regain control of our lives. And this is precisely why we should love stress!

Stressful events are thrown in our path as roadblocks, obstacles to our happiness, barriers to our Purpose and to our Values. Without them, however, we would never grow, renew, change and commit even more strongly to our Mission. If life had no bumps, we would never know or enjoy the ride on the smooth pavement. Without encountering difficulties, we would never develop the strength of character, the satisfaction of achievement and the enjoyment of success. Stress demands us to make choices, to take action and to be in control. The end result is to be fully human, to be alive and in control of our life.

Why do I get so easily upset about everything?

I think, therefore I am. These five words from Rene Descartes are perhaps the strongest words about the human condition ever uttered by a mortal man. James Allen expanded upon Descartes centuries later by adding, *As he thinks, so he is; as he continues to think, so he remains.* The wisdom of these philosophical writers is profound, for in those words we have been given the key to managing stress and ensuring our happiness. Simple words, yes, but for some reason we have made their meaning difficult to comprehend. If we could control our happiness by our thoughts, why do we resist it so fervently? If we could just flip a switch in our minds and be happy, then why don't we? The reason is that we lack faith. We basically don't accept nor understand any solution that can be that simple.

Let's explore how this works in more detail. It is a fact that our capacity for happiness rests in our expectations for that happiness. It was once said, *The man who believes he can do something is probably right, and so is the man who believes he can't.* If we perceive an event or situation to be bad, that is exactly what it will be. If we sense turmoil and confusion, it is because we don't believe we are in control, that we are helpless in altering the reality that confronts us. Conversely, if we feel that we do have control over the event, we will experience greater contentment and happiness.

We can say, therefore, that happiness is really the same thing as being in control, and having control is simply a matter of attitude and perception. J.S. Mill reminded us that our minds determine our condition when he wrote, *No great improvements in the lot of mankind are possible, until a great change takes place in the fundamental constitution of their modes of thought.*

An event, in itself, does not produce unhappiness. It is our response or reaction to that event that determines how we feel about it. We cannot always change the event that creates negative emotions like fear and anxiety, anger or resentment, but we can change our modes of thought and, thus, our emotions. They are entirely within our control.

We have learned that stress means having to adapt to events. Our sense of stress escalates simply because we don't want to adapt, change or alter our perspective or our attitude. But this is precisely the reason we fail to overcome our problems. We don't trust our ability to control the situation through our minds and our thoughts, that we can change our perspective on the reality that confronts us.

Descartes was the first to put the full responsibility on our shoulders. His natural law of happiness states that our minds (our thoughts) dictate exactly what we will receive out of life. Somerset Maugham added, *It is a funny thing about life; if you refuse to accept anything but the best, you very often get it.* We alone determine whether we are happy or not by deciding and acting upon the event to produce whichever outcome we expect.

The diagram below illustrates the dynamics of stress based upon our perceptions of control and responsibility over events that occur in our life. If we feel that we are directly controlling the outcome of the event and have commensurate responsibility for it, then we will experience a low level of stress. Conversely, if we feel that we have don't have any responsibility nor control over what will happen, then we will experience a greater level of stress. The critical component for us to remember is that our feelings and attitude are the main determinants of our perceptions of responsibility and control over the event.

Again, the event itself should have little bearing on our feeling of stress. It is our reaction to the event that determines our level of stress. We must, first, adopt the attitude that we will take responsibility for the event's outcome and then second, assume control over what actually will happen. The more we can connect ourselves to the perception of this possibility, the more likely we are to manage the stressful event. The final secret to taking responsibility and controlling life's events is found in our commitment. It is easy to say that we will try to look at life in a better light, but our real power to do this comes from our commitment to make it happen the way we want it to!

The following diagram depicts this relationship between our commitment to Self-Control and Self-Responsibility relative to life's events. The less our commitment, the higher our stress; the greater our commitment, the lower our stress:

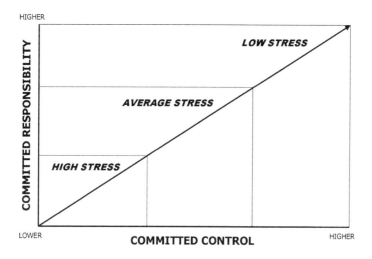

How can I commit myself to take responsibility and control over life's events?

As stress is linked to powerfully negative emotions, it would seem that if we could control them, we could control our stress. Our objective in controlling our emotions is to determine their actual basis and validity for existence. By rationally analyzing our worst emotions, we can often determine that there is little substance to support them. It is simply a matter of bringing logical and rational perceptions to what we think is stressful.

In their book, *A New Guide to Rational Living*, authors Albert Ellis and Robert Harper state, *People and things don't upset us. Rather, we upset ourselves by believing that they can upset us.* Their theories on Rational Emotive Therapy (RET) state that if we observe our own feelings and actions and analyze them objectively instead of moralistically or grandiosely, we can think straight and overcome the problems that we largely fabricate in our own minds.

Virtually all of us employ self-talk that *catastrophizes* a situation when the same self-talk, if it had been rational, would have led to a calmer, more intelligent perspective on the situation. In essence, we can perceive a situation as awful and it will be, or we can employ rational, straight thinking and more often than not reduce or eliminate the anxiety that was never justified in the first place. Ellis and Harper further argue that, *Humans do not get upset, but that they upset themselves by devoutly convincing themselves of irrational beliefs about what happens to them.*

Since our emotions are linked to our thinking, it would logically follow that a more satisfying life requires us to discipline our thinking. If we have emotions that are self-defeating, inappropriate or disorganized, it is largely because our thoughts were not tied to rational, logical analysis of the event or situation that confronts us. Clear reasoning, on the other hand, will block our negative emotions as we tie our response to fact rather than fiction.

Thus, any stressful event can be approached with one of two ways of thinking:

1. **The *emotional response*, which is often biased, prejudicial, subjective or blindly adherent to previous misconceptions;**

OR

2. **The *rational response*, which is a calm appraisal of the many elements of a situation, which will lead to an objective conclusion that more closely fits the reality of the situation.**

It is true that some events cannot be rationally responded to, e.g. the death of a family member or an immediate threat to our life by a mugger.

We have certain biologically based stimulus-response emotions that are programmed into our brain for basic necessities, most particularly our quest for survival. Experiencing the emotions of fear, or for that matter the joy of a beautiful sunset, are experienced feelings that we should not seek to eliminate. Nor do we suggest that we live our lives as robots where every event must be responded to after *Spock-like* analysis. If we solved all of our problems like computers, we could never enjoy the pleasures or satisfactions that add to the quality of our lives.

Rather, our aim is to attempt to place our reaction to most negative events and our most negative emotions - such as guilt, anger, denial, anxiety, depression and rage - into a box of rational analysis and clear thinking. This self-analysis should be based upon our ideological belief system. The point is that we can change, alter or control our emotions by observing and changing our underlying beliefs that create our most inappropriate feelings. It should be obvious that if we take a negative situation and review it thoroughly in our minds, we may come up with mental responses that are different than the first ones we developed. Thus, we need not respond negatively to an event if that event has little rational basis for being responded to negatively.

Let's clarify this with an extreme example. The most profound, stressing event we face in life is the death of a loved one. Assume our spouse just submitted to a long battle with cancer and died. This would naturally cause us to feel a severe deprivation. We may woefully upset ourselves to the point of wailing, moaning and despairing. It is natural to feel this grief and to feel that life is unfair and unkind. However, we will eventually find that our self-flagellation has done nothing to bring our loved one back; nor will our ranting and raving made us feel any better about our own future. Is it not better to ultimately view this event for what it is, bad but not catastrophic; that it is reality; that it has happened and there is nothing, like it or not, we can do to change it? We could decide that there is a good reason for this event, that we are thankful for the time we had with our loved one and that our own life and health continues. Yes, we can feel sorrow, grief and regret for the situation having occurred but we need not feel defeated by this event. We are still responsible for our own life going forward so the more effort we make in lamenting the situation, the less effort and time we will have to discover ways to overcome our grief and get on with our life.

Who said life has to be fair, kind and nice to us? Life can be difficult, and the sooner we recognize and accept this fact, the easier our life will become. In fact, just acknowledging this statement somehow makes life's burdens easier for us to bear. As humans we crave perfection of ourselves, of others and of the world in which we live. We wish not to see death, famine or disease. We even wish that we would never run out of gas, get fat or have our children talk back to us. But this is not the way life works. The entire universe is very much out of our control. Living with these constant imperfections frustrates us. However, once we accept the premise that life is difficult, that life's events are not always going to be in our control, then we can relax, learn to accept instead of resist and get on with the creative, intelligent management of our lives.

To overcome this burden of having to constantly deal with the unfairness of life, we must first, accept this unfairness and second, rationalize how we are going to deal with it. We cannot let life's unfairness defeat us. Rather, we need to conquer these unfair situations by designing our own set of responses to them. Life's events may largely be out of our control, but we do have control over ourselves. If we can effectively apply rational thoughts to an event as severe as the death of a loved one, imagine how many of life's smaller obstacles will be easier for us to handle.

We cannot deny our emotional feelings as they are as real as the event that precipitated them. Our challenge, however, is to redirect our thoughts to create feelings that are worthwhile and uplifting, not demoralizing and self-destructive. The idea of re-channeling our thoughts is known as a *reference reframe*. By adopting a philosophy that is rational and based upon our highest Values and beliefs, we can reference reframe our emotions into more productive directions. We only need to reframe our self-beliefs and our attitude toward life. As we expect it to be, it will be.

The key to reframing our thoughts and attitudes is to take a different view of those events that we deem to be stressful. This requires us to literally re-program our mind to see the event from a different perspective. Our mind, left unattended, is quite capable of conjuring up negative images of a situation. For some irrational reason we tend to get locked in on our worst thoughts because of their power to control and push out the positive thoughts.

When we allow this to happen we are engaged in thinking that is known as *awfulizing,* where we only see the worst possible outcomes in our minds. Over time, this process of *awfulizing* is very debilitating, leading to pessimism, anxiety and depression. Eventually, we give in to these self-beliefs and cannot see any other positive solution to our problems. Instead of self-empowerment, we become victims to self-imprisonment.

To avoid this scenario, we must break our cycle of negative thinking at the earliest opportunity. When we sense that we are falling into this trap of despair, setting ourselves up for failure, we must immediately engage in some self-administered shock treatment to our minds. We have to stop the tape running in our brains that is filling it with negative pictures and replace it with a new tape filled with optimistic, affirmative pictures. The fact is that we are equally capable of focusing on positive images. Our capacity for constructive thinking is already programmed into our minds. Knowing that the faulty tape is simply a function of faulty thinking, we must re-program it and run the correct one.

According to Maxie C. Maultsby, Jr., M.D., in his book *You and Your Emotions*, we tend to engage in four faulty habits of irrational thinking:

1. Thinking what you don't mean and meaning what you don't think and believing every word of it.
2. Listening to others but hearing only yourself thinking.
3. Believing what is not worth believing.
4. Having contradictory beliefs without knowing it.

Our objective is to know when we are doing this and stop it! The solution is to *reframe* our thoughts around a rational basis of understanding, that is, becoming specifically aware of the cause of our wrong thoughts or beliefs. To accomplish this, we must ask ourselves why we are thinking the way we are. According to Maultsby, there are five questions to ask ourselves to determine the basis of a rational thought:

1. IS THIS THOUGHT BASED ON OBJECTIVE REALITY?
2. DOES THIS THOUGHT HELP ME PROTECT MY LIFE AND HEALTH?
3. DOES THIS THOUGHT HELP ME ACHIEVE MY GOALS?

4. DOES THIS THOUGHT HELP ME FEEL THE WAY I WANT AND NEED TO FEEL?
5. DOES THIS THOUGHT HELP ME PREVENT SIGNIFICANT CONFLICT WITH OTHERS?

Our emotions are always determined by our self-beliefs. If we irrationally believe in something, we will self-determine irrational outcomes in our life. As there are an infinite number of outcomes to every situation or event, we only need to project the outcomes in our mind that we want to happen. The outcomes we anticipate will determine our self-beliefs; our self-beliefs will determine our attitude; and our attitude will determine which actions to take to ensure the outcome we seek. This is self-empowerment in its highest form!

How can I manage my self-beliefs?

Our self-beliefs literally create our reality. According to Todd Duncan, a master sales trainer and speaker, *Believe first in what you want to accomplish, what you want to become, and if you sustain those beliefs, they will become reality.* He also proclaims that *believing is seeing*, that is, we will see the results we want once we believe in our *Self* and our abilities.

Our self-beliefs and our actions, not the circumstances of our life, will ultimately dictate the outcome we will experience. In order to defeat our self-destructive set of beliefs, we must let go of our old beliefs, substituting new beliefs that will create the outcomes we are expecting. Our non-productive thoughts will only stand in the way of the results we are seeking.

In essence, by defeating old beliefs we establish new beliefs that ensure the correct outcome. We then become what we are thinking about and doing with our life. Our future depends upon little else if we put this power of self-believing to work. Our Purpose, our Vision, our Values, our Mission, our Behavior and our Results are all predicated upon this power of self-beliefs. Who we think we are, and who we think we can become, is the most powerful force available to us for life-long accomplishment.

It is important to recognize that holding the right self-beliefs is the catalyst for action, but simply believing in ourselves and not taking action will leave us at the starting line. We must transfer our self-beliefs into purposeful decision-making and specific behaviors for us to recognize our goals. Our self-beliefs create the motivation for us to act, but we are also required to carry our self-beliefs onto the battlefield. As we do, we learn from our mistakes, modify our self-beliefs if necessary and re-enter the battle.

Accordingly, we should adopt the following process:

1. **Reflect:** We need to take time on a regular basis to consider what results our actions are creating for us. Evaluation of our accomplishments and failures allows us to isolate the correct behavior for us to follow in the future. The essence of self-renewal is to learn from our mistakes and transform into new ways of thinking.

2. **Respond:** We can then develop the appropriate tactical changes to our behavior to ensure that we will be able to duplicate positive results and eliminate negative results. Our objective is to internalize self-beliefs that will keep us doing the right thing the right way and at the right time.

3. **Restart:** After evaluating the results of our past behavior and developing our tactical plan for future action, we must then jump back into the battle and *make it happen*! Our Purpose must be put to work!

When we choose not to take action against events that create stress in our life, we will have adopted a self-belief of powerlessness. This inaction on our part leads to anxiety, a mental state of worrying about an event, even to the point that we no longer know what we are worrying about. This worrying or feeling anxious literally shuts down our sense of control and responsibility over the perceived event. When this occurs, we really have only one solution: We must turn the worry into a problem! Once we have reframed the worry into a problem, then we have something tangible to deal with.

By re-identifying our worry as a rational and specific problem, we can literally launch an attack against it. This modifies our original self-belief of powerlessness to one of control and responsibility. Thus, we will fix the source of our worry through developing a proactive plan of action.

We will feel in control again, most likely eliminating or diminishing the worry to manageable proportions. At the very least, we will have turned our negative psychic energy into a purposeful attitude of control, which, in turn, bolsters our commitment and inner strength to overcome the problem.

As we discussed earlier, commitment is the key to responsibility and control. We cannot manage worry and stress nor achieve our life's goals without a real commitment to the process of self-renewing our beliefs. This means we are taking responsibility for ourselves and deciding to control the life that we want to experience. Continuous self-renewal of our beliefs is based upon this cycle of reflecting, responding and restarting. As we discover success with this process we will possess the momentum to carry us on to continued success. We, thus, will become self-empowered to manage the stress of life's conflicts by believing in ourselves and what we are doing. The more success we have, the more self-esteem we possess which in turns motivates us to further success.

Our belief, according to Daniel Webster is *a state or habit of mind.* The more we nourish this state of mind with positive self-beliefs, the more self-empowered we become to manage every aspect of our life. It is really very simple. Failing and succeeding are equal, but contradictory, states of mind; We only need to settle on one or the other as the pathway we will choose to follow. Paraphrasing Henry Ford, *We either believe we can, or we believe we can't.* Either state of mind will produce the results we are seeking.

The key to choosing the right state of mind means we must consistently align our thoughts with the outcome that we are seeking. We find our alignment by matching our Purpose and our Values with the Results that we want to achieve. This alignment becomes a state of mind and literally creates the path for us to follow.

By visualizing the outcome we want, we are compelled to act in the direction that increases the possibility of that outcome. Visualization is a powerful tool in the mind-behavior-results connection. Our *minds-eye* is a state of thinking where we see the final result and then understand the actions that are required to turn it into reality. We literally imagine the outcome and then, almost mystically, carry ourselves toward that outcome.

We, thus, master our self-beliefs by mastering certain tools for thinking and acting. In every life situation, we can learn to guide our thoughts and our actions by modeling those techniques that have long been employed by highly successful, happy and productive people. Self-mastery of our minds and self-mastery of the events that we face in life are within our power. As we gain mastery over these techniques, we also begin to understand and relate to our *Higher Self,* where we adopt even stronger techniques for self-empowerment.

In the next chapter, we will learn the significant rewards of:

> **Focusing** - Where we become highly conscious and aware of Purposeful decision-making. We will learn to take complete control of ourselves, setting the stage for all aspects of life management.

> **Flowing** - Where we create our self-designed experiences for living. This allows us to deeply enjoy our life through immersing ourselves in our efforts.

> **Centering** - Where we return to balance and control when we feel distracted from our Purpose. This allows us to defuse and manage the stressors of life's negative events.

Each of these tools work harmoniously with each other and are powerful resources for living with Purpose, but most importantly, they give us the strength to *make life happen.* Through the formation of these self-created beliefs, attitudes and positive actions, we can be in charge again!

CHAPTER ELEVEN

Where Do I Find My Inner Strength?

Self-Empowerment: Focusing, Flowing and Centering

Make no little plans; they have no magic to stir men's blood and probably themselves will not be realized. Make big plans; aim high in hope and work, remembering that noble, logical diagram once recorded will not die.

Daniel H. Burnham

Self-empowerment is inspiration moving in a consciously positive direction. It is that feeling of a distinct passion stirring within, an inner strength where we no longer perceive any obstacles in front of us. When we feel self-empowered, we sense the calling of Purpose, where our energy level soars and we channel all our resources toward a decisive goal. Our previously perceived barriers seem to fall mysteriously by the wayside. We become so intensely focused in our effort that time stands still, and we almost float above the ground, not sensing any other reality than the objective at hand.

This is a rare feeling for most of us. If we have ever experienced it, we will know it. It is that moment of such intense focus we seem to be flowing with an invisible current. It is a sense of being that is not stressful nor difficult; but rather, a natural state of being where self-knowledge meets motivated self-determinism. It is where we are one with our *Self*, consciously *self-knowing and self-living*!

Why do I seldom feel this happening?

Unfortunately, we rarely sense this total manifestation of our *Higher Self*, where we are in that focused zone of self-empowerment. It is a more common and uniquely human trait to spend our life swimming upstream, rather than self-directing the flow of life's currents. We typically make up our minds to *make life happen* only when we sense some degree of pressure to act, rather than acting before we sense the pressure.

While we may know what our planning calendar tells us to do - our programmed activities for the day - we tend to approach these tasks from a sense of obligation instead of focused will, much less with purposeful desire. As a result, what gets done, just gets done. And what we are getting done rarely leaves us with a great sense of satisfaction, internal pride or a feeling of valued accomplishment. Over time, we begin to sense that only one thing has really happened: That much time has passed but very little else!

With a lack of self-empowerment - where we are *not making life happen* - we often find ourselves drifting into a rut of indifference. Doing little of what is most important, we will often go long periods of time totally unaware of what is most meaningful and significant to us. After awhile, we will actually begin to go backwards, where life becomes nothing more than waiting to *see what happens*! We may refer to this as indolence, procrastination or even laziness, but we could more properly label it as a lack of Purpose.

This is because we are basically lacking any will or focused reason to act. Due to our inability to focus on what should be most significant to us, we allow other people or events to create that sense of urgency or pressure that compels us to act. By not focusing on the important, we have given up our right to act or make choices to external forces. We don't exercise any control over ourselves because we actually find it easier or more expedient to let outside events or other people dictate to us what it is we should do. Therefore, we tend to exist in a sort of mindless existence, tending to our daily needs much like the bridge tender waiting for boats to pass.

This may sound like a harsh indictment of the quality of our life, but for many of us this assessment is uncomfortably true. This is not to imply that our life is without merit or validity; it is rather a statement on our life lacking true meaning due to our lack of concerted focusing on what is most important to us. If we are doing anything less than making every moment count toward the fulfillment of our Purpose, then we should conclude that we are aimlessly drifting through the motions of life. We are *sacrificing effect for lack of cause.*

When we fail to act in a purposeful way, we are lacking focus. When we wait for something to happen, we are really saying that nothing is happening inside of us. When we literally don't know what to do with ourselves other than engage in mostly mundane, uninspiring activities, we are failing to see more opportunity in how our time should be spent.

By not focusing, we are *allowing life to just happen* rather than us *making something happen in life*. We are simply not recognizing any reason to do otherwise. Admittedly, we may go to work, manage our chores and take care of our bills. We may even squeeze some leisure time into our day, however, these activities are rarely the result of focused effort. The fact is that what we mostly do is based more upon perceived obligations rather than planned intentions.

Paul G. Thomas told us, *Until input (thought) is linked to a goal (purpose) there can be no intelligent accomplishment.* We can only state that our life has true meaning if we are consciously pursuing the life that we have designed and have chosen to live. Lacking focus is not living in accordance with our Purpose, our Vision and our Mission. By not focusing, we have given up control of these vital mandates in our life to the rest of the world.

However, when we do focus our life around what is most important to us, we are driving our own behavior and self-determining the results that we are seeking. Thus, the entire point of focusing is self-empowerment. Focusing gives us the power to manage every aspect of our life and to put every action into the context of our *Higher Self*. Our *Higher Self* is totally dependent on self-empowerment. By knowing our Purpose, our Vision and our Mission, we know who we are and where we are going. Focusing our actions around this knowledge assures us of getting there.

How do I know when I am empowering my *Higher Self*?

Perhaps the best way to understand self-empowerment of the *Higher Self* is to revisit Abraham Maslow's concept of *self-actualization*. His pyramidal hierarchy of needs suggests that we all have fundamental requirements for the fulfillment of the *Self*. Our most basic needs are physiological (food, shelter, sex, exercise, etc.) and safety (protection and personal security). These needs are our most elementary requirements and while critical to our survival, they only serve to fulfill our needs for physical existence.

Once these needs are satisfied, we require more personal fulfillment, such as a feeling of belonging and self-esteem. These needs distinguish us as humans, but the ultimate manifestation of our *humanness* requires a feeling of *self-actualization*. The following diagram represents this concept:

Maslow's Pyramid of Needs

SELF - ACTUALIZATION

SELF-ESTEEM

BELONGING

SAFETY

PHYSIOLOGICAL

Self-actualization is a sense of *Being*, where we are connected to who we are (our *Essential Self*), what we are here for (our *Purpose*), what is most important to us (our *Values*), and where we are going (our *Mission*). When we have reached the pinnacle of the pyramid, we have reached the essence of our *Being*, where we are self-empowered and living our *Higher Self*. This is the goal for all of us who believe that life's richest meaning and significance is worth the effort of attainment.

But how do I do this?

If we chose to exist at the bottom of the pyramid, we are indistinguishable from basic animal life - simply surviving day to day on whatever comes our way. As humans, we will automatically recognize this to be insufficient for a meaningful life. Our higher intelligence tells us that there must be more to living than basic survival, so we seek out self-acceptance by *Belonging* to a society or a group. We then feel the need to raise our level of self-worth by adopting self-images that promote our *Self-Esteem*. Again, this is virtually automatic for all humans and requires minimal effort on our part. The higher goal for each of us - the one that seems to be our most challenging barrier - is to a*ctualize* our *Being* into its highest sense of Purpose, where we are connected to our *Higher Self*. This is where self-empowerment is fully realized.

By choosing to live at the bottom of the pyramid, we are saying that our basic needs are being met, that we are satisfied with what we have, and that we have little motivation for anything else. We are allowing *life to happen* to us rather than us *making life happen*. This is also where self-empowerment is least realized. As we choose to live at higher levels of the pyramid, we are beginning to *make life happen* through our own conscious decisions based upon our greater sense of Purpose. By climbing the pyramid of self-empowerment, we move from simple *Having Needs* to *Doing Needs* with the ultimate reward the realization of our *Being Needs*.

The following diagram shows our climb to greater self-empowerment:

The Path to Self-Empowerment

BEING NEEDS
Self Actualization

DOING NEEDS
Belonging and Self-Esteem

HAVING NEEDS
Physiological and Safety

Using the above perspective of Maslow's pyramid, we can see that our basic physiological and safety needs are *Having Needs*. Belonging and Self-Esteem are *Doing Needs* while Self-Actualization serves our *Being Needs*. If we only base our life upon *Having* or *Doing Needs*, we are not living in accordance with our Purpose and are limiting our potential for growth, self-renewal and self-actualization. In essence, we will have locked the door to our *Higher Self*. Conversely, if we sense that our lower needs are being meet (and they must be for us to call ourselves human), we have the freedom to pursue the highest form of human existence, a pattern of living which we truly sense to be meaningful, worthwhile and successful.

How does this relate to my potential for success?

We all seek greater personal and professional success in our lives. Unfortunately, we confuse the meaning of the term *Success* as often as we confuse the term *Purpose*. Thus, our achievement of success will always remain elusive until we clearly understand what it means. Most of us identify success as the attainment of fame, fortune, power and prestige. We see the outward manifestations of success in Rolls Royces, Rollexes and mansions. We would also say that certain people are successful because of their titles, positions of influence or recognition factor on the covers of magazines. Bill Gates is successful because he one of the richest people in the world, but was Mother Theresa successful because of her work with the poor? The Green Bay Packers are successful because of their Super Bowl titles, but is the local high school team that wins their district championship? George Bush is successful because he became President of the United States, but is a single working mother equally successful by balancing jobs, children and a home?

We all have different concepts of success, and for this reason alone we have difficulty knowing when we have achieved it. The one undisputable fact, however, is that most people who have reached the so-called pinnacle of success will still admit that a void exists in their lives. Despite the trappings and outward appearances of their success, most never seem to feel it really belongs to them. There is always something more, something else, something missing in the lives of most *successful* people. Where does that leave us then for a definition of a successful life?

There is a fundamental difference between false success and true success? *False Success* is living at the bottom of our pyramid of self-actualization. We can abundantly satisfy all of our *Having Needs* (physiological & safety needs): a mansion for shelter, fine cuisine for food, mink coats for warmth and armed gates to protect our possessions and our need for security. We can also clearly satisfy our *Doing Needs* (self-esteem & belonging needs) by living in the most posh community, belonging to the most elite clubs, and having outwardly prestigious careers. But unless we satisfy our *Being Needs* (a feeling of self-actualization through the manifestation of our Purpose), there will still be some void left in us, a lack of feeling *True Success*.

Therefore, we must endeavor to satisfy our highest need of living a purposeful life before we can attain a sense of *True Success*. Rather than spending our lives in a continuous pursuit of *Having* and *Doing*, we must shift our consciousness to the pursuit of B*eing*. At the highest level of *Being*, we are in touch with our Purpose and consciously in pursuit of our Values with our focused Mission to guide us toward self-actualization (to fulfill our *Highest Being Needs*). At this level, we are becoming fully human, exercising all of our creative powers and fulfilling our destiny through the realization of our full potential. In essence, we will become one with our *Higher Self* through conscious decision making based upon our knowledge of who we are, what we are here for, and what we want. We will be self-empowered to the fullest in everything that we do, taking control of our life and ensuring our ultimate success.

What steps must I take to accomplish this?

Ben Stein wrote, *the indispensable first step to getting the things you want out of life is this: decide what you want.* He could have added that the second step is focusing, that is, after deciding what we want, we must be pursuing it. Orison Swett Marden came closer to the concept of focusing and self-empowerment by writing, *When a man feels throbbing within him the power to do what he undertakes as well as it can possibly be done, this is happiness, this is success.*

We need to organize our lives around this feeling of *power throbbing within* as it gives us the clear focus to pursue what is most fundamental to our happiness and success. Our goal should be to break our old habits of unconscious, unfocused living where we wait for *life to simply happen*, where we only live our perceived obligations of life. Our *Higher Self* will know its intent; it will make no excuses and will act with clear Purpose and resolve. The only way we can master ourselves is to have a focused state of mind that tells us exactly what we want, and we then become fully determined to find it.

There are three elements to having this intense focus in our lives:

1. **The self-awareness of our Purpose, our Vision and our Mission. This self-knowledge tells us what we are here for, where we want to go, and how we are going to get there.**
2. **A defined commitment to self-empowerment. This gives us the strength to embrace our Values, the confidence of our self-beliefs, our self-image, and our will to act.**
3. **The self-mastery of our daily behavior. This provides us the opportunity to choose our own course of action where we decide what to do, rather than allowing external events or outside influences to make our decisions for us.**

With these three concepts at work in our daily life, we will possess the clear focus we need to act in a purposeful manner. We will act with a clear conscience, effectively manage our time and enjoy the rewards of living a meaningful life. We will no longer drift on the tides of the rest of the world; rather, we will steer our life on the heading of our own choosing. We will savor the knowledge that we are managing our own destiny from the moment we arise each morning to the moment we retire in the evening. We will become connected to our *Higher Self* and be focused in our thoughts and efforts at all times. We will be living a life of our own choosing, a life with hope and promise, a life without regrets.

Sounds wonderful, but wouldn't focusing this much on my life make it even more stressful?

No… Just the opposite! If we are immersed in our pursuit of what is most important to us, we will experience the most liberating, stress free existence possible. *Doing* is what living is all about. It is the gateway to our

Being. Doing is also the manifestation of *focusing*, where we truly sense the feeling of *Being. Doing* is a physical act, however, it has more to do with the mind than the body as our thought processes govern exactly what it is we will do. Our mind is our regulator, the machine that turns us on or off; the gray matter command post that signals us to action or to shut down and rest. It is where our thoughts, feelings and emotions either get all tangled up or work together in perfect harmony. It is important to master the mind for that is how we learn to master ourselves.

Mastering our *Selves* is the art of *doing* those things that create the optimal experience of inner peace and happiness while *not doing* those things that create confusion and inner turmoil. Our mind tells us which things to do that are most satisfying as well as those things not to do that are most distressing. It would make sense, therefore, to get actively involved in the former while eliminating the latter. And the more involved and committed we are to our most satisfying experiences the more likely we are to continue pursuing them.

This sounds so reasonably simple it would be hard to believe that so many of us avoid doing exactly this. Many of us are self-exiles in the world of joy. We are too often apathetic, prone to inactivity or laziness, or simply too intellectually dull to think about any commitment to that which would give us an even higher level of satisfaction. We tend to settle for less, focusing on the unimportant and responding only to the urgent. We are mistakenly of the belief that anything worth pursuing would require too much of our time and effort. It is much easier to let life take our hand and lead us around. We act because we have to act, not because we want to act!

But this attitude is not what living is all about. Living is *doing!* It is active, not passive. It requires our focused participation, not our detached observation. And our greatest happiness will derive from challenging our minds to take us to the highest levels of involvement and commitment to this thing called life. Through our immersion in those things that we deem to be most important, we will find ourselves in our most contented state. We will discover that when we feel that we are control and are doing what we most enjoy and desire, we will attain a feeling of complete satisfaction with our lives.

Mihaly Csikszentmihalyi states this feeling to be the optimal psychological experience, that, *we feel a sense of exhilaration, a deep sense of enjoyment that is long cherished and that becomes a landmark in memory for what life should be like.* In his book, *Flow*, he describes the optimal experience as something that we make happen, where we make order in our consciousness such that we directly control the experience of happiness. As Samuel Smiles has told us, *Life will always be to a large extent what we ourselves make it.* We must, therefore, order our consciousness to *flow*, much like a river that knows its direction and intent.

This process of *flowing* is also vitally important to our sense of *Self.* By recognizing this concept, we can manage our lives to create happiness almost at will. To understand this, we need only to think for a moment about those times when we were so in touch with what we valued that we literally became one with that Value. Let's think about a past goal that we wished to accomplish so much that we became totally consumed by it. It may have been a difficult challenge for us, but we desired it so greatly that we blindly pursued it with incredible energy and excitement.

We should think about the last time we were so wrapped up in an intriguing novel that we couldn't put it down to go to sleep. Remember that score of music that enchanted us to the extent that we played it over and over in our head. Or recall that time in an athletic event were we felt so *zoned* that we performed flawlessly and effortlessly. Or remember being lost in deep concentration while we were working on some project or task - building a boat, writing a poem, coaching a team, arranging old family photos, or even preparing a new dinner dish. We were completely captivated by our involvement, perhaps so caught up in what we were doing the world around us didn't seem to even exist.

Whether leisure or work related, difficult or easy, we can all recollect those times and events where we were completely mesmerized by our total, unconscious participation in those events. We remember that they brought us incredibly intense pleasure or happiness, or at the very least, our worries and complaints about the rest of our lives were temporarily put on hold. In fact, being in this state of intense participation is analogous to being in suspended animation, not it the sense of unconsciousness, but rather in a state of extreme consciousness where we are vitally alive and the harsher realities of the world seem to disappear. We are literally lost in our own self-created happiness.

According to Csikszentmihalyi, we need to possess the following to achieve true enjoyment and happiness:

1. We need to feel that in whatever we attempt to achieve, we have a chance of actually completing it. In other words, we must feel capable and competent to achieve our goals.
2. We must be able to concentrate on whatever we are doing or hope to achieve. We need the feeling that we can focus on our goals without distractions.
3. We must be able to undertake tasks that are based on clear goals. We have to know the goals that we are seeking and not have vague or ambiguous interpretations of them.
4. We must have immediate feedback on our efforts. We need to know that the tasks we have undertaken to achieve our goals are producing specific results.
5. We need to act with deep involvement free from our daily worries. We must be able to act without the interference of life's daily frustrations.
6. We must feel that we are in complete control of our actions, and that we are in charge of what we are doing.
7. We must lose our sense of *Self* in the act of what we are doing. We essentially become unaware of our *Self* due to our total immersion in our activities.
8. We lose all awareness of time as we are engaged in our actions. We literally discover that time becomes a *non-event* as we become so engrossed in what we are undertaking.

The above components of total enjoyment are experienced as a result of our achieving the *flow experience*. We can actually teach ourselves to achieve this optimal state whenever we choose. With practiced effort we can seek out our happiness by putting ourselves in a flow mindset. Common activities such as reading, athletic endeavors, socializing and taking on challenging situations can excite us and gain our total involvement and focus. Even events like going to the dentist, doing housework or homework can actually produce satisfying psychological experiences if we apply the principles of flow to these situations. We have long known that *going with the flow* is a feeling of stress free existence. However, we must recognize that *flowing* is not the absence of stress, but rather experiencing situations that are deemed so worthwhile and enjoyable that stress seems to be irrelevant.

As we think about our Purpose, we must recognize that for life to be lived to its fullest, we must intensely focus on our Values and our Mission. We must take charge and deeply commit to the achievement of our Goals. Our actions must be congruent with our Values to ensure the rewards we seek. And to make this process as enjoyable and as exhilarating as possible, we must order our consciousness to *flow* with our efforts.

Thus, we need to organize our daily lives into a pattern, not of jerky, anxious, tenuous, and haphazard activities, but of a pattern of deeply concentrated and connected efforts. We will find our focused involvement produces euphoric states of awareness of who we are, what we want and what we most enjoy doing. Our Mission will be achieved and recorded not merely through a documented scorecard but through the greatest feelings of inner peace and harmony that we can imagine.

What will keep me focused and flowing in the right direction?

Let's revisit our *Wheel of Life*, where we became focused on our Values (what is most important to us) and our Purpose (the center of our effort). The spokes of the wheel were our Values and the hub was our Purpose. When we felt that we were not meeting certain Values in our life, the wheel became wobbly and unsteady. We had to adjust our behavior to return equilibrium to our Value-system. If we were successful in focusing on what was most important, the wheel turned smoothly, achieving for us a feeling that we were balanced and flowing forward in a positive direction. But as in life, there are bumps in the road. As we encounter them, our wheel loses its stability. It falters and shakes requiring us to re-center it before it crashes in a ditch along the roadside.

Thus, in conjunction with the concepts of *focusing* and *flowing*, we need to master the process of *centering*. This is a self-empowered process that restores an orderly management to our life before we crash land in the ditch. When we are out of synchronization with our Purpose and our Values, we tend to lose our sense of *Self*. When we become too distracted or consumed by the chaos that surrounds us or simply ignore the balancing of our wheel, we are ultimately heading for the ditch. When we *center*, however, we regain personal balance, emotional stability and a feeling of calm reflection within ourselves.

The chief threat to instability of our Purpose is the overwhelming number of events and situations that want to override our inner *Self.* Our consciousness can process only so much information or competing demands at any one time. When we attempt to absorb and manage all of the events that can come into our life, either directly or indirectly, we flounder in confusion as to what our minds should process or not process. We then become over stimulated and get the distinct feeling of losing control. We have already learned that we lose control by having to adapt to too many events. To eliminate this potential for stress, we need to *re-center* or order our consciousness only around that information or set of events that we want to manage.

We can easily recall those many instances where we felt an *overload* in our lives. We felt helpless trying to manage all of our self-created obligations as well as those that were imposed on us by outside forces. Over time, we became exhausted and our psychic energy was depleted. Left unattended, we will eventually experience anxiety in its mildest form to a total *burnout* or a nervous breakdown in its most extreme form. Our risk increases as we lose sight of ourselves, our Purpose, our Values and our Mission. We would be allowing life to manage us rather than our taking control, thus, reordering our life and our mental beliefs around those things that we can effectively manage.

The lament of modern society is that too many of us falsely believe that we must run harder and faster just to keep up. The proverbial treadmill is the greatest threat to our sense of *Self* as it takes us away from what is really most important to us. The mind has been scientifically proven to be capable of processing only so much information at any one point in time. There is a limit to our consciousness, and when we push that limit we are effectively shutting down our brains with an overload of *psychic garbage.* Our goal should be to filter this *psychobabble* out, before it gets a foothold in our minds. We must always recognize it for what it is: useless, non-urgent, non-productive data that crowds out the meaningful information that will bring more satisfaction to our lives.

We will not be able to effectively screen out all of the worthless information that flies in front of us demanding our attention, but we can choose to relegate it to its proper place. We can perceive it for what it really is and not allow it to assume any degree of importance in our minds. Simultaneously, we can choose to direct and order the information that does enter our consciousness. We don't need to be victims of information overload if we keep our minds clear, focused and *centered* on that informational matter that is congruent with our deepest Purpose and Values.

The process of *centering* is an acquired skill. We must learn to *center* ourselves in much the same way we learn to ride a bicycle. As we attempt to steady and balance ourselves, we cannot allow too many extraneous thoughts to interfere with our efforts. As soon as we relax and keep a calm Purpose, we will discover that the bicycle seems to take off on its own. If we clutter our minds with the advice of those telling us what to do, we develop self-doubts, begin to wobble, and quickly find ourselves heading for the ditch. Our life should encompass the similar process of *focusing, flowing and centering* ourselves on our bicycles. Our decisions should be based on the calm reflection of our Purpose, to keep our gyroscope spinning smoothly and not allow the forces that wish to derail us to have their way.

The following diagram depicts the self-empowerment concepts of *focusing, flowing and centering*. As life's external events (our obstacles) invade our sense of Purpose, we must refocus on what is most important (our Values). We take control by attending to our chosen path (our Mission) and by regaining the feeling of flowing effortlessly toward our goals. If we feel stress or imbalance in this effort, we must re-center to what is most motivating and meaningful to us (our Purpose). Let's carry a mental picture of this diagram in our minds as a guide to the process of self-empowerment.

Our Purpose Wheel

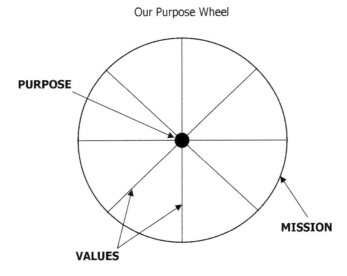

Focusing, centering and flowing are three life skills that once cultivated and mastered will allow us to control the subjective aspects of our reality. Masters of Yoga and practitioners of meditation are excellent examples of *focusing* one's objectives, *flowing* one's thoughts and *centering* one's consciousness. While we cannot spend our entire lives in the lotus position chanting *OM's,* we can still relate these practices to daily living. We can order our consciousness around that which is important and vital to our sense of *Self,* while filtering out what is inimical to our goals and our Mission in life. It is important that we learn to step back, take a deep breath and *re-center* our *Selves* on what will give our lives the greatest harmony and inner peace.

Our *Centering* is often accomplished by going into a *quiet room* in our minds when we feel overwhelmed by our choices, our decisions and even our circumstances. For the same reasons that we sleep, take vacations or play games, we need to learn to retreat from time to time from the daily stresses of living. We can master the mental image of retiring to a safe place in our thoughts where we feel protected and secure. We can literally *park our brains* when we become overloaded with irrational thoughts or incongruent behavior.

LaoTzo defined this state of being as, *An integral being knows without going, sees without looking, and accomplishes without doing.* Thus, we may often find that the fulfillment of our Purpose is better accomplished not through active involvement but through quiet detachment. As Deepak Chopra tells us in The Seven Laws of Spiritual Success, *Grass doesn't try to grow, it just grows. Fish don't try to swim; they just swim. Flowers don't try to bloom; they bloom. Birds don't try to fly; they fly.* Realization of our Purpose is, therefore, not always a result of intense effort but rather a matter of minimal effort. When we find that our efforts are creating such tension and strain that we are going nowhere, it is time to back off and re-center ourselves in a more relaxed, gliding mode of thought and action.

Living a purposeful life requires us to balance these three components of self-mastery: *focusing, flowing* and *centering.* They are integrated into each other at all times, without each taking any precedent over the others. Self-management is to know when, where and how each tool is employed in daily living. *Focusing* will keep us on target with our Purpose, *flowing* will allow us to intensely experience our life, while *centering* will keep us in check and in balance at all times. Our objective should be to apply all three principles diligently and thoughtfully. With our continuing knowledge and application of these life-living principles, we will ultimately be synchronized with our Purpose and our *Higher Self.*

CHAPTER TWELVE

How Do I Find More Time?
Managing Our Greatest Endowment

One hour of life, crowded to the full with glorious action, and filled with noble risks, is worth whole years of those mean observances of paltry decorum, in which mean steal through existence, like sluggish waters through a marsh, without either honour or observation.

Sir Walter Scott

The quest for time should be equal to our quest for life. In reality they are one and the same, with each deserving the same reverence and respect. Our time should be viewed for what it really is, a finite resource. We cannot create more of it; we cannot live it over; and we cannot save it for another day. It happens and then it is gone. It is the ultimate equalizer for all of mankind, with kings and paupers being allotted an equal amount, to either use wisely or to waste.

Our difficulty with time mastery is due to its internal paradoxes. We live as if there are infinite tomorrows, then mourn the fact there is never enough time to do all the things we need to do today. We set aside time for ourselves; then squander it relentlessly. We plead for more of it; then procrastinate until there is no time left. Time seems to race when we are enjoying ourselves and then tediously plods along when we must do something we dislike. As children, we sense it moving slowly, then as adults complain at how quickly it passes with each new birthday.

Thus, the quest for time remains one of our greatest challenges. We never seem to know how to get a grip on this thing called time, even though it has been around since day one. With generations of experience behind us, we should be time management experts by now. We have learned how to relate to it by measuring it with clocks and calendars. We read time management books, go to seminars and buy time organizers to plot out our daily priorities. We know about time from seasons, from bodily functions and from scientific inquiry. We know from physics that time curves through space and we know how fast light travels in one calendar year. We even have clichés and rules to guide our use of time, such as *a stitch in time saves nine, time stands still for no man, time is of the essence* and *there is no time like the present.*

Yet with all of our insights and with all of our rules, we are still dissatisfied about our use of time. Our inability to manage time in our lives is not through our lack of knowledge nor in the manner of how it affects our lives. Our poor time utilization is simply due to our inability to equate our needs with our time requirements. Our failure in time management often stems from our doing too much, from taking too little or too much time to do it, and even from doing things at the wrong time. But most importantly, we are not doing the things that matter the most to us. Essentially, our time clock is not synchronized with our Purpose, our Values and our Mission. Once it is, we will find that we have plenty of time.

So what is the secret to managing my time?

Our first and only mistake in time management is that we are trying to manage time - when we should be managing ourselves! Time manages itself. We have no control over that, but we do have control over ourselves. Natural laws govern our lives, from the movement of the planets to the movements of our bodies, our minds and our feelings. Time, as well, is made up of natural laws which we have little power to alter or manipulate. However, there exist certain principles of managing time that are largely within our control, as we are in control of ourselves.

Purposeful time planning (Self-Management) requires us to heed the following fundamental principles:

1.) **Equate our time with our Values;**
2.) **Plan our time according to our goals;**
3.) **Balance our time with our natural harmonies; and**
4.) **Control our time through our daily actions.**

Let's briefly examine each:

EQUATE TIME WITH OUR VALUES

Purposeful time management means that we must be masters of managing our Values. We have examined the power of our Values in previous chapters and identified them as those priorities that are most important to us, essentially our highest wants and aspirations. What better way to spend our time is there than in achieving our highest wants and aspirations? For us to spend time pursuing anything else is to spend time that has little meaning… and should be considered as a waste of time!

If we value our family and time is spent away from them, we are losing precious hours that we cannot recapture later. If we value health and our time is spent in front of a television eating chocolate bars, we have robbed ourselves of an opportunity to get physically stronger. If we value our spiritual awareness yet we are too busy to devote any time to meditation or prayer, we have weakened this Value in our lives. If we value recreation and leisure and stay too busy to ever take a vacation or a walk in the park, we will become frustrated over our lack of free time for this. Whatever we choose our Values to be, time must be devoted to their pursuit and fulfillment. To not allocate some measure of time to our Values, we are cheating ourselves out of life itself.

We often like to say *that time is money.* This is true if wealth is one of our supreme Values. But we can also say *time is anything we want it to be.* Perhaps time should be our most supreme Value. Without question, time is the only Value that makes all of our other Values possible. The more time we have, the more likely we are to realize the other wants and aspirations that are important to us. Therefore, as a Value, time makes all things possible. But since we all have the same amount of time, it follows that the management of this time supersedes the Value of time itself.

PLAN TIME ACCORDING TO OUR GOALS

Without a time plan for our lives, our goals are nothing more than a roadmap without a destination. If we have destinations to reach, we need to know our milestones, our directions and the amount of time needed to reach our destinations. We cannot plan on leaving Atlanta after breakfast and arriving in Miami for dinner unless we know how long it will take us to get there. If our destination is early retirement, we must know how many years we must work to achieve the necessary financial means to retire. If our destination is physical health, we must budget so many hours per week for exercise. It is an inescapable truth that nothing can be accomplished without attaching some time element to its achievement.

Since all of us get the same twenty-four day, those who achieve more will be those who are better users of time. The process of goal achievement is simply the process of time management. This does not happen by itself. It requires our active intervention, a taking charge of our lives by taking charge of our time. The best place to start is to review the *Commitment Statements* that we discussed in *Chapter Nine*. These statements were the pledges that we made to ourselves to achieve certain goals. If we know what we want to achieve, we should be able to put a time-line on the process that we will use to get there.

A practical and time honored method for turning our *Commitment Statements* into practice is to block out the overall time line needed to achieve our goals, then take one day at a time and prioritize the actions that will support those pledges. We can utilize a complex daily organizer system to achieve this, or we can put our ideas on the back of a paper napkin. It doesn't really matter as long as we follow our plan. The key is to write our actions down so that we may visually review our commitment to ourselves. We can prioritize our actions mentally, but they are more likely to be followed if we assign values such as A,B,C or 1,2,3 to these events. The key is to always do them in the order of their importance.

We do not, however, need to be a slave to this process. If we get off track due to external influences, we need not chastise ourselves for failing. It is much like a diet. If we set a goal to lose ten pounds and then have the *death-by-chocolate* dessert at dinner tonight, that does not mean we have abandoned our goal of losing ten pounds. We simply have to restate our priority that tomorrow's menu will have less carbs or fat. Live is to be lived, not fully programmed!

It is equally important that we not plan our goals around a daily schedule and forget the big picture. Depending on the goal, we must schedule larger references of time in our mind. As we think of our daily activities, we need to take the long view of what it will take to accomplish certain tasks. Therefore, we need to block out time lines before blocking out daily events. Many of our goals will never have an ending point because they are a lifelong commitment. We don't just get healthy one day and say that we no longer have to practice a healthy lifestyle.

BALANCE TIME WITH OUR NATURAL HARMONIES

We are physical human beings. There are natural biological rhythms that govern our best utilization of time. We need to recognize the times of day when we are most energetic or most lethargic. Some of us work better in the evening; some of us are morning people. Even certain seasons of the year dictate when we are more productive. Some of us literally shut down in the summer heat while the same conditions seem to revitalize others. We also get the flu and severe colds when we are physically tired or under stress. We get hay fever and feel miserable when pollens are in the air. We slog through the entire day after staying up late at a party the night before. And we recuperate from accidents and surgeries from time to time. The list of physical setbacks is endless because we are human.

It is the conventional wisdom of eastern cultures to *go with the flow*. As contrasted with western societies that are governed by schedules, computers, time clocks and deadlines, eastern civilizations believe in the natural harmonies of the inner self and their relationship to the ebbs and tides of the universe. Biological research supports this view and medical science recognizes that illnesses and stress are usually by-products of doing too much when the mind-body connection says to do less. But the opportunities for having positive energy and vigor are significantly greater than the down time experiences in our lives.

The key is to recognize within our *Selves* those moments in time when we feel productive and take advantage of the opportunity. And when we feel like *checking out* for a while, we should allow ourselves the freedom to do so. Time continues on regardless of how we feel or how much we choose to participate. Sometimes we will be content to be passive observers of time. And sometimes we will want to grab every second that is available to us. This is life. We should respect our biological heritage and not fight the inevitable. We should recognize those moments when we are at our peak and go for it. And we should recognize those times when we deserve a break and just lay back. Life is not a race to the finish line.

CONTROL TIME THROUGH OUR DAILY ACTIONS

We cannot use the argument that we don't have enough time. It's all in how we use it and how much time we really believe we have available to us, as aptly stated in old German proverb, *Who begins too much, accomplishes little.* Let's start with the premise that all of us have the same amount of time in a given day, week, month and year. Even if we subtract ten hours from each day for *physical maintenance* - the necessary time for sleep, eating and exercise to keep us alive and healthy - we still have approximately fourteen hours left in the day to do whatever we choose to do.

Of the fourteen hours we have left, most of us spend about ten hours each day doing our *daily business* - about eight hours at work and another two hours in basic chores and necessities like commuting, going to the bathroom, walking around the house, reading the newspaper, daydreaming, etc. Subtracting these ten hours from the fourteen we called *physical maintenance*, we are still left with four hours each day for ourselves. We may gain or lose one or two hours from this four hours depending on how long we stay at work, the length of our commute and if we combine reading the paper with going to the bathroom, but over the course of a year there are approximately four hours per day on average that we can always call ours.

Four hours a day doesn't sound like much, but over a year that equals 1,460 hours or 60 days to use at our discretion. Add a little more time for weekends, holidays, vacations, etc., and we get about 80 - 100 days per year to use anyway we please. We could call the balance of the year our time also if we value our time working, eating and sleeping, but for simplicity we should look at the fact that we have a great deal of time to ourselves even if we have other mandatory requirements.

These four hours per day is where we can grow, change, innovate, experience, create, and challenge ourselves in any manner we choose. Most of our goals will be attained during this period. Over a lifetime, this adds up to around twenty years of *free time* that nobody else controls. If we slept one hour less every day, worked more efficiently or combined work and play with achieving our other goals, we may even gain another twenty years that are exclusively ours. We cannot use the excuse that we are too busy to achieve our goals in life. The key is in using our time productively instead of wastefully.

How would I know my time was well spent until after I spent it?

This is a good question! We cannot predict the future and don't usually know if we did the right thing until sometime after we have done it. One popular sage put it this way, *The more sand that has escaped from the hourglass of our life, the clearer we should see through it.* Wouldn't it be great if we could see the future and correct our mistaken use of time? Consider the following possibility:

Picture yourself seated at the controls of your own time machine - a sleek, polished capsule that only you can control. You stare at the dials of time, trying to decide if you want to journey back to the Jurassic Age or catapult forward a few millenniums to a world you cannot imagine. But the time dials of this machine are different; they are preset for only an eighty-five year period, from the day of your birth to the day of our death. You know the day you were born, but for the first time you actually know the day of your death. After your initial disappointment that you can't venture back to see any dinosaurs, you think this could still be quite interesting.

Why go back, you think to yourself. You already know your past. Let's go forward and see what is in store for the rest of your life. You push the time throttle slowly forward and after a few lurches your time machine moves slowly into the future. As you watch the monitor of your future life, you see clearly every event, every decision and every happening that still lies ahead of you. As you observe, you find yourself laughing, crying, even getting a little bored at times, but you eventually learn everything there is to know about your future life. After reaching the end of your life and seeing which of your friends show up at your funeral, your time machine automatically resets itself to the present. You step out of your craft into the bright light of the day, walk to a quiet place by the lake and sit under a shady oak tree to think about what you just witnessed.

You now possess total knowledge of your life, from beginning to end, and although the mystery is now gone, you must now decide if you spent your remaining time in the absolute best way possible. As you ponder the events that will take place for the rest of your life, you come upon a brilliant realization. You remember reading in the instruction manual of your time machine that events can be changed by simply exiting the craft and doing whatever you wish to do differently at the time the event occurred. The manual strongly discouraged changing events in your past, but said you could change anything your heart desired for the future as this time had not yet actually occurred.

What an opportunity! You literally get to design your future the way you want it to be. Now you cannot fail at anything! Just decide how you want it to be and it will automatically be that way. If you forgot to send your mother a birthday card, you can correct your future faux pas! If you made the wrong career change later in life, you can simply switch to a better choice. If you bought the wrong investment, you could switch to a better one. With complete knowledge of the future, everything will be perfect!

The alarm clock rings and you wake up. It was all just a dream. Now the future is as unknown and enigmatic as it ever was. You grumble, get out of bed and head to the shower, thinking about the day that lies ahead. You have decisions to make, people to see, places to visit, appointments to make. All these choices! And you won't know the outcome of any of your actions until after you've made them. Seems unfair, doesn't it? No time machine… no crystal ball… no way to really know what the future will bring.

This is the way of life for all of us. We never really know what to do with our lives unless we have our roadmap of Purpose, Vision and Values. With these, we can design our Mission and know what Behavior to follow to achieve the Results we are seeking. There is simply no other way to satisfactorily predict our future. These elements make up the fuel for our Time Machine. The better we know what they are, the more likely we are to design the best future for our lives.

So what would you do the next time around?

If you knew the future and knew exactly the results of your decisions, what would you do differently? Assume you could not fail. The outcome is guaranteed. Would you commit to studying one more hour each night if you were told in advance that you would get all A's on you report card? Would you stick to your diet if you knew you positively would lose ten pounds this month? Would you be more inclined to write a novel if you knew you already had a publisher and a large advance for your next one?

Write down 5 things you would do today if you knew the outcome was guaranteed:

1.
2.
3.
4.
5.

So why don't we do the things we listed above? We don't do them because we don't know the future. We think our effort might come up short. We think we want these things, but we might change our minds later. We only have a hazy, vague notion of what it is we really want. We will commit to it when we think we have the time. We are afraid we might fail. We feel we don't have the skills, don't believe enough in ourselves or don't think we can. Basically, we don't have any guarantees.

The reasons are numerous as to why we have more excuses than we have convictions. But we do have choices and every time we decide to do nothing, that is in itself a choice. However, what if we made a different choice to attempt to accomplish those five items we listed above? What could possibly happen? We could actually discover some of them turn into reality! What could possibly happen if we don't attempt to achieve these goals? They won't happen! Guaranteed!

Now if we want a guarantee in our life, we've just discovered how to achieve one. We can be assured of a guarantee for failure if we fail to act. Nothing will happen unless we make it happen. Let's now re-board our time machine and fast-forward again to the end of our life. Right before we witness our final departure from earth, we get to look back at all the choices we made. We will see that all of our life's events have fallen into one of three categories:

1. **We see where we tried and succeeded.**
2. **We see where we tried but failed.**
3. **We see where we failed to try.**

We may discover that we had a few of each category in our life. Which situations made us the happiest; remorseful, but maybe a little proud; angry and regretful? Did we gain more inner peace for making the effort, whether we succeeded or not? Or did we feel mad at ourselves for letting life slip by without making better use of our time? We should not wait until the end to make these assessments of the value of our life. The only way we can endeavor to set our future course of events is by writing the script ourselves.

What time is most important?

How well did we spend our time? After it is gone, how do we know our most precious commodity was utilized with Purpose? Was our time positively balanced or skewed in negative directions? Was our time based on clear choices and decisions or did we just allow time to happen without any conscious intervention? Was our time ours or did we give it up to chance? Did we always live in the past, the present or the future?

Unfortunately, we're only able to answer these questions from the perspective of the *Past*. As Ralph Waldo Emerson reminded us, *The years teach much which the days never knew.* Thus, we won't know how well we used our time tomorrow until tomorrow has come and gone. We may know how we planned to use tomorrow's time, but until it actually happens, we really don't know how we actually used it. This means that *Past* time serves only as a measure of our successful utilization of time. It is simply recorded and documented history and has no other importance to us (except when we just want to reflect on our memories).

Future time is really no more valuable to our happiness and success than is our *Past* time, since *Future* time exists only in our minds, hopes and dreams. Like *Past* time, *Future* time is not even occurring in our lives; these times are either coming or they already went, but they're not happening right now which is where our lives are - Right Now! Kay Lyons said it best, *Yesterday is a canceled check; Tomorrow is only a promissory note; today is the only cash you have - so spend it wisely.* This means that there is only one time that is relevant to our happiness and fulfillment of a meaningful life - *The Present*!

The *Present* is where we are really connected to our Values and our Mission in life. It is where we are right now - for me, writing these words, and for you, reading them. If you have a more valuable use of your time, then close this book and go do it! If learning more about yourself and how to approach life purposefully is important to you, budget your time to gain these insights. Reading and studying this book is valuable, but only if it fits within your overall allocation of precious time to meet your highest wants and aspirations.

If the *Present* is the only time where we can potentially be in control of our lives, then it makes sense to focus our lives here. The *Present* is where we utilize time management techniques. While we may have a daily planner that tells us what we should be doing today, tomorrow, next week, unless we do it all, the only thing we really possess is a bunch of words on a calendar.

Daily planners serve a wonderful purpose as they keep our *mind clocks* organized, giving us some focus on events to pursue. But unless we choose the right things to do and then do these things right, all we have accomplished is the expenditure of time and energy with little to show for it. We must plan for the future, organize our planner for the present, then make it happen each moment.

Norman Vincent Peale told us to, *Plan your work for today and every day, then work your plan.* But what is the right plan? There is only one right plan, the plan that is based on our Purpose (our reason for living); that reflects our Values (our highest priorities); that outlines our Mission (our goals and specific commitments to them); and then details our specific Behavior (our daily priority actions) to guarantee the Results (our rewards) that we seek. This constitutes the success pyramid outlined in *Chapter Eight* and must form the basis of any daily-planning system that we choose to use.

Why do I use my time so poorly?

Assuming that we have the skill to organize and utilize a daily planner, which is a major assumption since numerous seminars are conducted in this subject, why then do we have such difficulty following one? There are three key reasons:1.We don't distinguish between the vital and the urgent, 2. We respond to rather than control events, and 3. We fail to set priorities and do first things first. Let's briefly review each:

THE VITAL VERSUS THE URGENT

Do we really know the difference between the two? If the phone rings and we answer it, are we responding to something that is vitally important to us or to something that feels urgent to us? Perhaps if we were waiting for a job offer, the phone ringing might seem vital, but most often a ringing phone is an interruption in our lives. If we were having a great conversation with our family at dinner and the phone rings, we should decide to let voicemail or the answering machine do the job for us. Yet most of us would feel the urgency of the ringing phone and pick it up, thereby allowing someone else to control our time and our right to choose how to spend it.

Now let's assume that there is a classic book that we have been meaning to read for over a year. We know that it will be enriching, valuable and enjoyable if we could only find the time to read it. Yet it sits there on our bookshelf month after month. Why? One student of a Franklin Quest seminar gave founder Hyrum Smith the answer. *It is because books don't ring!* How appropriate an answer! We tend not to budget our time by choice but by response. Given the choice between the urgency of a ringing phone or a vital but dormant book, we find it more expedient to do the former and postpone the latter. Hyrum Smith suggests that, *Urgencies are not priorities; they act on priorities.*

Urgencies will always be there. They demand our time continuously during the day, often referred to as *time robbers*, e.g. interruptions, unnecessary meetings, demanding neighbors, etc. These urgencies impact our time and almost always are unexpected. They are demands that may expect our attention, but they are rarely vital to us. Our first task is to recognize the difference between the two. If we can truthfully distinguish between what appears to be important to us and what really is, we will be well on our way to a more productive life. Urgent tasks that are not vital must be controlled by our response to them as outlined in the following section.

RESPONDING VERSUS CONTROLLING

We either make things happen or they happen to us. We either control our time or our time controls us. This leads to our most common frustration in life - feeling out of control. As we stated earlier, time should be our most supreme Value as it is what life consists of. If we accept this premise, then controlling our own time should become our most important activity in life. As time is nothing more than a sequence of events that occur in our lives, does it not make sense that controlling these events is what life is all about?

This is also what time management is all about - event management through managing ourselves. Everything that happens is an event: Brushing our teeth, answering the phone, getting married, talking to our children, etc. Even the commonly accepted negative happenings in our lives are events, and with each of these events, there is a time element attached to them. As time is a finite commodity, it holds that it should be wisely spent.

Perhaps, we should think of our time as money. If we were given a million dollars at birth and were told it had to last a lifetime, how would we elect to spend it? Would it all be squandered away before the age of thirty, or would we make every dollar count on the most important investments? Budgeting our valuable time is just as critical. As we attempt to be in control of our money, we should endeavor to control our own time. Ben Franklin once said, *Dost thou love life? Then do not squander time, for that's the stuff life is made of.* Whenever events, people, or situations are allowed to control us we are bankrupting our storehouse of time. Only we should decide how to spend it.

If we allow events to control us, we are in a constant state of stimulus-response. Like Pavlov's dog, we become conditioned to respond on cue to every ring of the bell. It was once said that *the quality of life depends on what happens in the space between stimulus and response.* We cannot let others set our timetable and establish how we will react. We must always distinguish between what is expected of us and what we expect of ourselves. More importantly, if we allow others to govern our choices than we have given them the use of our time, our most precious commodity. When our decision is to respond rather than to control, we have just transferred a part of our lives elsewhere, a choice we must seriously consider before accepting.

Not every event in our lives, however, is controllable. We can't control the weather, the outcome of a sporting event, or even our mother-in-law showing up for the weekend. But what we can control is our response to these events. We can be frustrated or stressed out by these events or we can adapt to them. The key is to know which events we do have control over and then exercise our right to be in control. We do have absolute control over one thing - our *Selves* - and that is where our focus should be. When we are in control of ourselves, we feel satisfied, if not powerful. The more satisfied we are with ourselves, the more control we feel over our total life experience.

ESTABLISHING PRIORITIES

Everything that we choose to do with our time is simply a matter of choosing one Value other another. In *Chapter Seven*, we developed our hierarchy of Values. We decided that certain things were of higher priority in our lives than others. And now that our supreme Values have been prioritized, we should be able to *say no! when there is a deeper yes! burning inside.*

This is perhaps the most fundamental key to all time management systems - deciding to spend our time with our most important needs taking preference while letting go of the unnecessary. Walt Disney told us, *All decisions are easy once we know what our values are.* And as a wise scribe once commented, *The main thing is to keep the main thing the main thing.* Thus, prioritization of our Values and the subsequent utilization of our time in accordance with these Values is the basis for effective time management; and more importantly, effective life management.

The difficulty with acting upon our priorities is that we become sidetracked, reacting to events that are not important - whether urgent or not. As all events have elements of time, we must *react* only to urgencies that are important or *act* on events that are important but are not necessarily urgent. This may seem confusing at first, but as long as we learn to distinguish between events that are important or vital to us and those that are simply unimportant intrusions on our time, we will increase our probability of effective time management.

The key factor here is to *act* versus *react*. The more we take control of events rather than having events forcing us to respond to them, the more likely we are to have time to stick to our priorities. By establishing our priorities and organizing our time around them, the less likely we will have the time or the desire to react to any event that is not vitally important.

Everybody wants a piece of our time because of its tremendous value, and if we continually say, *Yes, take all you want,* we will eventually discover that there was little left for us. We often allow this to happen because we tend to measure our effectiveness by how busy we are. Many of us feel that if we are juggling numerous events or reacting to the demands of everyone else, we are somehow getting more done. This constant state of *crisis management* feeds our ego but usually little else. Generating self-inflicted stress without accomplishing our key priorities is hardly a measure of living successfully. Any short-term gains in productivity will invariably be wiped out by long-term inefficiency and ultimate burnout. After a few years of doing more for everybody else, we will invariably discover we are enjoying it less.

We must follow our inner voice and decide whose priority we are following. We know what our core Values are and how they should be connected to our daily behavior. We are stewards of ourselves and our actions need to be in concert with our priorities. Michele Collet Kriz of Tampa, Florida summed it up best, *If it's not a priority, don't do it. If it is a priority, get help. If you can't get help, make time. If you can't make time, it's not a priority.* By not making a conscious selection of what our priorities are and then doing what matters most to us, we will be eternally trapped in life's merry-go-round. We may be having fun, but we will only be going in circles.

When we feel that we are in control of our *Selves* and our time, we will feel connected with our Purpose. But there will be many days when our Purpose does not feel connected with our time. The difference lies in not allowing our *Selves* to be slaves to ourselves. Our *Wheel of Life* will not turn smoothly every day. We must learn to recognize the insurmountable pressures of trying to do too much for the sake of our Purpose. Even God proclaimed Sunday as His day of rest. If God needs a break, then maybe we as well should be entitled to some rest. Our Purpose should flow like a river, speeding up on the long stretches but then backing down around each turn and bend. As the river flows, our Purpose will always be going in the same general direction, but it will know when it reaches the fury of white water or the calms of the quiet pools.

A.L. Williams, the founder of the fastest growing insurance company in America tells us in the title of his book *ALL YOU CAN DO IS ALL YOU CAN DO… But all you can do is enough.* In other words, *what gets done, gets done… what doesn't, doesn't!* We only have to know that we lived with Purpose to be great time managers. There is no scorecard in life that judges us on how much we have actually done. The only scorecard is our own sense of how much meaning we put in our lives. We can develop our Commitment Statements, live congruently with our Values and accept the Rewards that come our way. Whatever we achieve, we should be thankful for. Whatever we don't achieve, we should be thankful for our opportunity to have strived for it.

Simple Living – The Secret to Purposeful Time Management

Somewhere, somehow and some time ago, we got off the track of *Simply Living* and *Living Simply.* Maybe it was during the industrial revolution or perhaps it was during the post war boom of prosperity and the ensuing *me* generation. Maybe it has always been this way, but since prehistoric man did not carry laptops and planning organizers, it is more likely that we lost our capacity for the simple life sometime during this century. One thing, however, is certain. There has never been any time greater than the present when so many people are feeling so completely dissatisfied with the value and quality of their lives.

As a collective society, we have become much more of a harried lot than a happy lot. Adding to our frustration is our seeming inability to do very much about it. We deplore the treadmill, yet we hop back on it each morning. We invent machines to do our work for us, then frantically search for another job to replace the one we lost to the machine. We commute for hours each week, endure lengthy meetings, schedule numerous appointments, read and consume volumes of information in our field, catch planes and taxis, send E-Mails, text messages and voice mails, surf the net, peruse reports, play office politics, and workout at lunch. Indeed, we are very busy people!

But despite all this *busyness*, are we truly aware of our reasons for doing these things? Are we allowing this insane *busyness* to control us because that is the way we believe *life is supposed to work?* Are we running the show anymore or is it running us? Many of us will quickly defend our hectic lifestyle by stating that these are the requirements of the workplace, that we need the job, that we have no other choice, and that, like it or not, we are powerless to do anything about it. Well, maybe to a certain extent this is true, but certainly not to the extent that we have carried it.

Laurence Shames, in his book, *The Hunger for More: Searching for Values in an Age of Greed*, states that Americans are searching for alternatives to what is traditionally thought of as worth doing:

> ...that more money, more tokens of success - there will always be people for whom those are adequate goals, but those people are no longer setting the tone for the rest of us. There's a new set of more at hand. More appreciation of good things beyond the marketplace, more insistence of fairness, more attention to purpose, more determination truly to choose a life, and not a lifestyle, for oneself.

Without question, some of us really love our lives and careers and find them exciting, challenging, and, yes, even purposeful. For those of us that feel that way… well, congratulations! However, the overwhelming majority of us are not quite as convinced. There seems to be something missing in all this *busyness* for most of us. We never feel that there is enough time to enjoy what we really think is important. We don't jump from bed with enthusiasm each morning anxious to start the daily cycle over again. We feel that we should be doing something else but don't really know what that something else is. We are astounded that our bills and obligations don't ever seem to get any smaller, although we are working harder and harder. We never seem to have enough time for our family, our community, or the time to enjoy our hobbies. We would like to take up a cause or do volunteer work but just can't seem to squeeze it into our schedule. We want freedom from the monopoly of all this forced *busyness*. And we don't want to wait until the golden years of our retirement. We want it now!

The bad news is that we can't have what we want until we are prepared to give up something else. Unfortunately, we can't have it all. Even the idle rich amongst us quite often discover that they can't have it all. But the good news is that we can have a great deal of what we want… but we must first decide that it's okay to want less.

Too many of us give up too much of the most priceless possession that we do have - *Time* - to get more of something that we don't have, and for that matter, don't really need - *Stuff*! We should confess now: The single greatest contributor to any non-fulfillment that we have in our lives is the fact that we have created a forced sense of irrational *busyness* because we are too obsessed with our need for *Stuff*!

Why do I need so much *stuff*?

For some baffling reason, we have gotten caught up in an insatiable need for *stuff*! We seem to need all kinds of *stuff* - from clothes, cars, houses, electronic gadgets, toys, furniture and fixtures to new hairdos, pedicures and tummy tucks. We want to possess everything imaginable and never seem to be content anymore with the basics. According to comedian George Carlin, we even need to own *stuff* to put our *stuff* into. We like to take our *stuff* with us wherever we go, and when we get there we have to buy more *stuff* so we can take it home to be with other *stuff*!

Our fascination with *stuff*, however, is not the problem. It is the lifestyle that we must pursue to acquire, maintain and manage our *stuff*. All of this *stuff* is the antithesis to a sane, balanced and purposeful life. While we tend to believe that our happiness emanates from our possessions it is, in fact, these same possessions that become the bane and curse to a joyful and meaningful life. According to Elaine St. James, *Wise men and women in every major culture throughout history have found that the secret to happiness is not in getting more but in wanting less.* Only when we make it our Purpose to not make *stuff* the measure of our contentment, will we truly understand how simply beautiful (and beautifully simple) life can be lived.

Let's fully understand that materialism is not the source of our discontent. It is our unrelenting pursuit of material gratification that keeps us away from our Purpose and the realization of our *Higher Self*. It is not that driving a nice car, living in a nice home and having money in the bank is making us unhappy. On the contrary, we could be quite happy living a comfortable lifestyle. The real issue becomes: How stressful have we allowed our life to become due to the compromises we must make for attaining this *stuff*, not to mention how complicated the ownership of this *stuff* may be making our lives at any given moment after we have attained it. In other words, is the acquisition and maintenance of this *stuff* possibly keeping us from a life that could be considerably more fulfilling and purposeful?

We need to ask ourselves to what extent our total value system has been compromised because of an overriding sense that material *stuff* is the major source of our happiness. That is, what are we giving up to get it? How complicated has our life become due to our perceptions that *bigger, better and more of it* will somehow give us more inner peace and feelings of self-worth? Is keeping up with the Joneses keeping us from keeping up with ourselves? Have we sacrificed our *Self* and our most important Values by our own false impressions of the Value of *stuff*?

Countless medical and psychiatric studies have correlated the risk of health and mental problems with the stressors of the daily rat race. We are literally working ourselves to death! But for most of us, it is not the job that is killing us. Rather, it is our attitude that we have to produce, create, generate, and achieve in occupations that serve no other purpose than to provide us more *stuff*. We are simply slaves to our own material voraciousness. *But...* we say in self-defense, *We are not working to get mansions and Mercedes. We are working to just make rent payments and put food on the table for our hungry children.*

This is true; greed is a relative term, but we are all affected to a certain degree by our perception of what we really must have. Even some of our poorest ghetto-dwellers will crash store windows to get color TV's and Nike shoes because of the belief that they will create untold happiness. It is not the amount and the price of our *stuff* that is our enemy; it is the misplacement of our total value system that ensues from our blind belief in what is most important. Whether we are at the bottom of the food chain or we are Donald Trump, we are all equally obsessed with the idea that happiness comes from *stuff* and are willing to give up too much of what is most important to achieve more of it.

Let's be clear about what *stuff* is and which *stuff* is important. Stuff is anything that we consume. For example, food is important to our survival, while fine French cuisine is *gourmandish* entertainment. A coat is for warmth; mink stoles are for strutting. An apartment is for shelter; a Newport mansion is for gloating. A sunset is for glorification; a Mediterranean cruise is for self-aggrandizement.

Also, material items are inert objects that have no more value than what we place upon them. They are usually made of plastic, metal, glass, fabric, or other synthetic materials and are usually worthless in their raw form. We construct them in such a way that they give us pleasure by looking at them, playing with them or functionally utilizing them. The least expensive variety does the same thing as the more expensive, where the former is utilitarian (a pair of work boots) and the latter is ego/esteem building (Gucci loafers). While shoes are important, fashion is superficially individualistic, that is, more important to some than others.

What is unimportant, however, is our desire to place the wrong value on certain commodities, such that they consume our thoughts and effect irrational behavior. We all must have life's basic necessities and must produce a certain amount of effort to receive them. But when we become obsessively preoccupied with *stuff* such that we sacrifice a clear balance of Values, then we have lost the whole point of living. Again, *stuff* is not the villain in our lives. It is the wanting of *stuff* and the extreme sacrifices that we make to our other more important Values that we must diligently avoid.

Our goal, our mandate, our critical objective must be to keep an awareness of what is really important to us and pursue only that which is required to live a balanced, purposeful life. We must want less and need less, not to create abject poverty and austerity but to enjoy the true happiness that comes from the simple enjoyment of our most supreme Values.

What is a simple life?

A simple life is where we are simply living! It is nothing more and nothing less. When we are in touch with just the simple process of living, relishing in the uncomplicated pleasures that are abundantly available to us, we will find the inner peace that we are seeking. A simple life focuses on what we do have rather than being critical of what we don't have. It finds less joy in material possessions and greater joy in natural wonders, hearty laughter, warm embraces, stimulating conversations and long walks in the woods. It values ideas over things, peaceful meditation over argumentative debates, reading over television, quiet solitude over pushy crowds and lasting trends over temporary fads. The simple life favors giving more than receiving. It is to live humbly with pride, rather than ostentatiously without virtue. A simple life knows what is most important, content with the quiet conviction of lasting principles.

The simple life is not a lazy, uneventful life. It is often very busy, but its *busyness* is always self-directed. When we are living a truly meaningful life, we are active, not passive. We are in control of our destiny because we truly know what we are seeking. Our activity is purposeful and intentional, where we are *making life happen* rather than *letting it happen to us*. Our behavior is congruent with our Values and our goals are pursued commensurately with our self-beliefs. We measure the quality of life more from the act of achieving than from the checklist of our actual achievements. We know what we want, organize our lives accordingly and filter out the extraneous influences that compete with what we know to be most important.

When we live the simple life we find greatness not in being the best but in striving to be the best. It is the living; the doing; the being that occupies our attention and our efforts, not the expedient actions that gratifies us only for the moment. It is when we take the long view on life, disregarding the immediacy of the trees to savor the grandeur of the entire forest.

The world's greatest leaders, thinkers, artists, scientists and humanitarians, past and present, were and are simple people - from Jesus, Buddha, Gandhi, DaVinci, Thoreau, and Einstein to the Pope, Billy Graham and Mother Theresa. Their minds cut through the chaste, seeing only that which is critical and vital. Even the movers and shakers amongst us are not harried, stressed out people; they are calmly centered and focused at all times. Neither their desks nor their minds are cluttered. We, as well, will always think our best thoughts and do our best work when we are quietly reflective, not bouncing off walls responding to the myriad urgencies that life throws at us. We will always be more efficient and productive if we use our minds like a sieve, filtering out the nonessentials and the unnecessary.

Thinking and living simply is not a character flaw, a weakness of drive and ambition; rather, it is vigorous, inspiring, courageous and reflective of our conviction of Purpose. Life and happiness is not made from *stuff*; it is a state of mind, made from the interwoven fabric of purposeful attitudes and the belief that life, in itself and by itself, is sufficient and plentiful. When we adopt the philosophy of living simply, we will discover our greatness within the achievement of our *Higher Self,* and that the most meaningful rewards in life will always be the simplest ones.

CHAPTER THIRTEEN

What Makes It All Worthwhile?
The Ten Paths to Happiness

Happiness is not a state to arrive at, but a manner of traveling.
Margaret Lee Run

Has the promise of joyfulness and sheer bliss now gone out of vogue in our lives? Can we possibly think of happiness being created when we are surrounded by so many reasons to be unhappy? It does now seem that the human race does surprisingly little to put on its happy face. As we scan the headlines of the morning newspaper, we are immediately assaulted with misery and misfortune. We feel despondent as we view the horrid stories coming to us from all corners of the world. Terrorism is more newsworthy than charity; selfishness seems more interesting than compassion; exploitation appears more prevalent than benevolence. Even the sports and business pages, which should give precedence to triumph and achievement, save its boldest type for scandal and greed.

It may appear that the possibility for enduring happiness seems futile when considering the present human condition. Recent studies have shown that as a society we are more plagued with anxiety and depression than at any other time in our history. As Alfred Souza observed, *For a long time it seemed to me that life was about to begin – real life. But there was always some obstacle in the way, something to be gotten through first, some unfinished business; time still to be served, a debt to be paid. Then life would begin. At last it dawned on me that these obstacles were my life.*

Many of us share this same feeling that our *real life* is right around the corner, that it is about to begin, but the obstacles just keep getting in the way. And despite the promise of technology bringing enhanced freedom and leisure to our lives, as a society, we are more harried and frustrated than ever. While enjoying economic prosperity, we are faced with more debt along with the downsizing of businesses and the outsourcing of our jobs. The peace dividend of nuclear disarmament has never really materialized.

We still experience class warfare in our cities and dehumanizing systems of welfare. We feel less safe in our homes than our parents' generation and wonder if the next generation will not face crime problems that are even worse than ours. Does it not then seem that the basic nature of man is to be unhappy? Is the world obsessed with despair when it could as easily be preoccupied with hope?

So what indeed is there to be happy about?

The answer is obvious. Happiness is paramount to our survival and our progress as human beings. We are born with the innate desire to maximize pleasure and minimize pain. We truly desire happiness and will go to great lengths to achieve it if the opportunity is presented to us. The good news is that opportunities are abundantly available to us, both as individuals and as a society. All we must do is recognize our potential for happiness and discover the time and energy to create it.

If each of us give great purpose to happiness and share it with others, we will collectively evolve into a happier society. As James Barrie wrote, *Those who bring sunshine to the lives of others cannot keep it from themselves.* The consciousness of our entire world will naturally gravitate toward happiness if each of us makes a sincere effort, especially if we ensure the happiness of others before we enjoy it for ourselves.

But we must first embrace happiness as a central element to the achievement of our *Higher Selves,* that is, it must become intrinsic to our Purpose and the self-development of our higher consciousness. As we each tap our potential for inner happiness, we will create the desire and momentum to sustain our progress. By sharing every opportunity for the creation of happiness, it will spread like a joyful virus throughout society - beginning first with our *Selves*, then progressing to our homes, to our neighborhoods, to our city states, to our nation states and ultimately throughout the world.

Is this a ridiculous quixotic goal? Not necessarily. We actually embarked on this effort during the sixties and seventies as *Joy to the World* became our collective mantra. But as all good intentions face resistance, we mostly abandoned our ideals, returning to our egocentric needs for self-gratification. So is the human spirit doomed to repeat its failures in its pursuit of happiness? Would we not retreat again if we dared to make peace and love, instead of war and malice? Possibly. But not possibly forever!

It was once said that, *Of all our human resources, the most precious is the desire to improve.* We may never perfect happiness, but we can certainly bring it to new levels of being. It is doubtful, however, that we could ever eliminate all sources of pain and sorrow. It is also doubtful that such a utopian state would even be desirable. As all things in the universe must stay in balance, we can never completely experience one emotion without having the capacity to experience its complete opposite. In other words, the state of happiness would mean little to us if we completely forget the state of sadness. We should not even want to exist in a world where we strolled around all day in a euphoric trance as if we were on mind-altering drugs. As humans, the real reward comes from experiencing every dimension of living, even if we find the negative experiences to be difficult and stressful.

Our objective, therefore, is not to eliminate all unhappiness but rather to balance it with increased opportunity for joy. Buddha may have reminded us, *A hundred loves, a hundred losses. No loves, no losses,* but are we prepared to abandon the potential for love because we fear the potential for loss? Would there be any value in giving up our rights to search for a single sliver of happiness because we must first dig through a mountain of sadness to locate it? For that matter, would we not search for truth because it is hidden among deceit? Or would we not seek honor because we feel that it is surrounded by contempt? Or not seek courage because it is covered with cowardice? Or not seek morality because it is shrouded within an immoral society? Happiness is ours to discover despite the deterrents that stand in our way; it is our human right to be elated despite a world that flagrantly flaunts its despairing side.

Our Purpose, therefore, is to strive toward our *Higher Self* in a continuous and realistic pursuit of happiness. We will have reached our *Higher Self* when we have created a sense of internal peace within ourselves. This does not mean that we will live in perfect contentment but rather we will be contented with ourselves. The difference is that the former implies an unrealistic, stress free state of consciousness while the latter implies that we are in conscious control of our state of gratification.

Achieving our *Higher Self* means that we have attained contentment and happiness, that we are continually living in alignment with our

Purpose and our Values. We will feel it is possible to rise above the vagaries of unhappiness that may surround us. We will resist the feeling of being dragged into a maelstrom of discontentment because we will see ourselves as the calm center of the storm. And our joy will abound through our sense of calm Purpose being recognized and lived through our daily actions.

What are the right paths to happiness?

We should not confuse a state of happiness with a life that is simply euphoric or entertaining. *Happiness and fun really have nothing in common,* according to theologian Dennis Prager. He reminds us that the rich and beautiful people in Hollywood do have a great deal of fun with their parties, sexy lovers and exotic travel, but at the same time will confess their loneliness, drug and alcohol addictions and feelings of depression. He suggests that once we understand the things which really do bring happiness we will no longer envy those we perceive to be just having fun. Thus, the intensity of our self-created happiness will always be more dependent upon our Values and the level of Purpose that we are feeling in our lives.

The following *Ten Paths to Happiness* govern our feelings toward life and the degree upon which we feel it is worth living. Our objective should be to pursue and apply these natural laws to our lives as energetically and as passionately as humanly possible. As we sense these principles working in our lives, we will sense purposeful joy and happiness:

I. A SENSE OF LOVE

Nothing transforms the human spirit more than our sense of love. This is the greatest generator of happiness known to human civilization. According to Benjamin Disraeli, *We are all born for love. It is the principle of existence, and its only end.* As love is all encompassing to the human condition, we should recognize that there are infinite expressions of love in our lives. It is not simply the romantic version that we learn from novels and the movies. Love is the omnipresent sense of caring, sharing, giving - the feeling that our lives are filled with warmth and compassion.

Thus, love is at the epicenter of all happiness; for us to realize it, we must literally love everything that we encounter - including those who have the greatest needs and the least expectations of our love. We must love our enemies as well as our friends. We must love our earthly home and our natural resources, the animals and plants that surround us, beautiful sunsets and, yes, even our work. When we make unconditional, selfless love the basis for our Purpose, we will discover that our *Higher Self* becomes the principal beneficiary. We will witness our love bending back onto itself - when we give it away, it will consistently come back to us. It is the one thing that belongs to us that we should least keep for ourselves.

II. A SENSE OF CHALLENGE

A wise sage one said, *We act as though comfort and luxury were the chief requirements of life when all we need to make us really happy is something to be enthusiastic about.* The challenge of achieving is the principal motivator of life. We must recognize that it is not sufficient to merely exist, that without challenging ourselves, we will have little reason to exist. Self-challenge and our ensuing accomplishments are the greatest manifestations of our Purpose, for if we had no reason to enthusiastically pursue life we would have little rationalization for a meaningful life.

Being challenged is the path to discovery of our *Higher Self* as our feelings of self-worth and self-esteem are defined by our overcoming struggles to life's obstacles. The challenges we will face create opportunities for significant achievements, which in turn give shape and substance to our life. When we sense ourselves meeting our challenges, we will have provided the spark that is so necessary for the human spirit. According to one Olympic participant, *The point is not winning, but to actualize - to see how much you can get out of yourself.* Our efforts are what provide us a sense of Purpose, the most compelling reason for a meaningful and happy life.

III. A SENSE OF HEALTH AND VITALITY

An Arabian proverb reminds us that, *He who has health, has hope; and he who has hope has everything.* Our health and vitality is the sustaining force of our Purpose as it provides the will to live and the energy to successfully grow into our *Higher Self.* It is the one component of happiness that makes all things possible, for without it we have little capacity to acquire the other components. When we enjoy our health, we possess something far greater than any riches known to man.

How remarkable it is that we will sacrifice our health, both mentally and physically, to achieve wealth but then gladly give it all back again to regain it. We can never fully enjoy our happiness if we are preoccupied with the failings of our mind and body. Lest we take our physical state for granted and not nurture it to its full potential, we will suffer the consequences of an equal failure in our human spirit. But if we seek Purpose in our health, we will continually discover a renewed vitality of Purpose in our life.

IV. A SENSE OF FREEDOM

Some say *the best things in life are free,* while others say *there is a price to pay for freedom.* Regardless of how we prefer to view it, the absence of freedom is the absence of life. Our freedom is a God-given right, the liberty granted to us to make and enjoy our own happiness. Our Purpose is predicated upon this freedom to make choices and decisions. When we are denied this opportunity, we are relegated to a fate of hopelessness and despair, a state of being that is the exact opposite of the state of happiness. Happiness cannot coexist with the denial of our autonomy and our independence to choose our own lives. Thus, no one else should be allowed to control or dictate our feelings, our actions or our self-beliefs.

Our opportunity to explore options and to exercise the right to choose is paramount to enduring happiness; therefore, we must fanatically protect our freedom to live life as we desire. If we permit others or external circumstances to choose for us, we will have given up any remaining right to pursue our own happiness. Our sense of *Self* cannot survive without our sense of freedom. Only when they exist together can we create for ourselves a sense of happiness.

V. A SENSE OF HOPE AND DESIRE

The most profound difference between humans and the animal kingdom is the capacity for Hope. When we possess Hope and Desire for our future, we possess an unparalleled sense of happiness. While animals exist instinctively, humans have the ability to ponder the reasons why they exist. With Hope, we know that we can exist for a Purpose. And with Purpose, we possess a Vision for the future. Winifred Newman once said, *Vision is the world's most desperate need. There are no hopeless situations, only people who think hopelessly.* When we feel we are without hope, there will not be much capacity for happiness.

Thus, each day of our lives should begin with hopeful expectations. If our prevailing attitude is that life continually offers new possibilities, we will act with anticipation and excitement. Hope will create a willingness to explore life, to discover all that life can be. The door of Hope must be passed through first to gain access to all other doors of happiness.

VI. A SENSE OF CREATIVITY AND IMAGINATION

Nothing fuels the soul more than the creative spirit. J.G. Gallimore told us, *Image creates desire. You will what you imagine.* When we can imagine our possibilities, we can create the future we desire. As humans, we have the capacity to literally invent our lives before they even happen. Our imagination is the greatest force for happiness as it allows us to create the best visions of the future before we act upon them. We can ponder options, plan scenarios and manipulate events in our minds long before we embark on their realization.

When we are attuned to this creative power, we are able to dress-rehearse life before taking risks. By conceiving in our minds-eye all of our expectations and possibilities, we are able to critically choose the right path to take. Also, the creative mind is the best vacation destination in the world. We can see and feel art, music and poetry, allowing us to visit utopian worlds that we can construct into reality. By envisioning our life's Purpose and fulfillment, we literally create our own opportunities for happiness.

VII. A SENSE OF CONTROL

The antithesis to happiness is stress, anxiety and depression. These states of being occur when we lose our sense of control. Without the ability to control, we lose our capacity to perceive the possibility of happiness. While we will not be able to control every event or circumstance in our lives, we can control our reactions to them. It was once said, *happiness is not the absence of conflict but the ability to cope with it.* Our attitude is our source of control and the happiness we experience is simply a function of our attitude.

We will continually be challenged with difficult situations that will test our coping mechanisms but the power is within us to rise above them. Our objective is not to eliminate these daily stressors but to place them within the context of their real importance. If life seems uncontrollable, it is because we are reacting to situations rather than managing them. If we operate outside of a focused sense of what is most important to us, we are allowing ourselves to be controlled. If, however, we diligently control our Purpose, our attitude and our behavior, life's stressors will be reduced to manageable proportions. Our happiness is ensured when we make conscious choices based upon our Purpose, and when we feel that we are in control of ourselves.

VIII. A SENSE OF CONTRIBUTION

According to Eleanor Roosevelt, *When you cease to make a contribution you begin to die.* The corollary to her sage advice is that our unselfish contributions provide a rich Purpose to our lives. When we extend ourselves to others, we will discover a new dimension of happiness. Sharing our Purpose is creating meaning with our existence. What greater joy is there than to know that we are making a difference with our lives?

The opportunity to create happiness in others is available to us every day. Our choice is to either live selfishly inside of ourselves or to reach out with our hearts and minds to those in greater need. When we feel that our neighbors, our family, our fellow workers and our world society is just a little better off because of our presence, we will gain no greater satisfaction. While many components of our happiness are created by external events outside of our direct control, we are fully in control of our capacity to make significant contributions to others. We should embrace this opportunity daily.

IX. A SENSE OF HUMOR

It is virtually impossible to be happy and sad at the same time. Having a sense of humor and being able to laugh at ourselves and the foibles of the world ensures our right to happiness. Victor Hugo aptly stated, *Laughter is the sun that drives winter from the human face.* Almost every situation, even those that appear to be the most distressing, has a ring of humor to it. Our receptivity to the *comedy of life* will keep our spirits high even when we are faced with the melancholic events of daily living.

Like every other aspect of joyful living, it is purely a matter of attitude. Some of us will only see the tragic side of life and some of us will see hilarity in almost everything. Rather than wasting negative energy lamenting how bad things are, we need to loosen up a bit, relax and not take the serious things too seriously. It always takes more effort to frown than to smile, and we will find ourselves smiling at the world as long as we choose to. We must simply believe that this is a far better way to pass through this world.

X. A SENSE OF SPIRITUALITY

Many spiritual doors have been presented to us over the last several thousand years, from the worlds of the Far East, the Mideast, and the West. Whatever our religious orientation, all persuasions purport to arrive at the same conclusion: Our earthly happiness and peace of mind is predicated upon our being in touch with a universal power that will provide us a possibility for eternal grace.

Much of our happiness is diluted by our thoughts of old age, sickness and death. As we contemplate this dismal inevitability, we would seem to have little reason for joy. Without the possibility of somehow transcending this unavoidable destiny, life seems pointless and senseless to us. Why even get out of bed in the morning if life has no other meaning than to watch the calendar, counting down the days to the end of our actuarially predetermined life span?

The good news is that we are here for a Purpose. While we must decide how purposeful our earthly lives will be, we are also part of a larger Purpose, one that existed before us and will continue after we shed our physical selves. We are eternal beings and life does not stop simply because our bodies fail in their mortal forms. Recognition of our spirituality will serve as our greatest source of joy. We will eventually transcend our earthly presence as well as our earthly religions, but we will always exist as part of God's *Grand Plan*. We should accept this as our most wonderful gift for happiness.

Each of us should consider our own version of the *Ten Paths to Happiness,* such that they become core Values for our *Wheel of Life*. Our pursuit of these key principles to joyful living will add immensely to the quality and meaning of our life. Our happiness is not a mysterious force but rather a simple gift that we all possess. We will discover that it is not provided by money, power, status or prestige, but rather through the application of uncomplicated and unpretentious thoughts and feelings. We can discover it through the love of a pet animal, through the first smell of jasmine in the spring, or through the caring embrace of a child. It will come to us immediately if we open our hearts and allow it to enter.

Most of us, however, do not gain this wisdom until we reach old age. We take our lifetime of experiences and convert this into the wisdom that produces contentment and happiness. Unfortunately, many of us will also turn bitter and angry in our old age because of our cumulative experiences that led to a lifetime of regrets. The choice is ours as to which attitude will prevail, and whether or not we will find the wisdom of happiness before we reach an old age.

The secret to which attitude we take, according to University of Florida sociologist, Monika Ardelt, depends upon *our understanding and acceptance of the truths of life*. Her research into wisdom and happiness among the older population concludes that, *Wise people do not necessarily know more facts… but they comprehend the deeper meaning of the generally known facts.*

Thus, happiness emanates from our wisdom, that is, the perspective that we have on the *truths of life*. Wise people do not focus on personal needs, but rather on the sense of Purpose that they bring to life. Ardelt found that money, success, and sometimes even personal health had less bearing on happiness than having a high tolerance for adversity and a deeper perspective on what matters most in life. It is the attitude of acceptance of painful events that cannot be controlled while focusing on the deeper value of simple joys that are abundantly available to all of us. According to one of her older research subjects, *You have to work at living if you want to happy.*

The secret to happiness, therefore, lies in our natural ability to govern our feelings and our attitude toward life. If we elect to continue our journey into self-empowerment, we will need to learn how our life can be enhanced via the principles of attitude adjustment. Through mental mastery, we can become masters of our *Self*, knowing what we want and how to effectively pursue it. We must learn to reach our *Higher Self* through the application of our Purpose into daily living, where we can manage ourselves through our self-beliefs. Our happiness will always depend upon our ability to stay focused and centered on what is most important to us. This is wisdom at the highest level, a focusing of the *Self* on the *truths of life.*

How can I stay focused and centered on the *Ten Paths to Happiness*?

There is rarely any need for us to concentrate on matters that take us off the various pathways to happiness. But invariably, we do stray! The principal reason is from the clutter that we accumulate in our minds from our complicated, covetous lifestyles. The effects of the material world that we live in are anaesthetizing to our real Purpose and pursuit of happiness. Matthew 16:26 warns us of the fate of losing our chief Purpose in living: *For what has a man profited, if he shall gain the whole world, and lose his own soul?*

The point is that we are literally losing our way in the world with our mindless attention to insignificant matters and materialism. For enduring happiness, we must let go of all of the extraneous pursuits of life that conflict with what is really important to us. If we could only learn to live with an austere attention to what is significant and abandon all that is the antithesis to a quality life, we could rediscover our sense of Purpose and our true sense of happiness. The indispensable key for each of us is to keep life focused and simple. As a collective society we have thus far failed to realize this, but we must maintain our individual right to do so… *to march to a different drummer.*

CHAPTER FOURTEEN

Where Should My Life Be Heading?

The Unified Way through Life

Desiderata

Go placidly amid the noise and the haste, and remember what peace there may be in silence. As far as possible, without surrender, be on good terms with all persons. Speak your truth quietly and clearly; and listen to others, even to the dull and ignorant; they too have their story. Avoid loud and aggressive persons; they are vexations to the spirit. If you compare yourself with others, you may become vain or bitter, for always there will be greater and lesser persons than yourself. Enjoy your achievements as well as your plans. Keep interested in your own career, however humble; it is a real possession in the changing fortunes of time. Exercise caution in your business affairs for the world is full of trickery. But let this not blind you to what virtue there is; many persons strive for high ideals, and everywhere life is full of heroism. Be yourself. Especially do not feign affection. Nor be cynical about love; for in the face of all aridity and disenchantment, it is as perennial as the grass. Take kindly the counsel of the years, gracefully surrendering the things of youth. Nurture strength of spirit to shield you in sudden misfortune. But do not distress yourself with dark imaginings. Many fears are born of fatigue and loneliness. Beyond a wholesome discipline, be gentle with yourself. You are a child of the universe no less than the trees and the stars; you have a right to be here. And whether or not it is clear to you, no doubt the universe is unfolding as it should. Therefore be at peace with God, whatever you conceive Him to be. And whatever your labors and aspirations, in the noisy confusion of life, keep peace in your soul. With all its sham,

drudgery and broken dreams, it is still a beautiful world. Be cheerful. Strive to be happy.

Max Ehrmann

Much like the Bible, Max Ehrmann's *Desiderata* is perhaps one of the best self-help pieces ever written. *Desiderata* provides a pathway through life, a set of guideposts that mark the right course to take. If we could only internalize and live in accordance with *Desiderata*, we might find that we would never need psychoanalysis or self-help books. These guideposts serve us as a set of *Unifying Principles*, the self-governing beliefs or rules we can choose to live by. Collectively, they are the embodiment of our Purpose and our Values and serve to *unify* all of our feelings about life. They would become our most cherished principles, the laws that *unify* our worldview. And once adopted, they would serve as our gyroscope, steadying and balancing us as we confront the daily challenges of living.

The concept of *Unifying Principles*, is further clarified by examining a few of *Desiderata's* key phrases:

Go placidly amid the noise and the haste - denotes a belief in living calmly amidst the turmoil and confusion that surrounds us.

Listen to others, even to the dull and ignorant; they too have their story - states a belief in being considerate and open to everyone, no matter what their status in life.

Do not distress yourself with dark imaginings - says you believe in positive thinking, that you don't worry needlessly about things that are not real and only conjured up in your mind.

Beyond a wholesome discipline, be gentle with yourself - defines your belief in your own self-worth, that you seek to control any self-destructive actions and behavior.

Therefore be at peace with God, whatever you conceive Him to be - states that you have a strong belief in your spiritual awareness and are seeking your own spiritual fulfillment.

Desiderata is replete with these tidbits of wisdom in self-governance. This poem provides excellent principles to live by, however, we should endeavor to draft our own *Desiderata*. Our set of *Unifying Principles* should become our own personal code, our rules of self-governance that will produce a happy and fulfilling life.

However, let's not confuse these principles with our Values (our highest wants and aspirations) nor our Goals (the manifestations of our Values being achieved). Rather, our *Unifying Principles* are simply our self-beliefs, our innermost feelings about ourselves and how we choose to behave and interact with our total environment.

Defining our own *Unifying Principles* requires us to look deep inside of ourselves. We should begin by examining how our personality traits affect our principles or rules of living. Are we loud and boisterous or quiet and reserved? Are we easily angered or patient and considerate? Are we negative thinkers or eternally optimistic? Are we quickly aroused and excitable or are we contemplative and subdued? Are we resentful or appreciative? Are we envious or satisfied? Are we analytical or expressive?

Honest answers to these questions and many others will reveal our true persona. We each have innumerable character traits, most formed early in life. By having a good grasp of our basic personality attributes, we can adopt the principles that should govern our own behavior. This self-assessment determines which beliefs we will choose to follow or reject, making us better positioned to determine our personal laws of self-governance.

Our *Unifying Principles* then become our inner voice, the control center in our minds that tells us how to react to situations and how to go about the task of daily living. They will eventually become completely internalized, such that we seldom have to be reminded or even need to think about them. Residing in our subconscious minds most of the time, they spring forward much like the cartoon characters of good and evil that sit on our shoulders to advise us when we are confronted with a difficult situation. In essence, they become the invisible guidance system that directly affects our behavior, our actions and our reactions to everyday events.

We will continue to acquire our *Unifying Principles* much the same way that we derived our Purpose and our Values. They are assimilated by living, picked up like flowers along the roadside until we have a basket full of beliefs leading to our own system of self-regulation. Moreover, our *Unifying Principles* become the source of our self-esteem, our self-confidence and our self-reliance. They are, in effect, who we are.

How can these self-beliefs guide me ?

We must first and foremost be responsible to ourselves. Others cannot be the sole catalyst for our behavior and ultimately our true happiness. While others may play a role or provide assistance, any lasting, meaningful satisfaction must come entirely from our *Selves*. If we truly believe we are happy, we will be. If we see ourselves as miserable beings, then we will assuredly find very little in life to please us. If we think we are energetic and enthusiastic we will take on new challenges and find opportunities to be successful. Or if we believe we are lethargic and worthless, we will never rise to meet the wonderful offerings that life has made available to us. As we take stock of ourselves and know exactly what makes us tick, we will be able to translate our own self-beliefs into action.

The greatest benefit of living with Purpose is that it generates our world-view. Therefore, as we look within we must also take to time to look outside of ourselves. As we gain a greater understanding of our *Higher Self*, we will develop a greater sense of our place in the world and how to best interact with it. We can then create our *Unifying Principles* which will dictate our presence in the world community, providing us the capacity to unify or center all of our conscious actions. They will instruct us, lead us and provide us the stability we are seeking.

Our *Unifying Principles* clearly embody our Values. In an earlier section, we spent time identifying and prioritizing these Values which we then placed on our *Wheel of Life*. Let's now revisit our Values and see if we still feel strongly about our choices.

List again your eight most supreme Values. Have they changed?

1.
2.
3.
4.
5.

6.

7.

8.

From the Values list that we created, we can now begin to develop our *Unifying Principles*. Remember that our Values are the key priorities, our highest wants and aspirations. Our *Unifying Principles* flow from these Values and subsequently become the self-governing principles that we will choose to live by. They become our code of conduct, our set of self-beliefs upon which our rules will be adopted for interacting with the world in which we live.

We can utilize *Desiderata* to get our thoughts flowing freely but we should develop our own principles to guide us. To further assist us, let's think about our answers to the following questions:

- **How do I want to relate to my family, my co-workers or my community?**
- **What type of home environment do I want to create?**
- **How do I want to approach my career?**
- **What contribution do I want to make? And to whom?**
- **How do I want to be perceived by others?**
- **What expressions of love are most important to me?**
- **How important is money to me? Why?**
- **How independent (dependent) do I want to be?**
- **What will be my spiritual quest?**
- **What motivates me to succeed?**
- **What is my definition of success?**
- **What is important to me intellectually?**
- **How creative or challenging does my life have to be?**
- **What makes me feel comfortable (uncomfortable) with myself?**
- **Where do I want to live? Why?**
- **What level of self-discipline do I possess?**
- **What are my feelings about my health?**
- **How much fun or leisure do I need?**
- **How will I handle a crisis?**
- **How do I want to be remembered?**

This is a partial list of hundreds of questions that we could possibly ask of ourselves. The key, however, is to ask the questions. Honest answers will speak volumes about our *Selves*. And from our answers, we can begin to sketch out a picture of who we are, what our views are about ourselves, and how we will travel through this life of ours. Our *Unifying Principles* will emerge as our most powerful convictions about our role in this world. They will become our personal commandments to ourselves and will guide us in dealing with every event or problem that we may face.

Our *Unifying Principles* will focus us in life and allow us to remain in balance when the world around us seems to be troubled and in chaos. Our *Unifying Principles* will become our life's *Anchors*. And regardless of the severity of the storm, we will take comfort in knowing that we can ride it out.

Before we create our own A*nchors*, let's look at another example to clarify our understanding of this concept. Perhaps the most noteworthy list of *Anchors* is found in the Ten Commandments given to us by God. For clarification, let's take the liberty of modifying the King James text and change the reference from *Thou Shall Not* to *I will*:

I WILL NOT PUT ANY OTHER GODS BEFORE THE ONE, TRUE GOD.
I WILL NOT WORSHIP ANY FALSE GODS.
I WILL NOT MISUSE THE LORD'S NAME.
I WILL REMEMBER THE SABBATH AS A HOLY DAY.
I WILL HONOR MY FATHER AND MOTHER.
I WILL NOT KILL ANYONE.
I WILL NOT COMMIT ADULTERY.
I WILL NOT STEAL.
I WILL NOT GIVE FALSE TESTIMONY AGAINST MY NEIGHBOR.
I WILL NOT COVET ANYTHING THAT BELONGS TO MY NEIGHBOR.

Just as the list of commandments given by God to Moses established a covenant between man and God, our goal must be to form a covenant with our *Selves*. And as God's commandments were meant to be inviolable, our commandments must be equally held to their highest place of importance in our lives. If we think of living *God's Word* as our path to eternal grace, we may also think of living *Our Word,* the self-directed path to our *Higher Self.* We have the power within us to make our *Unifying Principles* the basis for *Our Word* to live by.

If we find it difficult to develop our own ten commandments, we must again return to our Purpose, our Vision, our Values and our Mission. Collectively, they form the foundation of our *Unifying Principles.* We can understand this more clearly by thinking of a simple flower and how it comes into realizing its full potential. A flower's Purpose is its deep root. It is its wellspring, the source of its *Being*. The flower's Values are the nutrients that make it grow. A flower's Vision is the strong stem that sets the direction or path in which it will grow. The flower's Mission is made up of its leaves as they, like goals, are continually changing and evolving as the seasons pass. And finally, we reach the flower's brightly colored blossoms, the Results from having actually lived its life the way it chose itself to be.

Yet the flower still needs something else: the sun and the rain, the vital source for keeping it alive and in its strongest state of being. The sun and the rain are the flower's *Unifying Principles*, for without them the flower may only exist in a wilted and stunted form. It will never reach its complete glory, for although it knew its Purpose was to be a flower, it never became all that it could be.

We are now ready to develop our own set of *Unifying Principles.* What will be our covenant to ourselves? Where will the sunlight and the water come from that will give *life to our life?* What are our personal commandments to ourselves? What will be *Our Word* to ourselves that will guide us and lead us to living a life in accordance to our Purpose, our Vision, our Values and our Mission? What set of rules will we choose to assure the blossoming of our own flower?

Unifying Principles govern organizations as well as our *Selves*. From college fraternities to service organizations such as the Shriners, Rotary and Kiwanis, all have their code of conduct to keep them centered on their Purpose and their highest Values. The Boy Scouts of America begin their meetings with the pledge of allegiance and the Scout pledge of strength,

character, cleanliness, holiness, helpfulness, etc. A Tampa, Florida chapter of the YMCA incorporates the following Unifying Principles into their character development strategies for young people:

FAITH: The substance of things hoped for, but not seen.
COURAGE: Standing for principle despite adversity.
TRUTH: The reality at the base of an appearance.
SELF-DISCIPLINE: Controlling oneself for improvement.
COMPASSION: Loving others the way you want to be loved.
KNOWLEDGE: The continuous quest for learning.
JOY: Gladness of heart through realizing the miracle of life.

Let's also reflect on some of the *Unifying Principles* that follow. These are some universal principles that many people live by and are presented here to give us some further direction in our own thought process. We need not make them ours, but we can think of them as valuable resources for living a valuable life.

1. I WILL LOVE MYSELF.
2. I WILL LOVE MY NEIGHBOR AS I LOVE MYSELF.
3. I WILL ACCEPT RESPONSIBILITY FOR MY ACTIONS.
4. I WILL DELAY MY GRATIFICATION AND ACCEPT SELF-DISCIPLINE.
5. I WILL ADHERE TO WHAT I BELIEVE IN AND STAND FOR MY CAUSES.
6. I WILL LIVE IN ACCORDANCE TO GOD'S WORD.
7. I WILL HONOR MYSELF AND MAKE MY BODY AND MIND STRONG.
8. I WILL ACCEPT CHANGE AND GROW WITH MY NEW EXPERIENCES.
9. I WILL SEEK OPPORTUNITIES TO GIVE OF MYSELF TO MY COMMUNITY.
10. I WILL COMMIT MYSELF TO MY PURPOSE IN MY DAILY LIFE.

It is now time to reflect and determine our own set of rules. Let's write down the *Ten Commandments* for our own self-governance - Our *Unifying Principles* for life:

MY UNIFYING PRINCIPLES

1.
2.
3.
4.
5.
6.
7.
8.
9.
10.

As we suggested earlier, it is desirable to carry a card with us always that states our Purpose, Values, Vision and Mission. Likewise, we should write down and carry our *Unifying Principles* with us at all times. The more we can reflect upon those things that bring the most meaning to our lives, the more likely we are to live them. Whether we keep these words in our daily calendar, on a card in our wallet or on the mirror in our bathroom, they must be constantly present in our life.

Life is undeniably complex and demanding. We know that if our lives were somehow more predictable, we could navigate it with a clearer sense of Purpose. If life was just less troublesome, we could get on top of it and stay on top. And it seems that we keep getting knocked off our feet every time we think things are beginning to run smoothly. In fact, we often give up on making our life more meaningful simply because we believe things won't turn out the way we would like them to. If we cannot control it, we think, why not just go with it and take what we get. We feel that if we cannot manage it with perfection and precision, we might as well accept whatever fate we are dealt. It is precisely for these reasons that we must find the strength to rise above the basic ironies of life.

Life owes us nothing. For that simple reason alone, we cannot expect to receive any more from life than what we decide to put into it. Our primary concern cannot be what life has granted us. We should not lament the forces that we cannot control, nor should we lament the negative outcomes of these forces. Rather, our focus should be on the greater gift that we have all received: The power within each of us to responsibly choose the life we will live.

We cannot blame circumstances for our situation in life. We cannot blame others for things not turning out the way we wish. We cannot blame the weather, our parents, our education, our luck or even God for what we receive from life. We can only blame ourselves if life is less than what we want it to be. Just as we are free to choose our own Purpose, we are free to choose what we will do with our lives. We are free to use our own wisdom, our own thoughts and actions, and our own talents and resources to decide what meaning or value life will have to us. Our life's worth then becomes our own responsibility. As burdensome as that may seem too many of us, therein lies its most wondrous benefit:

IT IS OUR LIFE!

We have been given that marvelous gift to do with as we choose. It is life itself that we should embrace. It is ours to live. Too often, we lose sight of this miracle called life. We take it for granted. We abuse it. We waste it. We criticize it for its difficulty. We believe we didn't get our fair share. We fault our opportunities and condemn our lack of good fortune. We feel that the best of what life has to offer rarely comes to us. But with all this blame and criticism of our life, we rarely believe it is our fault. We expect happiness to come our way, and if it doesn't, then the rest of the world is whom we indict for its unfairness. Yet, we alone create the good fortune that we will receive. We cannot wait for our ship to come in. We must swim out to it. We should not waste another moment agonizing over how unfair life can be; rather we should rejoice that it even exists.

Let's now acknowledge that there is no room in our life for blame, anger, denial, rage, prejudice, jealousy, contempt, envy, greed, avarice or selfishness. The precious time we have been given does not support the wastefulness of these self-destructive emotions. If we have been granted less than we think we deserve, we should always be thankful for what we do have. In the words of James Allen, we need to, *Work joyfully and peacefully, knowing that right thoughts and right efforts will inevitably bring about the right results.* Instead of depleting our energy by criticizing what we don't have, we must use that same energy being grateful for what we do have. If we can't always have what we want, we should always want what we do have.

Victor Frankl, the Holocaust survivor, decided that if he couldn't have physical freedom; he would have mental freedom. Likewise, if we can't afford shoes, we should be thankful that we still have feet. If our ears can't hear, we should be thankful that our eyes still see. If we can't have money, we should be thankful that we still have flowers, sunsets and laughter. If we can't have anything in life except for our five senses, we should be thankful that these gifts allow us to see, hear, taste, smell and touch the beauty of the world that surrounds us. Who are we to expect anything more wonderful than this?

Besides our five senses, life has given us the most important gift: *Choices.* We will always have the freedom to decide if one thing doesn't bring us happiness, then we can choose something else. There are infinite opportunities to find happiness and meaning in our lives. If we don't find it by taking one road, then we must pick another road. The good news is that life gives us plenty of roads. And we alone decide which roads we shall take.

Therefore, the way through life is to wake up to our possibilities. We wake up our lives by waking up to our choices. We can choose a life that has a clear sense of Purpose and decide what our supreme motivation will be. We can develop our own Vision and know in which direction we wish to lead our life. We can decide what is most important to us through deciding what our Values will be. We can map out our own Mission and commit ourselves to the goals we will pursue. We can decide how we want to live our life on a daily basis to seek our ultimate reward, that of having lived a meaningful and fulfilling life.

When we don't exercise our freedom of choice, we are living our lives recklessly. We will be living without respect for ourselves as we have denied our rights to choose, to grow, to fulfill our dreams. Without Purpose, we will have no self-direction and our fate will be out of our control. We alone must decide the way through life. We must appreciate our gifts, however insignificant they may appear to be, for our gifts will always be greater than we will imagine.

We will always have more causes to celebrate than we have causes to complain. Life does not owe us easy answers to finding happiness, but life has given us the opportunity to find our own answers. We have been given the power to chart life's rocky shoals by being our own navigator. The way through life takes courage and the conviction of our self-beliefs, but the path to our *Higher Self* is ours to travel.

The good news is that our choices are ours. Our time is ours. Our Purpose is ours. Our Life is ours. We should celebrate!

EPILOGUE

Can I Make A Difference?
The White Stone Promise

The end of history will be a very sad time. The struggle for recognition, the willingness to risk one's life for a purely abstract goal, the worldwide ideological struggle that called forth daring, courage, imagination, and idealism, will be replaced by economic calculation, the endless solving of technological problems, environmental concerns, and the satisfaction of sophisticated consumer demands. In the post-historical period there will neither be art nor philosophy, just the perpetual care taking of the museum of human history.

Francis Fukuyama
The End of History and the Last Man

Our world society is heading down a very dangerous path at an alarming speed. As a collective people, we are rapidly losing the essence of collective Purpose. If each of us live without Purpose, we all live without Purpose, suffering the consequences together. Perhaps, as Fukuyama warns us, we are approaching the end of human history. If we are indeed a post-industrial, cyber-techno society where crass commercialism and personal gratification exceed our desire to love, share and live with greater Purpose, then we will receive what we have asked for: the finalization of our right to exist as a human race. This is a harsh indictment of ourselves and an unpleasant proposition to consider but the evidence of this possibility surrounds us.

We are now living in a world dominated by greed, instant gratification, and weak cultural values. We are losing our ability to live with moral consciousness and belief in our Purpose and our *Higher Self.* We work ourselves to exhaustion, then have little more to show for our efforts than mounting debts and consumer products that are obsolete the next year. We educate our children; then lament their inability to reason, much less read. We have removed the front porches on our homes where we used to converse, moving inside to play with our electronic toys.

We are destroying our environment for profit and then complain that our fish have died, our beaches are gone and our parks are overcrowded. We embrace technology like a religion, then lose our jobs to the same machines that we created. We advance our scientific knowledge of ourselves while watching our inner cities decay. We sit mindlessly in front of true confession reality shows rather than read books or create art. We use video games to babysit our children, then complain that they won't communicate with us. We spend more money on prisons than universities; then wonder why our crime rates escalate.

Al Gore, before becoming Vice President, wrote:

We have constructed in our civilization a false world of plastic flowers and astro-turf, air conditioning and fluorescent lights, windows that don't open and background music that never stops, days when we don't know whether it has rained, nights when the sky never stops glowing, Walkman and Watchman, entertainment cocoons, frozen food for the microwave oven, sleepy hearts jump-started by caffeine, alcohol, drugs and illusions.

Yes, Illusions! Illusions of a better world for ourselves. It is no wonder that we are still seeking Purpose and meaning in our lives. We have become a people of paradoxes, a people without Purpose. It is indisputable that our problems have not been solved through advances in technology, science, medicine or government. We still chase inner peace and happiness, pursuits that evade us despite our progress in human engineering. Nothing has really changed with all the changes made to our *Selves* and the world in which we live.

The reason is simple: We have forgotten how to love, give, share, or live for higher causes than ourselves. We simply do not have a Purpose that extends beyond our own needs for comfort and personal satisfaction. We are not willing to give up ourselves for something that is infinitely more important than our gratification for the moment. Our children are becoming our greatest victims, and the world they inherit may not be the world we intended or wished for them. We are wasting our Purpose and our cultural values for our expedient desires of today.

Where did we go wrong?

We undoubtedly did not intend or plan for everything to turn out this way. We know that we have seen our *quantity of life* go up while our *quality of life* has gone down. We intellectually know that the value of our lives has not improved, but we feel that we have little control over our future. We feel the problem is simply too enormous for any one person to make any difference. We accept our fate and then feel miserable about it. We have lost the capacity to see that we can make a difference because we have lost the capacity to see where our individual Purpose can transcend to the larger community. We have abandoned the will to truly care, not only about ourselves but about others that we share this planet with. We do not have a cause to believe in - a cause to celebrate.

The reasons we lost our Purpose as a collective society are complex, yet understandable. Our Western civilization thrives on crisis management rather than purposeful action. We feel nothing needs to be done until it is a large enough problem. When we feel enough discomfort, our response is usually one of short-term, stopgap solutions. Our difficulty comes from thinking too much on a linear basis, where everything is supposed to happen sequentially. We believe that a simple application of reasoning and a couple doses of scientific principals will take care of the problem. We also arrogantly believe that we can somehow find the answer if we just study it and then throw a pile of money at it. And we think if we still can't fix it, then no problem, someone else will.

Eastern civilizations seem to have a little better handle on the solution of problem solving. They take a much longer view, feeling that conflict resolution is a matter of putting deep-seated principals to work over time. And rather than viewing everything as a series of problems to solve today, they believe that centuries old Values can still apply to life, business and social planning. To them, time is not a straight line; rather it is a loop that keeps coming back to itself. They feel that an investment of *right thinking* today will serve them well tomorrow, that by self-directing their future there is a greater possibility for success for the long term.

We cannot avoid the inevitability of history repeating itself, but we can avoid the loss of our moral Values and our clear Purpose in handling our problems the next time around. We must courageously face our problems by taking the longer view, or perhaps the bigger view, a view greater than ourselves where our Purpose extends out to the world in which we live. We can make our future a more pleasant place to live if we believe in the power of purposeful choice and decide to make a difference!

Where can my Purpose make a difference?

It is important to understand that our Purpose, while uniquely ours, is not fully manifested until we find cause to share it with others. We cannot find true meaning in life without connecting ourselves with something larger and more pervasive than we are. Existing in isolation of the larger world will only turn us inward, while our Purpose needs outward expression to find its fulfillment. It is said that *no man is an island* because no one of us can find lasting peace and happiness through any other channel than participation in the greater world in which we live.

Our Purpose can find expression along two major pathways: First, giving of ourselves to others; and second, having a cause to live for. Our greatest opportunity to feel totally alive and significant is to share ourselves to the larger community, to have something meaningful to believe in and stand for. We celebrate our Purpose by discovering the many ways in which our life can significantly impact and improve the lives of others. We will not have to look far for these opportunities. Likewise, if we possess a deep commitment to a cause, a crusade or a conviction that we hold fundamental to our Purpose, we will possess the most exciting, rewarding reasons to exist while ensuring great meaning for our life going forward.

We do not have to live in a world characterized by empty Values, unabated greed, hatred and unintelligent gratification at the expense of our collective well being. Not unless that is our Purpose, and we must believe that should *not* be our Purpose. Our Purpose should center upon our caring for the world that our children will inherit. We can find great Purpose in giving of ourselves with selfless love. Ralph Waldo Emerson wrote, *Love is everything. It is the key to life, and its influences are those that move the world.* If we cannot accept the world as it is becoming, we can make it our Purpose to change it.

Through giving of ourselves to others and to a cause that we deeply believe in, we will not only find our Purpose but also ensure that it thrives. Let's recognize that there are infinite opportunities to make our lives more purposeful by extending ourselves out to the world community. All we need to do is just look around…

IF WE LOOK AROUND, WE WILL FIND OUR PURPOSE

- *If we see hunger, our Purpose must be to find one family to feed.*
- *If we see hatred, our Purpose must be to offer kindness.*
- *If we see greed, our Purpose must be to counsel.*
- *If we see ignorance, our Purpose must be to teach.*
- *If we see pain, our Purpose must be to comfort.*
- *If we see pollution, our Purpose must be to cleanse.*
- *If we see sadness, our Purpose must be to cheer.*
- *If we see loss of hope, our Purpose must be to encourage.*
- *If we see helplessness, our Purpose must be to support.*
- *If we see chaos, our Purpose must be to calm.*
- *If we see deceit, our Purpose must be to inform.*
- *If we see war, our Purpose must be to make peace.*

We should not fail to utilize our Purpose because we believe that we are unable to make any impact. Our effectiveness does not have to be measured in grandiose terms. The simple, purposeful acts of each of us will collectively add up to bring our world back into better balance. If every one of us exercised our right to serve in a very small way, we could move the mountain together. An unknown monk in 1100 A.D. made this point about changing the world:

When I was a young man, I wanted to change the world. I found it was difficult to change the world, so I tried to change my nation. When I found I couldn't change the nation, I began to focus on my town. I couldn't change the town and as an older man, I tried to change my family.

Now as an old man, I realize the only thing I can change is myself, and suddenly I realize that if long ago I had changed myself, I could have made an impact on my family. My family and I could have made an impact on our town. Their impact could have changed the nation and I could indeed have changed the world.

Changing ourselves is the first step in changing the world. The mere act of each of us becoming more responsible about our own life will create a collective change for all of us. In fact, it may not even be our choice to do otherwise if we wish to maintain the right to exist with each other. New York Mayor Dinkins at the memorial service of Arthur Ashe said, *Service to others is the rent we pay for our space on earth. Arthur Ashe paid his rent in full.* Our Purpose should also be to pay our own rent in full, to give ourselves to our landlord, the world community in which we live.

Thus, we can never say that we can find no Purpose in our life when we only have to look around us and find needs that are greater than ours. We all have this opportunity on a daily basis should we choose to look beyond our own immediate gratification. To find our Purpose in life and the discovery of our *Higher Self,* we only need to *Wake Up* our consciousness to see where we can actually make a difference.

We should leave our legacy to those who inherit our world by heeding the words of John F. Kennedy, *I am certain that after the dust of centuries has passed over our cities, we, too, will be remembered not for victories or defeats in battle or politics, but for our contribution to the human spirit.* We, therefore, have a rather simple choice to make: Allow the world in which we live to continue in disorder or reach out and bring more harmony to it, to contribute to the human spirit for all future generations.

To discover our true Purpose, we must *Wake Up* and search for our own cause, to find the Purpose that extends beyond ourselves. St. Augustine wisely counseled us many years ago, *We cannot turn inward!* Thus, the discovery of our *Higher Self* is found only through turning ourselves outward, to the larger world of those in need. In fact, our *Higher Self* is only possible when we give up our existing *Self.* Our Purpose in life must be to make an impact, to extend ourselves out to make a difference. We must recognize that our simple survival is not the point of life. The point of life is to celebrate our life. We celebrate by celebrating our cause, so that others will know that we, indeed, did make a difference... and that we did have a Purpose.

THE WHITE STONE PROMISE

Throughout this book, we have laid the foundation for our *Unifying Principles*, the personal self-beliefs that will govern our actions going forward. We accomplished this by identifying our unique Purpose and clarifying our Value-system. We discovered our Vision and committed to our Mission by making personal commitments to achieve our highest goals. We learned that our Rewards are based upon self-directed Behavior that is congruent with our Purpose and Values. And we discovered new tools to *make life happen* as we choose, instead of *letting life just happen* to us!

Along the way, we gained numerous insights into personal growth, self-renewal and the benefits of simple, balanced living. We learned new time management techniques and self-mastery through rational thinking. We found new ways to make stress work for us and learned how to deal with the complexities of daily living. We revisited love and laughter, relationships, destiny and our spiritual being. Hopefully, in the process, we attained a better sense of who we are, why we do the things we do, where we are going and even how we are going to get there. Essentially, we took self-empowerment to its highest form - to the realization of our *Higher Self!*

Achieving our *Higher Self* is the key to being connected to the perfection of the universe. There is no higher nor more worthy goal for any of us. As we each strive to personal perfection, we can carry our Purpose to the world at large, such that we all collectively benefit. Self-knowledge begins our journey, but we must not lose sight of the fact that *We* are the journey. Our path leads to self-enlightenment where we are connected with our Purpose in everything that we do. The issue before us is to decide if we wish to make the trip!

For those of us that do undertake this trip through life, we must recognize that there is a price for anything worth attaining. The price of self-enlightenment - to reach our *Higher Self* - is personal faith, dedicated commitment and a belief that we can overcome the challenges that lie before us. In Revelations 2:17, we are told, *To anyone who overcometh, saith the spirit, I will give a white stone, on which a new name is written which no one will know except the one who receives it.* We must learn and live our Purpose each day of our life to receive our white stone.

Let's make the *White Stone Promise* to ourselves today! The small white stone, the symbol of our commitment, is ours to carry as long as we travel along the path of a purposeful life. It will be a personal journey for each of us. We should never lose sight of the path itself as the trip will always be our greatest reward. It is our destiny to create our own destiny. *To make life happen…* as it should!

CPSIA information can be obtained
at www.ICGtesting.com
Printed in the USA
LVHW082312230420
654358LV00011B/410